COLLABORATIVE WEB DEVELOPMENT

COLLABORATIVE WEB DEVELOPMENT

Strategies and Best Practices for Web Teams

Jessica Burdman

ADDISON-WESLEY

An Imprint of Addison Wesley Longman, Inc.

*Reading, Massachusetts • Harlow, England • Menlo Park, California
Berkeley, California • Don Mills, Ontario • Sydney
Bonn • Amsterdam • Tokyo • Mexico City*

Many of the designations used by manufacturers and sellers to distinguish their products are claimed as trademarks. Where those designations appear in this book and Addison-Wesley was aware of a trademark claim, the designations have been printed in initial caps or all caps.

The author and publisher have taken care in the preparation of this book, but make no expressed or implied warranty of any kind and assume no responsibility for errors or omissions. No liability is assumed for incidental or consequential damages in connection with or arising out of the use of the information or programs contained herein.

The publisher offers discounts on this book when ordered in quantity for special sales. For more information, please contact:

Corporate, Government, and Special Sales Group
Addison Wesley Longman, Inc.
One Jacob Way, Reading, Massachusetts 01867

Library of Congress Cataloging-in-Publication Data

Burdman, Jessica R.
    Collaborative Web development : strategies and best practices for
Web teams / Jessica Burdman.
        p.   cm.
        Includes index.
        ISBN 0-201-43331-1 (alk. paper)
        1. Web sites—Design.   2. Web publishing.   I. Title.
    TK5105.888.B855   1999
    658'.055276--dc21   99-36736
                                                                            CIP

ColorSafe, GIFMation 2.1, and Image Vice trial versions copyright © 1999 by Boxtop Software, Maben, MS 39750 (*http://www.boxtopsoft.com*). All rights reserved.

Dreamweaver and Fireworks™ copyright © 1998 by Macromedia, Inc., San Francisco, CA 94103 (*http://www.macromedia.com*). All rights reserved. Macromedia, the Macromedia logo, and each of the product names are trademarks or registered trademarks of Macromedia, Inc.

Microsoft® Project 98 120-day Trial Edition and FrontPage® 2000 45-day Trial Edition copyright © Microsoft Corporation, 1997–99. All rights reserved.

Milestones, Etc. 5.0 Trial Version copyright © 1999 by KIDASA Software, Inc., Austin, TX 78746 (*http://www.kidasa.com*). All rights reserved.

Text printed on recycled and acid-free paper.

ISBN 0201433311

2 3 4 5 6 7   MA   03 02 01 00

2nd Printing   January 2000

Contents

Preface

If you can't describe what you are doing as a
process, you don't know what you're doing.
– W. Edwards Deming

Those who cannot remember
the past are condemned to repeat it.
– George Santayana (1863–1952)

Over the two years that it has taken to conceptualize and write this book, many people have asked me what inspired me to write about Web development, and why is this book different from the many other books out there on the bookshelves? This book doesn't offer a single-minded solution to the myriad of problems and issues that Web developers face. It's not a solution in a box, or an "Idiot's Guide" to anything. It's naïve to assume that it would be possible to offer the single solution for Web development because of the many kinds of Web applications that exist: entertainment-based, information-based, commerce, or advertising. What this book does contain is a treasure of ideas, methods, devices, tips, advice, stories, and even a CD-ROM full of useful templates and tools to help you develop the Web team and Web development systems that best suit your environment and project objectives.

Who Should Read This Book?

This book is for a project manager or producer, or anyone who is responsible for putting together a Web team. It will help you understand what you need to know to build the right team for the project. It will also help you understand the Web development cycle, the issues you face with clients, be they internal or external to your business. This book will help you understand the costs involved in Web development, time lines, phases, and cycles so that you can create a process that suits your team and the needs of a specific project. The figure that follows this Preface will give you a "picture" of the book's organization.

Heading toward Sanity

Why did I write this book? Many reasons. I had produced more than 20 Web-related projects and at least half of them seemed akin to torture.

Through conferences and networking I developed a circle of friends and colleagues who were creating Web sites: the production manager at Cisco; the managing editor of the *Miami Herald*, the vice president of Snap! Online; producers at Red Sky, Novo | Ironlight Interactive, Ikonic/USWeb, and CKS Partners; and project managers at Netscape, Microsoft, and the Servinet Consulting Group. They were all saying the very similar things:

"Web development is crazy."

"Web projects are death-march projects."

"I need to take three months off to recover."

I began to develop a theory that the central problem with Web development is the lack of clear standards or methods for creating Web sites. There are many kinds of sites and applications. The people who are building Web sites today come from many backgrounds. On e-business sites, I worked with software engineers, security experts, information designers. In advertising, I met brand stewards, copywriters, graphic designers.

Each kind of site required a certain team and a certain methodology. There existed good practices that I could use from my e-business background, but they needed to be modified to fit with the needs of the team and the project. To try to enforce processes without the team's buy-in meant certain project failure.

This book contains interviews with people from the following fields: software development, advertising, multimedia, film, publishing, teaching, and writing. It shows how and why we, as Web project managers and developers, must create methodologies and standards for developing Web applications. Not every suggestion I offer will work for you; your organization will have to decide what works best for its Web team. But, it's important to work toward developing methods that your entire team supports, understands, and wants to use.

When you can do that, and when you are able to articulate the method, then you will start to gain some sanity around developing Web applications. Not that you won't ever experience a chaotic project again, you will. This book will, however, help you develop strategies to make those projects run as smoothly as possible, thereby reducing team burnout and, ideally, help your group achieve true job satisfaction and profitability whenever you take on such a project.

You can find the URLs for vendors and products mentioned in this book under "Links in Text" at

http://awl.com/cseng/titles/0-201-43331-1

Acknowledgments

First and foremost, I have to thank my team at Red Sky for giving me the inspiration and support necessary to write this book: Adam Kane, Alisia Cheuk, Beau Giles, Christina Neville, Greg Meyers, Deirdre McGlashan, Jill Badolato, Kristine Gual, Sophie Jasson-Holt, Stacy Stevenson, Willy Lefkowitz, Pamela Snyder, and Yelena Glezer. You guys are the best. Thanks to all my colleagues at Red Sky for cheering me on.

Thanks to the great project managers I've known: Susan Junda, Chelsea Hunter, Lisa Welchman, Sheila Albright, Amy Lee, Stacy Stevenson, Deirdre McGlashan, Pamela Snyder, Christina Neville, Jill Lefkowitz, Mike Powell, Dave McClure, John Kim, Peter Rosberg, Don Howe, Lisa Bertelson, Linda Waldon, and those who've introduced themselves to me at conferences and trade shows. This book is really for you.

Thanks to the writers of books that inspired this book: Edward Yourdon, Louis Rosenfeld, Linda Weinman, Tom DeMarco, Timothy Lister, Peter Drucker, Neal Stephenson, J. P. Frenza, Michelle Szabo, Phil Jackson, George Santayana, and Walt Whitman.

Thanks to the people who contributed to this book directly. Janine Warner gave me the original idea to write about Web teams, and she wrote the *Miami Herald* case study and most of Appendix B. Sophie Jasson-Holt, my friend and QA manager, wrote Chapter 7. Amy Lee, account manager at Red Sky, wrote the Absolut Vodka case study.

Andrew Klein, director of technology, and Gary Stein, account manager at Red Sky, wrote the Lands' End case study. Dave McClure, Peter Rosberg, Bayard Carlin, Dave Kendall, and Renay Weissberger Fanelli contributed to the Quicken Store case study. A big thanks to Tim Smith and Joel Hladecek for giving me a great interview.

Many thanks to the people who helped in the publishing process. For their thoughtful and helpful review of this book, my sincere thanks go to Heather Champ, Ken Trant, John Cilio, John Wegis, and Mitchel Ahern. Many thanks to my editor, Elizabeth Spainhour, who gave me support, supervision, and encouragement along the way. Thanks to Marilyn Rash's production team at AWL, Angela Stone of Bookwrights in Rockland, Maine, and Judy Strakalaitis of Bookworks in Derry, New Hampshire, for producing a beautiful book. Thanks to my agent, Margot Maley, for helping me find a publisher for this book.

Most of all, thanks to my family and friends, especially my husband Paul, for putting up with the late nights, early mornings, and weekends that I couldn't spend with you all while I was working on this book. Your understanding and support mean very much to me. And now that I'm done, bring on the beer!

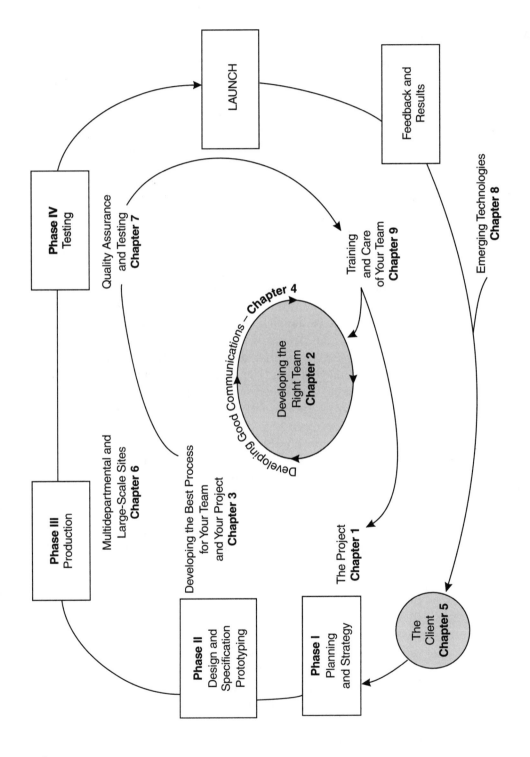

LAUNCH

Feedback and Results

Phase IV
Testing

Quality Assurance and Testing
Chapter 7

Training and Care of Your Team
Chapter 9

Emerging Technologies
Chapter 8

Developing Good Communications – **Chapter 4**

Developing the Right Team
Chapter 2

Multidepartmental and Large-Scale Sites
Chapter 6

Developing the Best Process for Your Team and Your Project
Chapter 3

Phase III
Production

The Project
Chapter 1

Phase II
Design and Specification Prototyping

Phase I
Planning and Strategy

The Client
Chapter 5

COLLABORATIVE WEB DEVELOPMENT

CHAPTER 1

The Project

You're about to take on a Web project. Where do you begin? It's not software development and it's not print production—it's the Web, a whole new medium. Therefore, a new approach is necessary.

I'm not saying that you, the seasoned project manager, can't borrow from the excellent methods you've learned doing software development or advertising production. In fact, you will see methodologies that I've borrowed from this field throughout this book. But the Web is different; development times are much, much faster, and the teams change on a project-by-project basis. Also, you might not be calling all the shots: You might be working with marketers and strategists as the Web becomes the advertising space of the future.

As I say in the preface, this book is about the new Web team, and it is dedicated to the project manager or producer who ultimately has to get the project built on time and on budget. This first chapter is on the project itself—getting your arms around it so that you can go forward confidently.

You will see boxes like the one at the top of the next page at the beginning of chapters. These boxes are designed to help you get the most out of the book by telling you where to look within the chapter if you have to get a task done immediately.

> IF YOU NEED . . .
>
> ◆ To create a budget, go to the section called "The Budget."
>
> ◆ To put a team together quickly, go to the section called "Finding the People You Need."
>
> ◆ A quick to-do list of initial project tasks, go to the "To-Do List."

Key Differences among Web, Advertising, and Software Project Management

I stumbled into Web project management from the software field, though not as a software project manager but as a technical writer. Right away I saw some important similarities between software project management and program management. I also saw some important differences, both in process (how the project was defined, planned, and implemented) and in perception (how both the team and the client understood the project's complexity). In order to manage a Web project, I had to be able to cull the most appropriate processes from both the software and the advertising fields, and I had to be able to explain what was different about Web project management to my clients and my account team. (Not that anyone really listens—usually it takes at least one project going seriously over budget to get anyone to listen to you, but we'll cover that later in the book).

Need a refresher course in basic project management? I recommend Weiss and Wysocki's book.[1]

Depending on your background (software, advertising, or internal corporate project management), you will see significant similarities between it and Web projects. However, knowledge of the differences will enable you to appropriately assess the risks of the project. I've noticed that producers who have worked in advertising have a hard time understanding the sheer cost of a Web project. As well, the technical complexity and in-depth requirements-gathering phase is something those advertising producers are not used to—on the technical side. For the software project manager, this is perfectly obvious; however, most software project managers who enter the Web project management field are surprised to find their teams completely inexperienced in such requirements gathering. They are surprised that the clients do not see the Web project as a software development project and do not understand the complexity and therefore the resources and time necessary to get the site done. Believe it or not, the project manager who comes from the traditional project management

---

1. Joseph Weiss and Robert Wysocki, *5-Phase Management: A Practical Planning and Implementation Guide.* Reading, MA: Addison-Wesley, 1992.

background and who understands the phases of project management will most likely be successful, because he or she will not bring preconceived ideas about software or advertising and will manage the project with the tools of project management: the budget, the schedule, the resources, and the project plan.

Table 1.1 outlines the similarities and differences in Web project management and software, advertising, and what I'll call traditional project management. Let's take a look at each of these characteristics next.

TABLE 1.1   Web Project Characteristics

Web projects	Software projects	Advertising projects	Traditional projects
Project managers are not always client managers.	Different	Similar	Different
Development schedules are dramatically short.	Can be similar; called "death march" projects	Similar, though manageable since there is no technical component	Similar
New, often beta, technologies are used, often without technical support.	Different	N/A	N/A
Scope changes occur during the implementation phase.	Similar, though not without dramatic change in cost and time	Different	Similar
A pricing model for Web projects does not exist.	Similar	Different	Different
Standards for Web production do not exist.	Different	Different	Similar
Team roles are less specialized.	Different	Different	Different
Clients are often unwilling to bear the costs of Web development, especially during the planning phase.	Different	Different	Different
The project manager's responsibilities are very broad.	Different	Similar	Different

1. *Project managers are not always client managers.* On a Web project, you might not be the person responsible for managing the client's expectations. This is especially true if you work in an agency where you have an account manager.

2. *Development schedules are dramatically short.* Most Web projects are "death-march" projects—projects with seemingly impossible develoment schedules.[2] The reason is that the Web is a relatively new development phenomenon, so people on both sides (client and developer) underestimate the time and resources needed to complete a Web project.

3. *New, often beta, technologies are used, often without technical support.* In the first commerce site I worked on, our commerce vendor had to work along with us to write patches for software bugs we unearthed while building the site. New software packages are used while they are in beta, usually because they are available and because they offer "new" and "cool" features that client and Web developer alike want to use.

4. *Scope changes occur during the implementation phase.* This is something that occurs on most Web projects and often in software projects, but this doesn't tend to happen in advertising because it is very expensive to change a print ad once it's gone to press. However, clients and Web project managers need to understand that scope changes during implementation phase are very expensive and must be tracked and managed.

5. *A pricing model for Web projects does not exist.* In the advertising world, costs are fairly modularized and budgets tend to be somewhat easy to create, once the campaign has gone through the creative phase. However, it's very difficult to cost out a Web project. There aren't ranges for "an e-commerce site" or "a series of advertising interstitials"; however, this is what clients tend to want.

6. *Standards for Web production do not exist.* In the advertising, manufacturing, and software development worlds, there are standards to follow that ensure quality. Standards, or best practices, can help a Web company gain efficiency and therefore realize some profitability. This makes getting the Web project off the ground a difficult task. One of the objectives of this book is to give you some standards to implement and a process to follow.

7. *Team roles are less specialized.* On a Web project, a server-side developer may also be an HTML programmer, and a producer may also be an information architect. Roles are less specialized, often because a Web project might call for someone who can create content in Flash, Real

---

2. See Edward Yourdon, *Death March: The Complete Software Developer's Guide to Surviving "Mission Impossible" Projects.* Upper Saddle River, NJ: Prentice-Hall, 1997.

Audio, and HTML. There isn't always enough work to have specialists in each category.

8. *Clients are often unwilling to bear the costs of Web development, especially during the planning phase.* In my experience, getting the client to buy into our planning and design and specification phases is hard. Clients want to see creative concepts as soon as possible and do not want to hear that a production budget is an impossible thing to give them until after they have signed off on a design and specification document.

9. *The project manager's responsibilities are very broad.* On a Web project, a project manager or producer might be responsible for anything from developing the schedule and budget to managing assets to acquiring talent and negotiating contracts. Depending on the kind of Web site, the project manager's or producer's role will be broad. For this reason, I prefer to t managers producers.

Need?

sk me what kind of skills are necessary to produce Web proj-
ver is complex, because it really depends on the individual
A person with no technical skills can produce a Web project
has experience as a project manager, understands the Web
are built, knows what questions to ask, and has a technical
m he or she can communicate effectively. In putting together
ion for a producer/project manager, I came up with a list of
quire in project managers:

or film project management experience
understanding of scheduling, budgeting, and resource

written and verbal communication skills
lead effective meetings
ented

se of humor
stay calm during disasters
nent or production experience in Web, multimedia,
or film

some project managers could lead a Web project without
a production or development team, these people are rare. I
k for people who have worked in multimedia or the Web as
a production or development person and then made the move to project

management. I also require that people know the core project management skills and have been trained in producing a work breakdown structure and a project plan. I recommend the American Management Association for training.

Now that you understand the difference between Web project management and other forms of project management, read on to find out how to begin a Web project.

Define Your Project

It sounds very simple, but your Web project's success really depends on your ability to define your project accurately. Defining a project means that you understand and communicate (on paper) the project's mission, objectives, risks, and requirements. A project can be defined quickly and easily by following the steps in this section before you present your ideas to your boss, your client, or your prospective team.

Write a Project Mission Statement

The first step in defining your project is to write a project mission statement. This will help you focus on the following three tasks:

- Identify the project's objectives.
- Identify your users.
- Determine the scope of the project.

A mission statement describes the solution to the problem that your Web site project is going to solve. It answers three questions:

- What are we going to do?
- For whom are we doing it?
- How do we go about it?

For example, Company X is creating an intranet and has this problem statement:

Company X needs to improve internal communication across its 10 locations. Global e-mail is not working and employees feel disconnected from the corporate headquarters.

Company X might have this mission statement for that intranet:

Our mission is to improve communication for our employees by providing a Web site that has the latest corporate and industry information and that is updated frequently. Additionally, subsidiary companies may participate in sharing information by maintaining their own individual Web pages.

Once you have a mission statement, you will work with your client to answer the three defining questions.

Identify Objectives

What are objectives? Objectives are results. They are specific, and most important, they are attainable. In his excellent book *Fundamentals of Project Management,* James Lewis[3] says that objectives must be SMART, meaning that they are

- ◆ Specific
- ◆ Measurable
- ◆ Attainable
- ◆ Realistic
- ◆ Time-limited

Of these five characteristics of objectives, the measurable and attainable characteristics are the hardest to determine. If an objective of a Web site is to increase brand awareness, how do you measure that? Two questions help you monitor progress of objectives:

1. What is the desired outcome?
2. How will you know when you achieve it? Answering this last question for all your project objectives, especially nonquantifiable ones like our example, is very important. This answer will help you establish criteria for objectives that cannot be quantified.

Who Sets the Objectives?

Clear objectives are probably the most important factor in the success of a Web project. Objectives help your creative team to design the best graphics for the site, they help the programmers understand how the Web site might grow, and they tell the writers what tone or information is critical to the site.

---

3. James Lewis, *Fundamentals of Project Management: A WorkSmart Guide.* New York: American Management Association, 1995, p. 33.

Who decides your site's objectives or goals depends on many things, but generally the person or persons who fund the project are the people, called stakeholders, who, directly or indirectly, set the objectives of the project. In the early days of Web development, when small software consulting companies were the primary providers of Web sites, this was definitely true. Now, however, the Web team has evolved to incorporate strategic marketers who may not be the primary stakeholders. These team members should play a very large part in helping the stakeholder develop the Web site's objectives.

Objectives need to be written down in order to be effective. The document that states the objectives is called many things: the goals document, the strategic brief, the objectives document. It doesn't matter what it's called. What matters is that it defines what you hope to achieve by creating the Web site. A sample objectives document can be found in the /templates/chapter1/ folder on the CD-ROM that accompanies this book.

Web Site Objectives

What are some common Web site objectives? As the Web evolves from a communications tool to an integrated business system, the objectives for having a Web site continue to evolve. I've worked on Web sites with the following objectives: sell products, ship goods, replenish inventory, increase brand awareness, improve corporate communications, and improve brand perception.

Identify Your Targeted Users

The kinds of content that you will create for the Web site will be determined by the users whom you want to visit the site. Though this makes common and business sense, often Web designers and developers overlook the degree of research that is required to identify users accurately. Clients often want to use site traffic as a measure of a Web site's success. However, site traffic is misleading. The only way to truly measure a site's success is to determine whether your objectives have been met. If your objective was to increase your Web sales through a new and improved ordering process, then you would look at sales figures before and after your new ordering process was implemented. If you did not increase orders, yet your site traffic increased, you would attribute the increased traffic not to the simplified ordering process but to a good advertising campaign (if you initiated one), a particular search engine, or pure luck.

How do you go about learning what your targeted users want to see on your Web site? What will make them purchase your product or use your service? The only real way is to ask them. In the next two sections, I discuss ways to reach your targeted audience.

Market Research

If you have worked for an advertising or public relations firm, you know how important market research is to the success of your campaign. Market research is equally important if you are going to create a Web site that sells products, services, or ideas. If you are looking for any kind of return on your investment (ROI) from your Web site, then it is critical that you understand exactly who your audience is and what it wants, so that you can provide it.

Many firms provide this kind of service to companies. If you are a Web designer working as a freelance consultant, you should think about developing partnerships with research companies that specialize in the new media so that you can provide this service to your clients. If you are building a Web site for your company, build market research into your budget if your company does not have a marketing department. If it does have a marketing department, then make sure the personnel understand how your audience interacts with the Web.

Focus Groups

If you can't afford the services of a market research company, then consider conducting a focus group. A focus group is a group of people who represent your target user or audience. Focus groups are used to get feedback on proposed ideas for your Web site or to understand how your target audience thinks. When I was putting together a Web presentation for a group of two hundred high school girls, I thought I understood what they wanted to know. After all, I was once a high school girl. I put together all my ideas and perceptions, and then I conducted a focus group. I couldn't have been more wrong about what they were looking for on the Web. Believing that you understand the target audience without any supporting data won't work most of the time. If you are going to be spending money on a Web effort, then spend some money up front and do the right level of research.

Understanding Intranet Audiences

If you are developing an intranet site, you have access to your audience; but you will find that each department or group within your audience has specific needs and desires that are related to their job functions. With such

◆ Meeting and Learning from Your Audience

It's easy to get off track and forget your over-all project objectives when you begin to meet with members of your intranet audience. Generally, when people find out what you're doing, they have lots of ideas and suggestions, many of which are excellent. However, you probably have time and budget constraints; so be sure to write down all the ideas and priori-tize them. To maintain a good relationship with your audience, make sure you can com-municate the project's objective and state that suggestions will be met either during the first phase or in later phases of your project. It's important not to alienate this audience. After all, the success of an intranet is largely due to whether the audience uses it.

varying needs, it's easier to focus your first planning effort for your in-tranet on the areas that affect every department or group.

The best strategy for understanding your intranet audience is to take the time to meet with each group or a representative of each group. After all your interviews, you will begin to see the connections among the groups and the kinds of content that will reach the widest audience. That's where you will start your planning process.

Determine the Scope

Many things can determine the scope of a project. Also, unless you are very careful, the scope of a project can change quickly, and, before you know it, your project is over budget and late.

The biggest mistake a Web project manager or producer can make is not nailing down the scope of the project in the beginning, with the proper supporting documentation and client approval. In order to nail down the scope, you must first understand the project completely. The next two sections will help you understand the process of understanding scope.

Factors that Contribute to Scope

The old project management adage says that scope is directly related to time and cost. This means that there is a relationship between scope, time, and cost—if one changes, it affects the other two. Nothing is more impor-tant to remember when you commit to a Web project. If you have a limited amount of time and a limited amount of money to spend, then, necessar-ily, the scope of your Web project should be limited to what you can ac-complish within the allotted time and budget. Specifically, it should be something you can do easily within the fixed time frame and budget so that you can make a decent profit if you are paying people by the hour to do the work.

This simple fact is often misinterpreted during a Web project. Why? For one thing, a Web site is perceived as being easily changeable. HTML doesn't need to be compiled and can be edited easily. Because the medium is open and accessible, clients may believe that changes are "not a big deal." Often, project managers are caught between a client who wants changes that seem easy and programmers who insist that changes are not as simple as they seem. Before you know it, you have committed to a change, and you have incurred extra costs associated with that change. What's more, if you didn't tell your client about the change, he or she might refuse to pay for it.

There are several issues here. Communication is by far the biggest. In chapters 4 and 5, I discuss how to communicate with your client and your team. Also, the project manager must fully understand the process involved in building a Web project. What I'm implying is that a Web site project manager must be someone who not only is skilled in project management, but also who has been part of a development team.

Determining Key Elements

Enough of the gloomy prophecy I put forth in the previous section. My objective is to help you avoid such costly mistakes. This section will help you figure out quickly those key elements that make up the scope of your project.

Your objectives document will help you focus on determining key elements of your Web site, as will the amount of money your client wants to spend and the date the Web site needs to be published, or "go live" as most developers say. Money is obviously an important factor in choosing how to implement an element. For example, if one of your site's objectives is to collect data from users and store it for later use, there are several ways to accomplish the task. Each possible way to accomplish the task has a different price tag attached to it. You could create a simple HTML form that uses a standard form handler to save the data into a flat text file. Then someone could import the data manually from the file into a database program and process it there. That would be a low-cost implementation. Or, you could create a Shockwave game that dynamically asked questions of the user. The game could have a hook coded into it that talks to a database and automatically stores the data in the appropriate database tables. That would be a relatively larger cost implementation, but it would meet the goal if the goal were only to collect data. If there was a contingency that the method of collecting data had to be entertaining, then the Shockwave game would be the best way to implement the element because it would be more in line with the project's goals.

The most effective way of breaking down the key elements is to outline the features that the Web site must have in order to satisfy the objectives. To illustrate this, let's create a fictional intranet project. Let's take the mission statement for the intranet in the previous section. In case you don't remember, here it is again:

> Our mission is to improve communication for our employees by providing a Web site that has the latest corporate and industry information and that is updated frequently. Additionally, subsidiary companies may participate in sharing information by maintaining their own individual Web pages.

From this mission statement, we have come up with the following objectives:

♦ Publish industry information weekly
♦ Provide access to human resource information and employee handbooks
♦ Provide a message from the president of the company
♦ Provide links to subsidiary company Web sites

Starting from these four objectives, you will need to investigate the effort necessary to satisfy the objectives. In traditional project management, this process is called developing the work breakdown structure (WBS). Figure 1.1 shows a breakdown of the objectives into tasks and subtasks that help you start understanding the scope of the project.

We have been looking at key elements from a "feature" standpoint, meaning that we are looking at the areas of functionality for the site. When determining the key elements of a Web site, you also have to include nonfeature aspects of the site, such as design, information architecture, copywriting, and quality assurance. Each of these features will have some aspect of these global Web site development processes. Hence, the key elements of this Web site include the objectives, plus the following:

♦ Site design
♦ Navigation architecture
♦ Copywriting
♦ Quality assurance testing

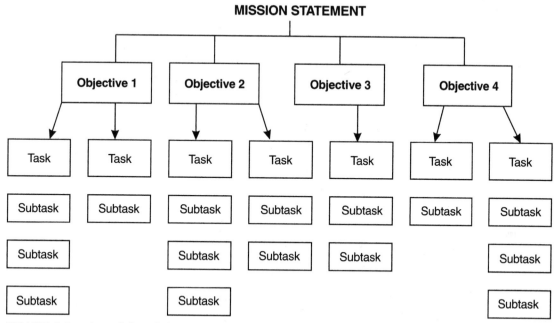

FIGURE 1.1   A work breakdown structure helps determine the project's scope.

In the next section, you will learn how to break down these elements further into information that will help you decide how to implement the features of your Web site.

Breaking Down Components

Be sure to track how many hours it takes you and your team to go through this process. Add this cost as a line item into the estimate you prepare.

Now that you have identified the key elements of your Web site, you are ready to investigate the time, effort, and cost associated with each element. You will be breaking down each element into tasks, analyzing the tasks and the time it will take to complete them and making some decisions about how to implement the features so that you stay within a budget and on schedule.

You might be asking yourself, How would I know what tasks each objective will require? You won't. The people who will be doing the work must help in this process.

On a large sheet of flip chart paper, begin your work breakdown structure as seen in Figure 1.1. Table 1.1 shows how the objectives might get broken down into tasks and subtasks. This list isn't meant to be taken literally; it's just to show you how you would go about breaking up the

TABLE 1.1 Key Elements of a Web Site in a WBS

	Key Elements						
	Design look and feel.	**Establish navigation.**	**Publish industry information.**	**Provide access to HR information.**	**Message from the president.**	**Add links to subsidiary Web sites.**	**Develop test plan.**
Task	Obtain site architecture.	Collect content list.	List industry sources.	Obtain employee handbook.	Ask company president to write a message.	Obtain list of Web sites.	Obtain functional specification.
Task	Draw thumbnails.	Draft site architecture.	Decide on industry sources.	Convert handbook to HTML.	Edit copy.	Add sites.	Write test plan.
Task	Get approvals on thumbnails.	Get approval on site architecture.	Write copy.	Design page.	Code page.		
Task	Design digital composites.		Design page.				

objectives into tasks. The next step is to estimate the time and duration it will take to complete each task.

The first two elements, graphic design and navigation, are the hardest to cost out. Why? It's very hard to put a dollar amount on how long it will take someone to come up with an idea and create visual representations of that idea. So how do you break down seemingly amorphous elements?

I've found that the best way to approach this part of the project is to agree with your client on a fixed amount of time, along with a price, for the design phase. During this time, visual designers, information designers, and application developers can create composites and models for the client to approve. Getting the client to agree to this phase isn't always easy; but in the long run, it will definitely reduce the risk of the project and often the cost as well. I talk more about this in chapter 3, "Planning and Process Development."

For the more tangible aspects of your Web project, such as "a method for collecting timesheet information via the intranet," breaking down the element into chunks of information is easier, but still requires a "design" phase of its own. The first thing you need is a brainstorming phase with your team to figure out the viable options for achieving this goal and the risks associated with each option. Then, you will work with the team members who are most qualified to determine the strategy for designing and implementing the feature to develop a list of steps, or tasks. Each of these tasks will have an associated time and cost and will become a line item in your budget. I discuss team responsibilities in chapter 2, "The Project Team," and chapter 3, "Planning and Process Development."

Writing the Scope Document

The scope document is the culmination of your effort to define the project. The work breakdown structure that you created is essentially the scope of your project. Your next task is to write up what your WBS illustrates. In your scope document, you reiterate the mission and objectives of your Web project along with the features that you will build to meet the project goal. Your scope document should be easy to follow and must include a sign-off page. The sign-off page is for you and your client to put in writing your agreement on the features of the site.

Some Web producers include visual sketches of the interface, or schematics, along with data models for more sophisticated Web applications, hardware and software specifications, and anything else that contributes to the development of the site. Others find that a simple write-up of the site's functional features is enough to determine the scope. My recommendation is that you can never have enough documentation. It helps eliminate confusion and scope creep; and it helps not only your client but also your team in keeping crystal clear the site's objectives and how you plan to meet those objectives.

The Budget

Your budget is your fully defined project with a price tag. The better you become at defining your project's scope, the more accurate your budgets will be. Creating a perfect budget is the Web project manager's lifetime project. It's almost impossible to do it; but each time you create a budget, you will get better at it. I don't know any project manager who has created the perfect budget. However, if you know when to adjust your budget appropriately and identify hidden costs that are often overlooked, you will be able to use your budget to help you effectively manage your team and your client, and, most important, you will make money doing it.

Budget Categories

Your budget categories come directly from your scope document and WBS. Every task that you outlined in your WBS becomes a line item in your budget, as well as your project plan (you will learn more about the project plan in chapter 3). If you follow this process, you will clearly see requests from the client that result in tasks that aren't in your scope document, and therefore not in your budget. If you perform the task, you put your project at risk of being over budget. It's a perfect time to alert the client that the task was not part of the original scope, and therefore you will need to negotiate for a change in scope and budget.

I've included some sample budgets in the /templates/chapter1/ folder on the CD-ROM.

Assumptions for Budgeting

Your budget is also a set of assumptions about things that are to be delivered not only by you to the client, but also from the client to you. Assumptions about the budget should be written up either as part of the scope document or in an appendix to the budget. The following are possible assumptions about the budget:

♦ All content provided by the client should be delivered in Microsoft Word.
♦ The client has 48 hours to approve design.

- The Web team will present two design concepts.
- Media buying is not part of the strategic plan.

Like the scope document, this assumptions document is very important because it helps you keep track of incidents that might cause your project to go over budget or past your delivery date. It's a good idea to make this document, along with your scope document, part of your contract with your client.

Hidden Costs

Every time you meet informally about your project or pick up the phone to discuss something with your client, you are incurring a cost. The costs may be small, but they add up. It's important that you include a cushion in your budget for these kinds of untraceable and unexpected costs. Some of the most widely forgotten costs are the following:

- Meetings with the full team
- Phone calls
- Photo or art research
- The WBS and scope document
- E-mail and administration
- Setting up the review site
- Setting up a development site (hosting)

It's a fairly common practice to include a 10 percent to 15 percent cushion for project management in a budget. I usually include two hours per week per team member for administration and other costs, such as meetings and phone calls.

Tools

Every project manager has his or her own set of preferred tools. I have several tools I just can't live without:

- *E-mail with integrated task management*   I use Microsoft Outlook because I can assign tasks to people and sort those tasks by project. Outlook is integrated with my calendar, so I can switch back and forth easily between my calendar and my task list.
- *Microsoft Excel*   I use Excel to keep track of my budget.

♦ *Microsoft Project*   This program is my best friend. I use it to keep
track of the project time line and to measure estimated task durations
against the actual task durations. It also gives me a project budget
for tasks, but I create a higher level budget in Excel that includes the
cost of sales and other costs that Project doesn't track easily.

References

It's great to read about what it takes to build a reasonable budget, but it's
hard to write one, especially starting from scratch. To help you get a jump-
start, I'm including several sample budgets for different kinds of Web projects. I've used the standard rate sheet that is on the CD-ROM, in the
/templates/chapter1/ folder; but you can use your own rates. I'm also including a spreadsheet of some ballpark prices for certain kinds of Web
sites. Remember that these are ballpark figures. You may find that prices
are lower or higher, depending on where you live.

Ballpark Pricing

One of the most difficult things a Web project manager faces is the justification of the project's costs. As discussed in the preface, managing a Web
project is not like developing software. It doesn't have the same barriers to
entry. Therefore in many people's minds, it's easy to develop a site for the
Web because most people can learn HTML from reading a book. However,
the real costs of Web development are high. How high? That is the question the Web project manager has to answer. While it's impossible to
say exactly what the cost will be, you can provide ballpark estimates to
your client or stakeholder. Once you have completed your design phase,
you should be able to provide concrete estimates of the costs to produce
your site.

To get a sense for what people are charging for Web sites, check out the
NetMarketing's Web Price Index at *http://www.netb2b.com/wpi/index.html*.
The Web Price Index (see Figure 1.2) gives ballpark prices for small,
medium, and large Web sites with various features. Keep in mind that
costs should be adjusted upward if you are in New York City, Silicon
Valley, the San Francisco Bay Area, Chicago, Seattle, or other major ur-
ban areas.

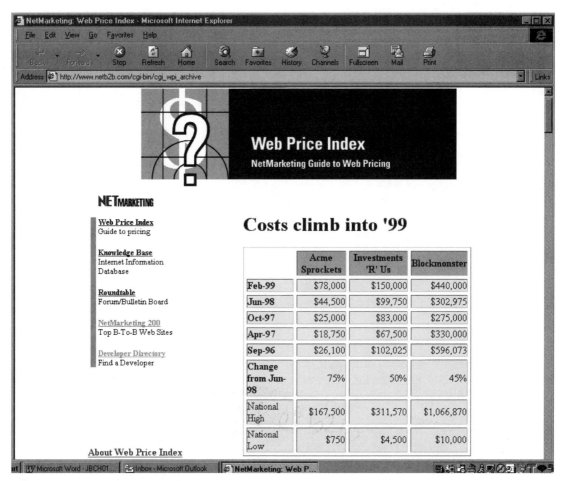

FIGURE 1.2   The Web Price Index.

More Preliminary Planning Issues

While you are scoping and budgeting for the project, you need to be thinking about two things: your team and your infrastructure.

Your infrastructure is the supporting environment for your project. It consists of your communications system (e-mail), your tools (software, hardware), and any other tangibles or intangibles that are important for providing an environment in which to build your Web site. Some things you can do are listed on the next page.

◆ Using the Subject Line to Communicate Effectively

One of the best conventions I've seen for communicating about a project is the use of the standardized e-mail subject line. I owe this convention to Richard Hoefer, an information architect with whom I worked on a Web project with an extremely tight delivery schedule. All the team members received an average of 25 e-mail messages per day. To make sure we prioritized mail about this project, Richard developed a convention for the subject line that looked like the one in the next column.

PROJECT NAME/ Team. Subject of the e-mail. Date.

Some of us used the filtering feature of our e-mail systems so we could have all mail that pertained to this project automatically sifted into the e-mail folder for that project. Team members who didn't filter mail could easily sort their inboxes and look for mail about this project.

- ◆ Set up an e-mail alias for your project.
- ◆ Develop an e-mail convention for your subject line, so that all team members (see sidebar) can easily recognize e-mail pertaining to your project.
- ◆ Make sure you have all the documents you need for client sign-off. These could be legal contracts, non-disclosure agreements (NDAs), or your own scope document.

If you are developing a Web site for a client, you will also be thinking about where the Web site will live and making some preliminary inquiries into your client's existing information systems (IS) organization, if the site will live at your client's place of business. To help you assess your client's Internet infrastructure, I've included a sample questionnaire, a "needs analysis," that you can give to your client. You can find the questionnaire on the CD-ROM, in the /templates/chapter1/ folder.

Finding the People You Need

If you have a large organization and you are responsible for creating your Internet or intranet site, you will probably be looking for people internally to help you develop the site's content. You might be discussing this project with your IS manager or systems administrator. At this point, you don't know the exact skills you require, but it's a good idea to start thinking about where you will look to find the people you need.

For most Web projects, the two most important people on your team will be the creative lead and the technical lead. The creative lead will develop the visual design of the site. The technical lead will be responsible for setting up your site's network infrastructure and hiring the right people to build the Web site.

There are several ways to find qualified people to help build your Web site. As you flesh out your site and its requirements as you write your scope document, you will be able to hone your search to those with the specific skills and experience you need. Finding the people you need is covered more thoroughly in chapter 2, "The Project Team."

Summary

In this chapter, you learned the key differences between Web project management and other kinds of project management. You were able to see how critical project management tasks like scope development and budgeting are approached, and you learned about skills you might need in order to take on a Web project. Now, plug the of tasks listed below into your calendar. In the next chapter, you'll learn about the Web team and the kinds of resources you are likely to need.

TO-DO LIST

- ♦ Write your objectives document with your team.
- ♦ Do a WBS with your team.
- ♦ Develop a scope document.
- ♦ Get a written sign-off on the scope document.
- ♦ Create a budget for your design phase.
- ♦ Identify existing human resources.

INTERVIEW Getting Your Arms around the Project

Stefan Fielding-Isaacs, CEO
Art and Science W3 Development, Ltd.

Stefan would like to have been born at the height of the Renaissance. Instead, he was born near the home of golf, St. Andrews, Scotland (prophetic given his abiding interest in the sport) in 1961 and educated in England and Canada, followed by university in the United States (Reed College).

Although San Francisco has become his home, he remains committed to the belief that the Web will allow one to work virtually anywhere. His romanticism sees him living on the Left Bank in Paris and studying the Parisians from the comfort of a seat at Les Deux Magots. Unfortunately, a successful Web business has intervened for the last few years.

His heroes are Admiral Nelson, Ben Hogan, and Winnie the Pooh. He and his cat still plan to move to Paris someday soon.

How do you set the goals or objectives for Web sites?

We go through the goal-setting process in several contexts. First, we do it in-house. We give some consideration to what we think the user of the Web site will want (in look and feel and navigation) and prioritize what we think the most important information in the site is. Sometimes this may be quite different from what the client thinks—often because they have never really prioritized it themselves or because organizational impediments prevent corporate-level prioritization (the client's divisions fighting amongst themselves).

Second, we request that the client come up with a set of goals for the Web site. Short-term, mid-term, and long-term (that's 3 mo, 6 mo, and 1 yr in Web terms). I'll often ask the primary decision maker or CEO how he or she would like to think of the site six months from now. It's a mental exercise. I ask him or her to imagine that the site is successful and is being evaluated six months in the future. What will it have accomplished for the company? It's a really worthwhile exercise because a lot of the noise and glitz drops away. In this sort of evaluation, results are what count and one quickly gets to the core of what the user needs.

Finally, we sit down with the client and hash out any differences between our approaches. Generally, we find that we can integrate our priorities (the need to make the navigation really shine, for instance) with their priorities (the need to build a dedicated audience, say) pretty easily.

How do you determine the scope of a Web project?

Scope determination is a funny thing. Scope as envisioned by us is rarely the same as that envisioned by the client. It used to be the case in the early days (1993–1994) that our vision always exceeded that of the client. Unfortunately, so did the budget many times. So we ended up trimming back the vision radically in some cases. More recently, client visions seem to exceed the available budget. Clients will come to us with grandiose visions of Flash-enabled, commerce-enabled sites and expect to pay $30,000 for a seventy-page site. Way out of line with the actual cost, and we then have to educate them about quality issues, support issues, maintenance, upgradeability, and so on.

Anyway, back to the question of determining scope. Budget is a major factor, as is the goal setting. The first task is to accomplish the goals agreed upon with the client. If in our estimation, we cannot accomplish the minimum goals within the budget of the client, we recommend that the client go elsewhere. I really believe that one is a fool trying to make a silk purse out of a sow's ear. It just ends up hurting both parties to engage in the process when there isn't a realistic path to a successful outcome.

If we can accomplish the goals within the budget, we come up with a statement of work that very clearly outlines the technology to be used in the site, the architecture of the site (sometimes going as far as a page count), and a set of specifications for the content of the site. How the audio, video, and text must be delivered. This is accompanied by a really detailed project plan (MS Project 98) that calls out the milestones for deliveries from the client and from us and outlines all the tasks necessary to complete the project. It pretty much details where every dollar of the client's money will be spent on the project.

Together with the scope of work document, it provides a really concrete basis for determining a project's scope.

How do you keep a project from getting out of scope?

That's a good question. Generally, it's an education process. We find ourselves needing to educate the project manager, the account executive (now that we are using one), and the client about scope issues. We're up front at the very start about "scope creep" being a primary concern to us. We discuss what it is, how it occurs, and how we deal with it in a professional manner. We have these meetings internally and externally with the client.

There are a couple of organic elements that can help prevent or reduce scope creep, and we harp on them constantly. They are schedule and budget. Often, we are working on a schedule, trying to accomplish milestones and get a product out the door by a certain date. We maintain and have been proved right lots of times that our project planning is very good. It's accurate and comprehensive; and we can demonstrate how adding functionality or content will frequently delay or otherwise impact the project schedule, thus threatening our making milestones or other deadlines. These delays, in turn, have financial consequences for the project. They can push the project over budget, and that is something we staunchly refuse to do.

I think concern for budget, and a quality job within budget, are pretty rare in our industry. So when clients find that we work really hard at educating them about project impacts and we are very concerned about staying within budget (as opposed to agreeing to the change and simply billing them an additional 10 percent), they respond pretty positively.

The big issue has always been educating our side of the team to remain steadfast in the face of pressure from the client to compromise on scope issues. We've gone so far as to include a clause in our standard contract that says that only officers of the company have the right to alter the scope of the contract, and then only with a signed authorization (a paper trail). We've had our share of poor project managers who made verbal promises to the clients, were fired, and then we had to meet the commitments they made. We learned pretty quickly that scope issues have to be watched really vigilantly. We also document all correspondence (verbal or written) with the client and will frequently post aide-mémoirs of conversations or agreement points on our extranet site so that we have a paper trail.

I guess I would say, education, education, and education when asked about how to solve scope creep. Some of my project managers think I'm draconian in my attitude, but then, they haven't been through what I've been through with clients trying to add a ton of features at no cost.

CHAPTER 2

The Project Team

IF YOU NEED . . .

♦ To learn about how Web teams evolve, go to the "Evolution of the Web Team" section.

♦ To see what Web teams look like today, go to the section called "Common Team Compositions."

♦ To find out which skills your team will need to produce different kinds of Web projects, go to the "Putting Together the Right Team" section.

♦ To learn about what you can do as a project manager to keep your team communicating with each other, go to the section called "Managing the Team."

It's certainly not like the old days when I was the project manager, interface designer, writer, and HTML coder. I worked with two people, a network engineer and a production artist. The best part of that team was that as long as we produced a nice-looking, easy-to-use Web site within the budget, our client was happy. And we made money.

The New Web Team

Times have changed. For one thing, businesses are no longer putting together Web sites because everyone else is. The Web is finally becoming a space for doing real business on-line, appealing to and communicating with consumers and entertaining users. The Web has grown up, and therefore today's Web teams must be able to perform a myriad of business functions, from business consulting and strategizing to setting up a secure network for financial transactions.

Evolution of the Web Team

Web teams began with Webmasters, people who did everything from coding the page to maintaining the Web server. Web development efforts were often grassroots efforts within companies, with a nondedicated staff comprised of anyone who could code HTML. Companies did not acknowledge the Web as a viable place for doing business, so people who worked on the Web site came from different departments all over the company and, if budgets permitted, from independent service vendors like design shops or application development shops.

As the popularity of the Web increased, companies began to recognize the need for a more formal, dedicated Web team. Service companies like advertising agencies, software development companies, and start-up interactive shops (multimedia companies turned Web companies) began to put together Web teams. Each company had its own team model; but at the core were a project manager, a graphic designer, and an HTML programmer. Chances were that these three roles would be consolidated in one individual. In the corporate world, marketing managers and information technology (IT) managers competed for control of the Web site, with marketing managers controlling content and IT managers controlling programming. This bipolar model does not foster alignment of the Web site with the business objectives of the company. Without clear objectives from executive management, these Web sites do little to extend real business objectives on-line.

The Web team is evolving because business leaders are beginning to understand that the Web is transforming the way business is done. Leaders are realizing the need to bring this medium into the overall, long-term business plan and treat it as they would any other significant component of their business.

Be it on the service side or the client side, the new Web team has a strong strategic component, strong content management and production

♦ **Types of Web Teams**

"Service-side" Web teams are Web teams hired by a company to develop a Web site. "Client-side" Web teams are part of the com-pany that is putting together the Web site. It's entirely possible that you will put together Web teams comprised of both these sub-teams.

processes, and an IT component that can handle doing business on-line. If you are in charge of your Web development effort, then this chapter will help you understand how to put together a team for a specific project.

Roles and Responsibilities

What are the skills your team must have? What are the roles of the team and how do team members interact? Team composition varies depending on the scope, audience, and level of complexity of your Web project. However, there are some key roles on virtually every project. This section focuses on the roles and responsibilities of the core team and discusses different compositions of teams based on certain types of Web projects.

Core (C), Extended (E), and Special (S) Team Members

No matter what kind of Web site you are producing, there are some core responsibilities and roles. For other kinds of sites, generally larger and more complex sites, there are extended team members. Extended team members are people whose skills might not always be necessary or who might have cross-functional roles. An example of this might be a network engineer who is also a security expert. Special team people are brought in to do work that is not part of your core or extended team but may become so. For example, in an interactive agency, there are team members who are specialists in audio engineering, security, or database architecture. However, the special members of this Web team might be core or extended members of yours, depending on what kinds of sites your company tends to produce.

> *Project manager/producer (C)*   The project manager/producer is responsible for scoping the work, developing the project plan, scheduling, allocating resources, budgeting, and managing the team. The project manager deals with all the political and business issues, including contracts, licensing, and other administrative issues. In the absence of an account manager, the project manager or producer

handles client management. The project manager interacts with all members of the team.

Account manager (E)   Part of the extended team, the account manager is generally present in agencies or companies who follow the agency model. Generally, this means that the company is responsible for a client's entire on-line business plan, which may consist of several projects. Usually, these kinds of engagements are time-based, and a Web company is held on retainer. The account manager is responsible for selling in different projects and providing the project team with the necessary consumer insight and information. The account manager generally interacts with the client, the project manager, and the creative lead.

Technical lead (C)   A technical lead oversees the project from a technical point of view. The technical lead assists the project manager in ensuring that the technical strategy is sound, manages the programmers, and chooses specialized team members such as security experts, database programmers, and other systems integrators. The technical lead prepares technical briefs and communicates with the project manager, technical team members, and members of the client's technical team.

Programmer (E)   A programmer develops applications for the Web project. These applications could be simple server-side scripts to database applications to java applets to shockwave applets. The skills a programmer needs, depending on the kind of programming he or she is doing, could be any of the following: an understanding of object-oriented programming, Java, JavaScript, Lingo, Visual Basic, VBScript, SQL, C/C++. A technical lead should directly manage the programmers on a Web project.

Network engineer (E)   A network engineer is responsible for setting up and configuring a Web server. Often, a network engineer is also a database administrator or security expert. A network engineer is also responsible for registering domain names and sometimes responsible for setting up e-mail servers as well.

Security expert (S)   A security expert is someone who provides security strategy for Web sites. This person knows and has implemented sites using various types of encryption and can discuss the pros and cons of each with your team and your client. As well, this person understands the processes involved in making financial transactions on-line and can advise on products and strategies from the security perspective. In companies that specialize in creating commerce sites, a network engineer or programmer is often also a security expert.

Web production specialist (C)   A Web production specialist is the person who integrates the site using HTML or JavaScript, and is generally the hub of the site. Often, a Web production specialist is called an HTML guru, HTML coder, or integrator. This is usually the person who codes the HTML pages, integrates Java or Shockwave applications, integrates images and animations, and hands the project off to the QA department. This person is also generally responsible for getting the project ready for deployment or delivery to the client. Web production specialists are also responsible for creating a production guide, which documents the production of the site. The Web production specialist communicates with all members of the Web team and reports status to the producer.

Creative lead (C)   The creative lead determines the creative concept for the site and is responsible for the site's design. The creative lead may not design the site herself, but acts as art director for the site. The creative lead interacts with the technical lead, programmers, and Web specialists to determine what is technically possible. The creative lead often reports status to the project manager and account executive.

Designers (C)   Designers create the look and feel of the site. The main tool of choice for this work is Adobe Photoshop. Web designers should have a good understanding of design principles, including information design and interaction design. A print designer will not easily slide into this role. Understanding how images need to be made for the Web is a key skill. Fortunately, there are many books on the subject, and design for digital media is becoming a core component in the graphic design curriculums. The designers are managed directly by the creative lead. In reality, a designer is often also the creative lead.

Information architect (E)   An information architect understands how to display information visually so users understand how to interact with the site and find the information they need. An information architect would be responsible for site architecture, navigation, search and data retrieval, and interaction design. As well, the information architect would be responsible for key messages to users regarding errors, service, technical needs of the site, and privacy messages.

Copywriter (E)   It would be great to have a dedicated copywriter on a project, but often copywriting is a luxury. The information architect might also double as a copywriter. Often, the client supplies copy and the information architect or designer makes it Web-readable.

Production artist (C)   A production artist transforms the artwork that the designer creates into Web-ready art. The production artist obtains Photoshop files from the designers and cuts up the files into individual graphics, and then optimizes the graphics into Web file formats. The production artist must be skilled in color-reduction and image-compression techniques. On small teams, the designer is also the production artist.

Quality assurance lead (C)   A quality assurance lead should be a core person on your team. This person makes sure that the product you deliver meets the criteria specified in the scope document and functional specification. The QA lead is objective and that's why QA should not be done by developers. The QA person interacts with developers during bug-fixing time and with the producer to ensure that all bugs are addressed and resolved when the project is delivered.

Tester (E)   A tester tests the Web project based on the test plan that the QA lead writes. On small teams, the tester might be the QA lead.

Audio engineer (S)   An audio engineer designs sounds for Web sites. These sounds could range from music to sounds that happen when the user does something. The audio engineer usually interacts with the creative and technical leads.

Video engineer (S)   The video engineer creates video images and delivers them in digital format to the creative lead or the Web production specialist.

3-D modeler (S)   A 3-D modeler creates artwork that is in 3-D and usually works with the creative lead.

Web cast specialist (S)   A Web cast specialist is usually a third-party vendor who specializes in Web casts.

Media buyer (S)   A media buyer is usually part of the client's advertising agency. If your project is an advertising campaign, the producer will interact with the media planner to obtain specifications on the media buy so that the Web team can create advertisements based on the sizes in the buy.

Strategic planner (S)   A strategic planner is the person who delivers the consumer insight to the team. This person generally
conducts market research on the client's audience and delivers a
brief to help the creative team understand the mind of the target
audience.

Common Team Compositions

Although there are all kinds of Web projects, it is possible to acknowledge
certain types of teams and determine who is likely to be a part of the team
based on the type of project. Table 2.1 lists some typical kinds of Web development efforts and the likely composition of your team.

TABLE 2.1   Common Team Compositions

Type of Web Site	Team Composition
Interactive/marketing	Account manager, project manager, creative lead, designer, copywriter, technical lead, lingo programmer, Web production specialist, production artist, quality assurance lead
E-commerce	Project manager, technical lead, information architect, creative lead/designer, database programmer, systems integrator/server-side developer, security expert, network engineer, quality assurance lead/testers, third-party vendors for customer service and shipping
Data-intensive	Project manager, technical lead, creative lead/designer, information architect, database administrator, database programmer, server-side developer, Web production specialist, quality assurance lead, testers
Intranet (static)	Project manager, technical lead, creative lead/designer, network administrator, Web production specialists, quality assurance lead, content providers
Advertising campaign	Account manager, Strategic planner, project manager, creative lead/designer, production artist, Web production specialist, media buyer

Putting Together the Right Team

The "right team" is the team that will fulfill your Web site objectives most successfully. It's easy to choose the wrong people for Web teams, especially because some of the tasks involved with putting up a Web site can be perceived as easy. For example, you've probably heard many sales pitches for "a Web site in an hour." Maybe you've even bought some of the hardware and software packages. If you have, you've seen that installing server software and creating some HTML pages is not rocket science. However, those tasks are only about 1 percent of what it takes to create a successful Web site that meets business objectives, is profitable, and is of the highest quality possible.

Identifying Necessary Skills

As I said in the previous section, there are some core skills that your team must have in order to plan, design, build, and deploy a Web site. This core skill set is the base of your Web team; depending on your site's needs, you will need more specialized team members. When putting together your team, make sure that the following skills are covered:

- *Project management skills*   The ability to see and communicate the big picture to the team and your client (executive management or the paying client) and make sure the site gets built according to specification, on time, and on budget. This infers that you have strong executive support for your project if you are a project manager for a corporate Web site for your own company.

- *Information design/architecture skills*   The ability to design a usable and useful user interface that includes how the user will interact with the interface and navigate the site.

- *Graphic design skills*   The ability to transform the information design into a visual design.

- *Graphic production skills*   The ability to create Web graphics that are fast-loading and that look great on all browsers.

- *Content development skills*   The ability to develop both written and interactive content for Web sites. This includes copy, video, audio, and anything that is not part of the user interface.

- *Programming skills*   The ability to create Web pages using HTML, JavaScript, and other client/server scripting languages.

◆ *Technical/network infrastructure skills*   The ability to understand the requirements for serving a Web site on the Internet and to recommend the best strategy based on the client's or stakeholder's needs.

It is entirely possible for one person on a team to have two of the skill sets above. In fact, as you will see later in this chapter, it can be more profitable for a dedicated team.

Assessing Skills

It's a big risk when you hire someone specifically for a Web project and it turns out he or she doesn't know Photoshop as well as the résumé said. The best way to find out if someone is qualified for a job is to watch him or her do the job. Sometimes, however, you need to hire someone quickly. In this case, common sense says that you should check references, see samples of work, and go through a rigorous interview process.

Building a Team

Finding the right people is a difficult task, but an even more challenging task is matching team members both to the task and to each other. If you are managing multiple Web projects, then you have probably faced the dilemma of choosing the right combination of people for a particular project.

There really isn't any golden rule for doing this. People are people; that means they are not robots whose energy can be predicted and modulated at your whim. However, as you study your team, you will begin to see pairings that make sense.

You might find yourself having to choose between similar people to do a certain task. To make a good choice, it's important to think about several things:

◆ Is there a critical deadline for the task? If so, choose the person with the better track record for meeting deadlines. This will reduce the risk of missing the deadline.

◆ What risks do I take if I put this person on this task? If you know that one person is more prone to mistakes, then you can assign him or her tasks with lower risk.

◆ How does this person interact with the rest of the team? If either person has a history of not getting along with one of your team members, then you can decide whether to take the risk of having to manage interpersonal problems as well as project-oriented issues. (Chances are that you already do this. If you have a team member who consistently has issues with other team members, it's time to assess the risk of confronting this team member or letting the team member go.)

You'll find that certain pairings work well. On my team, since all my production artists also code HTML, they are exceptionally valuable to the higher-end programmers who often don't have time to do cleanup of HTML code. Once they build their scripts or applets, they can hand over the code to the production artists who drop in the artwork and then make the modifications necessary for the page to function up to its specification.

Managing the Team

Some people say that one of the unique aspects of project management for Web teams is that development times tend to be very aggressive. I'm not sure how true that is; it is a well-known fact that time lines for some software development projects can be just as aggressive.[1] I do think that, because the industry is so young, there are many more unknowns and risks than there are in more predictable production environments like the print production environment. It's important to remember, especially if you come from the advertising world, that Web production teams are very different from print production teams. There are many, many more risks because there are more unknown factors and development times can be longer and more costly. If you remember this early on, you will have success in managing your Web team.

Multiple Projects

One of the more challenging aspects of Web project management is managing human resources—from different departments or different teams, on one project or over several projects. Here's an example. You are the Web project manager for a company that makes plug-in DVD players. Suppose you have an internal project, such as developing a new area on your existing corporate Web site. The job scope is to shoot and capture video of a

---

1. For a classic book on hellish software development cycles, see Edward Yourdon, *Death March: The Complete Software Developer's Guide to Surviving "Mission Impossible" Projects.* Upper Saddle River, NJ: Prentice-Hall, 1997.

user installing a player and then design a small site around this feature. You have a central Web team who is busy on a redesign of your main site. You have to put together a Web team for this project, but your resources are tapped out.

Leverage the Central Web Team's Skills

You are faced with parallel Web development efforts and limited resources, including your own time and expertise. You can't clone yourself or other people, but you can structure the teams and projects in such a way that you extend your core team's expertise across the multiple projects. Being able to leverage your core team, the people who can manage different aspects of the Web effort, such as design, content development and coding, will simplify the effort needed to manage multiple projects.

Let's explore how you might handle the problem outlined in the previous section. You have a central Web team busy redesigning the corporate site. You have just been given the task of adding a whole new section to the Web site, which includes doing a video shoot and capture and designing an interface around this shoot. Your obstacles are the following:

- You don't have people on staff who shoot video.
- You need to have the new site designed.
- You need to have the new site coded.
- You cannot interrupt the project in process.
- You have a small budget for the second project, but you can cover the cost of video shooting and production.

Let's also assume you can't hire another project manager and Web team (that would be too easy). Here's one way to approach this task. First, since you are managing the efforts, you must schedule the second effort to begin after the planning and design phase of your first project. You want to do this for two reasons: to leverage the designer in your central team so that he or she is available to work on your second effort, and to leverage your management expertise which is the most critical in the first phase of Web project development. While the first project goes into production, your design team begins to work on the smaller site.

Then, you will need to hire someone who can both shoot and digitize video for the Web. Don't be confused by the many resources out there that shoot video and then deliver the digitized video to you on a portable hard drive. You don't have the time to have someone on your team play around with figuring out how to digitize video, though the impulse to do so is

◆ The Development Process

Here's the production method we use to produce Web pages and artwork from Photoshop files. Macromedia's Fireworks program is also worth considering for this purpose.

- ◆ Once the design is finished (see Figure 2.1a), a senior HTML coder will create a grid over the design (see Figure 2.1b), which is created in Photoshop. The grid is a separate layer in Photoshop. The grid helps the coder identify where to cut the graphics and how the table that holds the graphics will be structured.

- ◆ When the grid is done, the coder gives the Photoshop file to a production artist who cuts the page into separate graphics. The production artist names the graphics and gives an unoptimized copy back to the coder. These are placeholder graphics.
- ◆ While the coder codes the page with the unoptimized graphics, the production artist optimizes the graphics. When finished, the production artist gives the optimized graphics to the coder to integrate within the site.

Figure 2.2 shows this production method.

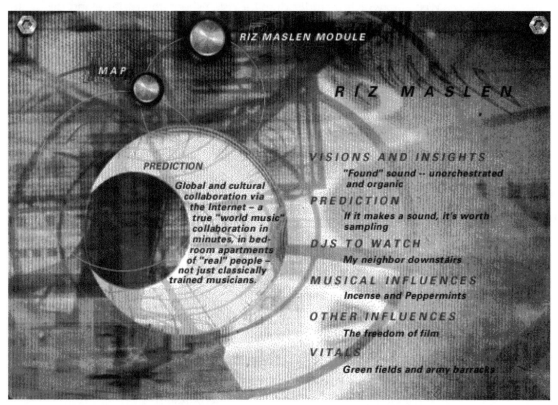

FIGURE 2.1a   The composite artwork.

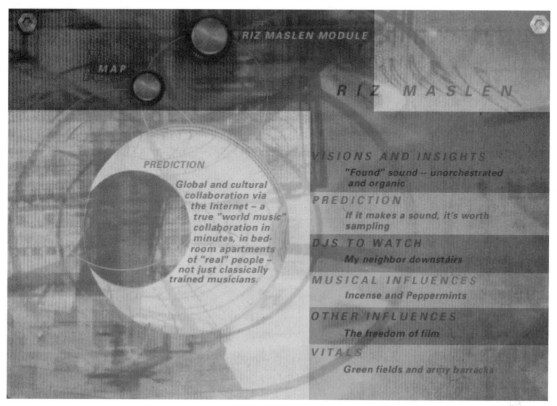

FIGURE 2.1b The grid layer over the design shows the coder where to cut.

high because of all the free beta software out there. Doing this would put your project at risk because the time in learning to digitize video is a large unknown. Instead, you want an accomplished shop to do this for you, and you want to see samples of their work. A good shop will be able to set up the whole shoot for you. All you should be required to provide is a detailed scope document of what you would like to receive, the DVD player, and, if necessary, a person to appear in the video.

While the video is being shot and digitized, your designer is designing the interface and must communicate the size of the frame required to the video shop. When the design is complete, you will need to determine when you have a production person available to create the Web pages and produce Web-ready graphics. At my company, we have developed a methodology for production so that it is easy to produce HTML and Web graphics once the design is done. This way, those precious production people can work on multiple projects at once.

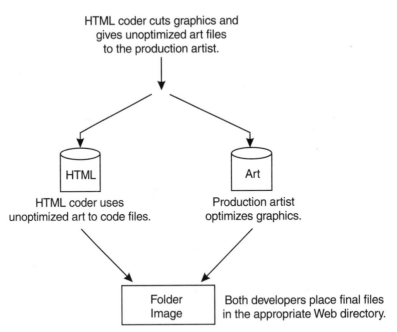

FIGURE 2.2   The production method.

Develop a Fast Production Method

It's important to develop processes that each team member follows. When you have a method of doing things, people get more and more efficient and save time. It's a "mass production" mentality; but, as we know, that's where you make money and ensure consistency. Once you get past design and into production, it's essential that your team be able to work efficiently.

As you can see, a production method is pretty important in leveraging resources and managing time lines. You need to know what's happening at every step so that you can pull resources between projects at noncritical times. We will discuss more about methods in the next chapter, "Planning and Process Development."

Cross-Functional Teams

A cross-functional team is made up of individuals who perform different functions within the team. For example, a producer might also be an information designer. A designer might also be an HTML coder. A production artist might also be a production assistant. The benefit of the cross-functional team is that depending on the types of projects you have, your resources can perform one function for one project and if that job does not take up 100 percent of their time, they can perform other functions on other projects. Also, one person can perform two functions on the same project, thereby reducing the number of resources you will need on a project.

Team Dynamics: The Unique Issues

Virtual Management

There will ultimately be occasions where your Web teams will be in different locations, working simultaneously on a Web project. If you find yourself managing resources at different locations, be prepared to travel a lot. Here are some reminders to help you manage and support your team.

Set Clear Guidelines

When members of a team are scattered in various locations, nothing becomes more important than a clear understanding of what everyone's roles are, including who does what, when, and how. It's critical to provide team members with information about the other team members, what their roles and deliverables are, and how they will deliver their piece of the project. A clear scope document and a description of the process, or methods, for executing the project is an absolute must. A production guide is also critical if more than one person is going to be producing HTML pages, graphics, and multimedia elements.

Set Up a Review Site

A very important tool for the virtual team is the review Web site. This is a Web site that lists everything about the project, from contact names and addresses to the scope document, schedule, and schematics of the site. As well, it has a link to the staging site, which is where your team will work collaboratively on the site. You will learn more about the staging site in chapter 3, "Planning and Process Development."

You manage the review site; or if you are fortunate enough to have a production assistant or an associate producer, you can delegate this task. It should be updated regularly with changes, news, and the latest additions to the site-in-progress.

The last reason to have a review site is so that you can conduct remote reviews with your client or stakeholder. Your stakeholder can view the site in progress, give feedback on a design, get your pager number, and check the schedule. This gives your client the feeling that you and the team are available, which is a very important perception.

Working with the Client's Resources

In your career as a Web producer, you will undoubtedly work with members of your client's internal team. These unions can be very productive, or they can be lethal to your project.

The most important thing for you to do as a project manager is to be open to using these resources. Never refuse to use them. Doing so would only cast you in a negative light to your client. The right thing to do is to find a job for them. If they are IT people or employees who have learned Web production, then pair them with people from your team and give them low-risk tasks to do. If they prove themselves to be competent, then you have just earned another resource, and you can use your own team resource on another project. Above all, give them the respect they deserve. You will benefit from their approval of you in the long run.

If you are working with marketing staff, then you will be responsible for making sure their vision and insights into their customers is reflected clearly in the concept and design that your design team creates. Don't assume that since you have been building Web sites for years, you know more about consumers than your client's marketing team. It's okay to contribute your suggestions; they should expect this of you as a Web professional. If you see a critical risk in the success of the project due to a marketing idea that doesn't seem sound based on your experience or research, then you can broach the subject with the facts, not your opinion. If the marketing team still wants to go through with the project, you can then assess whether this high-risk situation is the best situation for your team. If the success of the project directly impacts your potential revenue from the project, then this might be a project you ultimately turn down.

Outsourcing or Working with Vendors

Every now and then you will need to work with an outside resource on a project. Either you will need to hire a specific resource, such as a coder or designer, or you might need to form a partnership with a vendor to provide services to your client that your Web team does not provide, such as networking infrastructure, production, or strategic planning.

Many companies are forming strategic partnerships. For example, TBWA Chiat-Day uses Red Sky Interactive as their interactive agency for one of their clients, Absolut Vodka. Red Sky works with TBWA Chiat-Day to develop Web sites and CD-ROMs for Absolut. It's a mutually beneficial relationship. You can read more about the relationship and the team in the case study in chapter 10.

Where to Find People

If you are looking for contractors to do design and production, there are several resources on the Web. Digital Talent Agency (*www.digitaltalent. com*) has locations in both San Francisco and New York and can provide art, programming, and production resources. If you have Internet user groups in your area, chances are you can find programmers. Also, through third-party vendor software you can often find partners who specialize in deploying solutions for a specific suite of applications. Microsoft's Solution Provider Program is one of these organizations, so if you need application development help on the Windows NT/2000 platform, you can call 1-800-SOLPROV. Oracle also has a development program, as do many of the big e-commerce software companies, such as BroadVision and Interworld.

Make sure whomever you hire will be able to do the job you need them to do. Always check their work for quality. If you can't determine the quality of the work (such as the code of a Java coder, unless you are a Java coder), then find someone you trust to make an assessment. Always check references. If you are going to use resources from a third-party vendor, such as an e-commerce vendor, ask for a client referral list. Find out how the team worked and if team members were able to partner with existing resources and teams.

Sorting Apples and Oranges

Finally, remember that all members of your team don't work the same way. Your responsibility is to develop an environment of communication and production systems that help your team do the best job possible. To do this, you need to understand how the different members are used to working.

How Programmers Work

Programmers are solitary beings. They are used to getting a requirements document, designing a specification, and then coding. They don't respond well to having to write documentation, but they know they have to. Some programmers will not speak up and will defer to the loudest voice. Others won't. Be sure to listen carefully to programmers' concerns. Always ask them questions about potential red flags and risks.

How Designers Work

I've worked with designers of all types. Some are quiet and solitary. Some are gregarious. All are perfectionists. Because they are ultimately responsible for how the site looks, they are very visible. Often their sense of value is at risk. Wanting to be perfect can cause your project to go over time and budget, so it's important to develop a method for making sure your design team can do the best effort in the shortest amount of time. Being empathetic, and yet a strong leader, is critical. A clear iteration of the marketing goals and key consumer insight can be invaluable in helping a designer get the concept right on the first try. Giving the designer a production assistant to do photo research is also a good idea—this way the designer does not spend too much time getting artwork and can focus on sketching and design.

How Writers Work

Writers need to know who the audience is and what the project's objective is or they will be writing in a vacuum. Your creative or strategic brief should contain what the writer needs to develop copy that is appropriate for the audience. Writers are also solitary beings. Some writers need to write at home. Be flexible.

How You Work

Finally, how are you used to working? It's your job to motivate, support, and drive this team to your ultimate goal: to deliver a project on time and on budget. You must know yourself and your shortcomings so that you can identify them and not let them sabotage your project. Are you impatient? Do you tend to compare members of your team to yourself? Are you too lenient? Take a good look at yourself, accept yourself, and keep the project's goals in the forefront of your mind. Remember not to sweat the small stuff. Give perks to your team when they need them, and take a few for yourself.

Summary

In this chapter, you learned about the Web team and the different roles and responsibilities of its members. You learned what skills your team will need for various projects, and you learned how team members need to interact. Also, you saw how a production method could help your team in crunch time. In the next chapter, you will learn how to plan your Web project.

TO-DO LIST

♦ Take an assessment of your current team. Do you have the core skills necessary for your Web project?

♦ Make contact with some freelance people. Bring them in for informational interviews. Keep a record of their skills in an easy-to-find place—not buried in your "résumé" file.

♦ If you will need to work with members from your client's team, make sure you have a process in place where you can communicate easily, whether verbally, on paper, or through your review site.

♦ Make sure all roles and responsibilities are outlined at the start of the project.

♦ Set up your review site.

Bringing in the Special Teams

Steve Kirsh, Partner and Director
of Sales and Marketing
Digital Talent Agency

Paul Smith, Partner and CEO
Digital Talent Agency

Steve Kirsh has worked with Robert Abels's pioneering digital media group, creating highly publicized projects, including Picasso's "Guernica" and Kurosawa's "RAN." He has worked with AND Communications and was Red Sky Interactive's first producer and then senior account executive. He has managed strategic relationships with high-profile clients, such as Goodby Silverstein and Partners, Weiden and Kennedy, Nike, Sony, and Microsoft.

Paul Smith has worked in the Internet and new media realm for more than 10 years. First, he developed software at McDonnell-Douglas's Advanced Technology Lab, then designed consumer educational titles, and prior to starting Digital Talent Agency (DTA) with Steve Kirsh, he was director of technology and production at Red Sky Interactive. Together with the business development team, he set scope, time lines, and budgets for major accounts and ran internal planning and production meetings.

What kinds of services does DTA provide?

We're matchmakers. We help clients—corporate clients, entertainment companies, advertising agencies—locate and evaluate vendors when they execute their brand strategies across a full set of digital media. That includes Internet, intranets, broadcast, and broadband. We offer a "banners to broadcast" solution for these companies.

Why did you start DTA?

We saw that there was a lot of confusion for clients. With technology becoming more and more complex, it's getting harder and harder to tell whether a bunch of guys are the next Pixar or a garage shop that might be gone tomorrow. By being industry insiders, we can tell the difference and make recommendations to the clients. On the flip side, there are many boutique and midsize studios that are really good at their work, but are not as good at selling or representing themselves. We can help them, by acting as an extension of their business development departments.

There must be hundreds of shops that offer digital services. How do you screen these shops and make the best match?

We have a huge database of shops ranging from strategic brand consulting to e-commerce and EDI services. Through our process of Natural Selection™, we are able to draw up a short list of appropriate vendors from which our clients can choose.

We conduct what we call a DTA Interactive Review™ in which we do an in-depth needs assessment on the client side. Then, we go to our database and files and put together a long list of vendors, usually one to two dozen. We handle all nondisclosure paperwork and ensure that each vendor provides an organized response to the client's request for information.

After we review the vendor's response, we choose a short list of vendors to respond to a specific Request for Proposal (RFP). The RFP outlines a specific project that will serve as a test case to assess the candidates' approach and capabilities. The client then chooses the vendor from this short list with our assistance.

What does this cost the client?

The cost to the client is nothing. We take a small percentage from the vendor that is awarded the business.

What are clients looking for when they contact you?

They basically need some assistance in narrowing the search. Obviously, if there are only one or two contenders, our services aren't needed. We might save the client some money, but we aren't critical. Where we really make a difference is when a job could be done by one of hundreds of multimedia companies or might even take a team of them. For instance, when a company wants to set up their site for e-commerce, a smaller firm might do it faster and cheaper than a larger vendor. Or for a major national campaign across many media such as Internet ads, webcasts, AOL, videos, promotions, and trade show demos, one studio may not be able to handle it. However, we can bundle a team of vendors.

Clients are also looking to us to make judgment calls for them. They might not be able to see the differences among shops. Since we have worked in this industry, we are able to give them very informed choices. We're sometimes called the "Consumer Reports" of the multimedia industry. We really want both sides to win. Since we receive no fees from the client, we have no hidden agendas. We know what doesn't work in the industry, and we want to save others the battle scars.

As more and more companies begin to bring their core Web teams in-house, do you see a continued need for your services? (Core Web teams

are an account executive, a producer, a creative lead, a technical lead, and production resources.)

Without a doubt. The technology keeps growing and changing, and no in-house team will be able to stay on top of the many technologies out there. And new vendors keep appearing and disappearing each week. Doing technical, creative, and financial background checks is more than a full-time occupation. I think that more and more companies will need our services in the future.

Are there requests that you hear over and over again? What is the most sought-after expertise right now?

Clients definitely need help figuring out the technical side of things—what e-commerce vendor should I use? Which product, from the scores of software solutions out there, should I invest in? So right now, e-commerce is a hot request. However, we are constantly keeping on top of emerging technologies and innovations. What seems to be an obscure development today could change the needs for digital talent in the future. We need to see that coming and be ready to provide solutions.

CHAPTER 3

Planning and Process Development

IF YOU NEED . . .

♦ To present a strategic plan to your client, go to "Early Planning."

♦ Tips on managing the creative process, go to "Creative and Content Planning."

♦ Tips on understanding technical requirements, go to "Technical Planning."

♦ Tips on setting up a production methodology, go to "Production Planning."

♦ Templates and ready-to-use planning documents, go to the CD-ROM and look in the /templates/chapter3/ folder.

♦ To have a quick to-do list of planning tasks, go to "To-Do List."

If you are going to invest in a Web site, the money you spend in the planning stage is the best money spent. It's the only way to ensure that your Web project will accomplish what it must in order to achieve your business goal. However, clients don't always want to pay for planning. Sometimes the client will have certain aspects of the Web site planned long before you are hired to build the project. It's up to you to decide at that point if that particular project is right for you and your team.

Some companies are fortunate enough to have an entire department devoted to strategic planning. This group determines the best use of the Web for the client, based on the client's business objectives. It's a level of planning that is new to the Web industry, specifically because some Web developers can create a Web site in a week. Only in recent years have businesses started to combine business strategy and Web-site strategy.

This chapter discusses the types of planning that occur for the different phases of development of a Web project.

Early Planning

In chapter 1, I discussed how important it is to define your project in terms of the objective, including the client's expectations and the user's needs. In this section, I will discuss the steps you can take to accomplish that goal.

Getting to Know Your Audience

If you don't know your audience, you will not be able to build a successful Web site, because you won't understand what the Web site must contain in order to meet your client's goal. As I discussed in chapter 1, there are many ways to get to know your audience, and the route you take to accomplish this depends on the kind of site you are building.

In the next few sections, we will discuss some tactics you can use to get to know both Internet audiences and intranet audiences.

Interviewing

A thoughtful and well-planned interview with your client and/or department representatives and team members is the best way to fully understand what kind of experience you will need to create in order for your Web site to be successful. You will most likely be able to conduct such an interview if you are creating an intranet.

Before you set up the interviews, you need to do some hard thinking about what you need to learn. Here are some points to consider:

♦ You are trying to find out what your users need in order to meet the objectives set forth by the stakeholders. Make your questions broad but still related to the objective. If you ask a narrow question, you will get a narrow answer like "yes" or "no," which won't tell you much.

◆ Who Is the Decision Maker?

Setting objectives when your client is internal is often very difficult. If you are trying to manage an internal Web project, you probably have experienced a lot of frustration just trying to identify the person who has ultimate sign-off authority. In an internal project, it seems that everyone has an opinion and personal agenda to push. It's a complicated and difficult task, often with internal budgetary pressures and sticky political situations. Try to remain neutral, identify the stakeholders (by budget, usually), and make sure to stay focused on what you perceive to be the critical objectives. It's also a good practice to look for the 80/20 rule—you provide 20 percent of the content that reaches 80 percent of your audience.

◆ Be open to ideas about Web-site features, but remember that each feature has a cost associated with it. You will need to weigh carefully each feature against your client's objective and the amount of money he or she wishes to spend.

◆ Bring a tape recorder and, if possible, an assistant to take notes. You should focus on listening carefully and not be distracted by taking notes.

◆ Use a questionnaire to help you strategize for your interview. I usually draft questionnaires that are specific to the objective of the site. These questionnaires can be found on the CD-ROM that accompanies this book, in the /templates/chapter3/ folder.

Focus Groups and Market Research

If you are creating an Internet site, chances are you don't have access to your targeted audience. Focus groups and market research services can help you understand your target audience. Please see chapter 1 for a more in-depth discussion of getting to know your target audience through focus groups and market research.

Gathering End-User Requirements

Focus groups can help you understand the mind set of your target audience, but you also have to ask the client how the site is supposed to function for the user. Do your users need to download software? Do they need to get to data quickly? Do you want them to sign in? Do your users need a fast modem to access content? Do they need a certain browser? These are things your focus group won't necessarily tell you. End-user requirements are important parameters that you must follow in order for your site to be usable to the people who visit it.

There are some consistent requirements that you need to address for all kinds of Web sites. These requirements have to do with users' connection speed, browsers, and browser versions. The kind of experience you offer on your Web site depends on these requirements. In the /templates/ chapter3/ folder on the CD-ROM, I've included an end-user requirements analysis form to help you focus on getting these questions answered.

Other requirements have to do with the kind of site you are building. Depending on the objective of the site, you will need to ask "What is the experience supposed to be for the user?" Are the users going to need to get information from the Web site? Will they be finding important data? Do they need to interact with a game? These kinds of end-user requirements are specific to the Web site, so they will be different for each kind of site you create.

When you have gone through the process of gathering the end-user requirements, you will need to list them all in your functional specification, which we will talk about later in this chapter.

Defining Development Stages and Strategies

It's important for you, your client, and your team to understand what the stages of development will be. It is very easy to miscommunicate when everyone is saying words like "strategy" and "design phase" and "production guide." These terms may mean different things to different people. Therefore, one of the first things for you do to with your client and your team is to meet and define exactly what your phases of development will be and specify the deliverables that will result from each phase.

The four-stage development process works the best for my team, but it may not be realistic for you. I encourage you to try this process and then modify it based on team and client feedback. This process is shown in Figure 3.1 and outlined next:

I try to negotiate a fixed time line and fee for the first two phases, based on the resources necessary to produce the deliverables for each phase.

Phase I: Strategy   During this phase, either a strategic planner, account executive, or project manager and/or the client is determining the objective for the site based on a dedicated research effort. The culmination or deliverable of this phase is the creative brief, which clearly outlines the objectives, requirements, and key insights of the target audience. The creative brief provides a foundation for every team member's work.

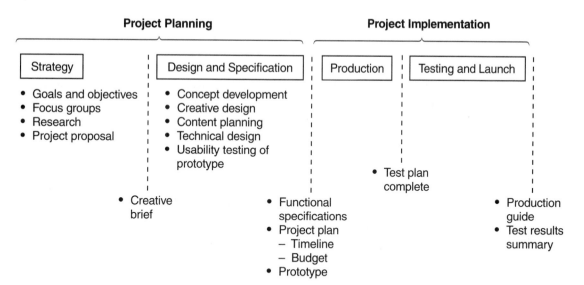

FIGURE 3.1   Web project development phases. A standard Web development process follows a strategy similar to that for software development.

In my contract, I note that if we exceed the fixed time line due to a client's change in initial requirements, there'll be an additional fee.

Phase II: Design   During this phase, the creative and technical teams are doing a parallel design of the site. The creative team is designing the user interface and interactions, and the technical team is designing the back-end and applications that will be used on the site. The culmination of this phase is the functional and/or technical specification, site architecture, schematics, and designs of the site. Sign-off by the client is critical to proceed.

After the design phase, I can give a realistic estimate for producing and testing of the site.

Phase III: Production   During this phase, we are building the site. Any major changes in functionality and features have to be monitored closely. If the client requests a change at this point, a change order is issued. The culmination of this phase is, of course, the site, which will go into Phase IV. A production guide is also created during this phase.

Phase IV: Testing   During this phase we are testing the site and getting ready to publish it on the live, or production, Web server. Our QA manager develops a test plan based on the scope document and functional specification and tests against this plan. Bugs are reported and fixed. The site is ready to go live at the end of this phase.

Identifying the Development Phases

At the end of the strategic planning phase, you might find a discrepancy between what your client wants and what it is possible to deliver in the required time. When this occurs, meet with your client to present your position and offer alternatives that you can develop within the required time.

If not handled correctly, this can be a very critical and project-ending discussion. Negotiations of this sort are not for the amateur project manager. You need to be able to frame to your client what you can deliver and why it is the appropriate way to proceed. You need to convince your client that this is the best choice for her, and you need to believe it yourself in order to convince her. Managing clients is an art, especially when telling them you can't give them everything they want up front. For more information and tips about effective client management, see chapter 5 and the interview with Louis Malafarina, president and CEO of Ripple Effects Interactive, located in Pittsburgh.

The objective of this conversation is to agree on phases for development. For example, if your client wants a storefront like Amazon.com, but needs it in a month, you will need to be able to negotiate a first step for that eventual goal. There are lots of options. You will need to research them with your team and then present them to your client, along with a solid recommendation. If you don't think you can deliver, it's time to back away.

Writing the Creative Brief

The creative brief is the document that defines the objective of the project, along with a description of the audience and the key insight into their mind-set. It is the foundation of the site and should be what the Web team uses to ground and focus them as they design and build the site. The creative brief (see Figure 3.2) should contain the following section headings:

- *The Project*   This section describes the project.
- *The Objectives*   This section describes the project's goals.
- *The Target Audience*   This section describes the target audience and gives demographic information about it, including targeted browser, platform, and connectivity.
- *Personality*   This section describes site's desired personality and tone.
- *Current Mind-set*   This section describes auidence's mind-set.
- *Key Target Audience Insight*   This section gives an insight into the mind of this Web site's consumer—often one of the most important factors in developing a concept that will reach the target audience.

♦ Template for a Creative Brief

Client Name: _____   Date: _____

Project Name: _____   Client: _____

Product: _____   Original Author: _____

The Project
(What is the scope of the assignment?)

The Objectives
(What are the business and marketing objectives of the project? Short- vs. long-term?)

The Target Audience
(What are the demographics and psychographics; buying and usage habits; values, attitudes, and lifestyles?)

Personality and Tone
(What is the tone and manner? What are the overall personality traits the project must communicate?)

Current Mind-set
(What does the target think now relative to the brand, its products, and current project, if applicable?)

Key Target Audience Insight
(What is the most compelling thing we want the target to think after they experience the project?)

FIGURE 3.2   The creative brief informs the creative team about the user's mind-set.

This template is included on the CD-ROM in the /templates/chapter3/ folder.

Brainstorming

With the creative brief in hand, you can conduct a brainstorming session with the entire team to discuss the features the site must have in order to meet the objectives. From this discussion, you can write the creative document and the functional specification for the site. If you haven't written the scope document yet, this is when you should begin to focus in earnest on the exact scope of the project. (For more information about the scope document, see chapter 1, "Determine the Scope.") If you have written the scope document as part of your business proposal, then after the brainstorming session and preliminary creative planning phase you would write a functional specification, which explores what the functionality of the site will be. This document is best written after your team develops the site architecture and schematics, which I talk about in the "Creative and Content Planning" section.

Creating the Review Site

David Siegel[1] talks about the use of a project Web site to keep clients aware of the progress of the Web site in development. Earlier, I referred to this as the review site. No matter what you call it, this excellent communication tool functions both as a way to keep clients apprised of the progress of the project and to keep all team members up-to-date on all aspects of the site. On a typical review site at Red Sky Interactive, Web project managers are responsible for coordinating and updating the project site. The following information is available:

- Roles and responsibilities of the project team
- Contact information for all team members
- The project mission
- The creative brief
- Site architecture
- Schematics
- All design reviews
- The project schedule
- A link to the staging site

Figure 3.3 shows our project review for one of our clients, TBWA Chiat-Day/Absolut Vodka. You can read about this project in chapter 10.

Creative and Content Planning

Early planning usually culminates with the creative brief. The purpose of this document is to provide information about the customer or user to the creative team. In this section, you will read about the different kinds of creative planning that can occur in a Web project.

Creating the Concept

Every Web site needs a concept. The concept shapes the way the Web site will look, its tone, and the other kinds of features it offers. The most im-

---

1. David Siegel, *Secrets of Successful Web Sites: Project Management on the World Wide Web.* San Francisco: Hayden Book Company, 1997.

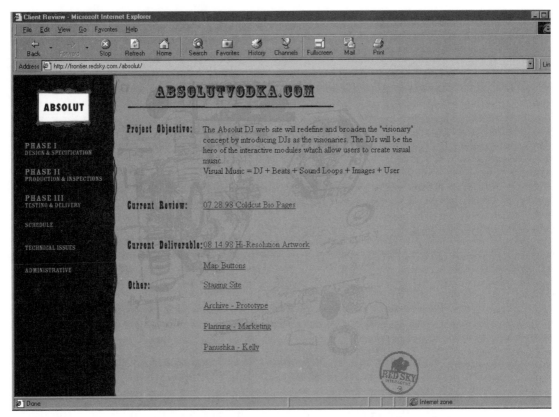

FIGURE 3.3   The review site for TBWA-Chiat Day (representing Absolut Vodka).

portant thing about a concept is that it must be able to extend itself throughout the site, in visual design, through copywriting, and even with regard to the kinds of technologies that are used to create the user experience. For people with marketing and advertising backgrounds, the idea and value of a concept is understood. But for the Web project manager who comes from a software development background, a concept can seem like a foreign and unnecessary thing. It's not. The concept, like the creative brief, becomes the primary focus for the visual execution and writing of the site.

Communicating the Concept

Once the concept has been thought out, it needs to be communicated to the rest of the team, specifically, to the design team that will be creating the look and feel of the site. Usually the creative director is responsible for leading the development of the concept, and so the creative director can choose the method that helps the design team understand the concept best. Some companies use storyboards, others use a more formal written document along with illustrations. It's important to give the design team a sense of the concept along with preliminary ideas for imagery and copy. One of the more effective methods I've seen is a simple sketch of the initial concept, along with a written paragraph on the ideas around the concept. Other companies write a creative document, which directly addresses the highlights of the creative brief. Doing this ensures that the creative team is in line with the objectives that were laid out in the early planning stage, a critical milestone to hit if you want your site to be successful.

Usability Studies

To learn more about usability studies, you can check out *www. alertbox.com*. Also some reference books[2] will help you understand the value of the usability study.

After the first round of design has been done, getting feedback on how well the user interface works is critical. Unfortunately, very few Web teams actually do this because the cost to the client can be prohibitive. To get this kind of feedback, you need to conduct a usability study by having actual users explore a prototype of the Web site you are building. Usually, an interface designer will lead the study and will videotape users as they click through the site. The interface designer will ask them to find certain areas of information and will then watch how long it takes a user to find the information. As well, the interface designer will look for patterns among users that might indicate a usability problem. For example, if the user is trying to find information about products and continuously clicks on a heading called "About Us" instead of "Crafty Gadgets," then the interface designer might conclude that it's necessary to rename the heading in order for the users to find the information they want.

Site Architecture and Schematics

When you are in the process of designing and developing content for a Web site, it's important to have a way of keeping all team members in the communications loop regarding the content of the site. This is especially true for large Web teams with multiple content providers, such as writers, designers, and audio/video creators. Content development is an iterative process. Your team brainstorms for ideas about what information belongs

---

2. Louis Rosenfeld, and Peter Morville, *Information Architecture for the World Wide Web: Designing Large-scale Web Sites.* Sebastopol, CA: O'Reilly and Associates, 1998; Jakob Nielsen, *Usability Engineering.* Chestnut Hill, MA: AP Professional, 1994; Jared M. Spool, *Web Site Usability.* San Francisco: Morgan Kaufmann, 1998.

on the site and you need a way to show your client or stakeholder the team's ideas. Once the client has signed off on what the site will contain, your team members, from designers to coders, will need to know what elements go on which page and how the pages link together. Two invaluable tools for informing everyone are the site architecture and the schematic. Both of these models will live on your project site, so that the entire team can have access to the information at all times.

A site architecture is essentially a diagram that shows how the pages of your site link to each other. Figure 3.4 shows a typical architecture.

While a site architecture gives you an overall view of your entire site's content, page schematics show you what elements of content live on each

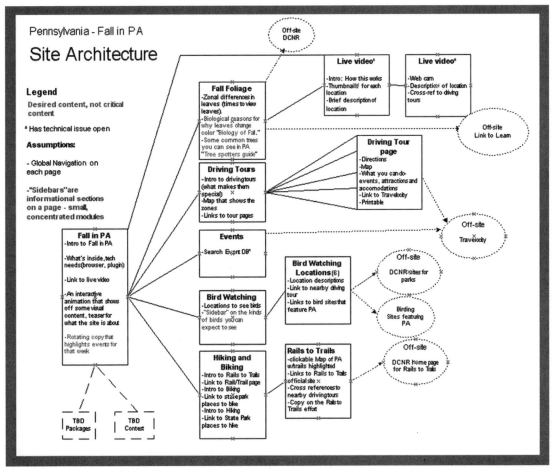

FIGURE 3.4   Site architecture for Fall in PA (*www.fallinpa.com*).

page. At Red Sky, we use Illustrator to mock up each page's content quickly. The different kinds of content might include:

◆ Copy
◆ Images
◆ Links
◆ Video
◆ Audio
◆ Shockwave
◆ Other media files

The value of the schematic is huge. Schematics help the designers understand the elements on each page so that they can appropriately design the pages, and they help the production staff track the assets needed for each page. The schematics help the client understand and contribute to the development of the content by providing a visual representation of the site long before the design is finished. This saves much development time because issues about content placement can be addressed before the design phase is complete. Finally, page schematics help you, the Web project manager, keep track of all the various pieces of information needed to build the site. Figure 3.5 shows a typical page schematic.

Software Programs

We use Visio to create our architectures, but you can use whatever software you choose. There are lots of programs to help you and your team create site architectures and schematics. Try to use a program that makes it easy for you to save your work as a .GIF file. A .GIF file is in a format that you use for images that you want to be able to see over the Web. I use Visio and Illustrator, but people also use Word, PhotoShop, FreeHand, and other drawing programs. Use whatever is easiest for you.

Technical Planning

Technical planning is the phase in which your technical team investigates the technical requirements of a project and develops a strategy for building features of the site such as databases, shockwave movies, transaction systems, and scripts of all kinds. As with all the other phases of development, the technical team must plan for not only the first rollout of the Web site but also the evolution of the site from a technical standpoint.

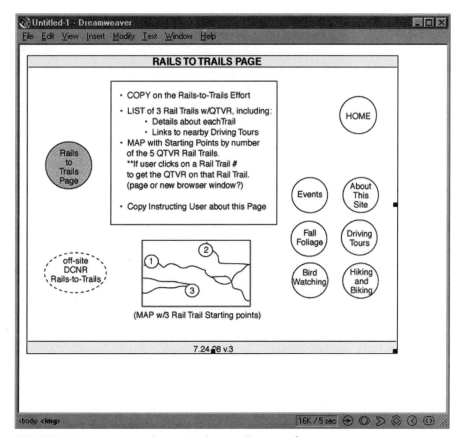

FIGURE 3.5 A page schematic shows all types of content on a page.

Identifying Technical Infrastructure

The technical infrastructure is the environment in which your Web site lives. By this I mean the server environment, which includes hardware, software, security, and connectivity. In addition, your technical team needs to provide both a development environment for your Web team and a production environment, which is where the site will live when it goes live. Ideally, these two environments will be mirror environments, meaning that the servers will be configured in the same way.

The purpose of this is to ensure that the live site will work perfectly in the production environment because you have built it and tested it in a development environment that was essentially the same as the production environment. By doing this, you eliminate the risk of dealing with unknown problems that can arise when moving the site over to the production environment.

One of the more important decisions your technical team will make is what platform and server software your Web site will run on. This decision should be based on the client's existing environment, their existing technical resources (why sell NT if they have a UNIX environment?), and their budget. I don't recommend any single solution. There is a "right" solution for each client and a particular vendor or platform is not right for all clients. The same is true for database solutions. It depends on the client's needs, resources, and budget.

Network Assessment

One of the steps your technical team can take in identifying the necessary technical infrastructure requirements is to use an assessment questionnaire. I've included a sample form on the CD-ROM, in the folder called /templates/chapter3/. Our form is basically for our clients, and it helps us determine what the existing network infrastructure is. Then the technical team makes the necessary recommendations to support the targeted features of the site.

Defining Technical Development Requirements

Your technical team will define the technical development requirements by reading the objectives document and participating in the creative brainstorming. The technical team should come away with a good idea of the overall functionality of the site. It then becomes their responsibility to make recommendations for how the actual technical features will be built.

As a project manager, you can do some risk assessment in this phase by asking your technical team members some key questions:

- *Will they be using technologies they haven't used before?* This is a very typical scenario since the Web and Web technologies change virtually from week to week. Risk increases when your technical team uses software or languages that are new and unexplored.

- *How different are the new technologies from those they have used?* It's a greater risk if they have absolutely no experience in a certain technology. However, if someone is trying out a new server-side scripting language and they have done many kinds of server-side scripting, the risk may be less. (But perhaps not that much less!)

- *Will they be using code that is already developed or will they need to create code from scratch?* Often, you will find that engineers can use the same code over and over again, and sometimes they can't. The development time will naturally be slower for code that needs to be written from scratch.

♦ *Will they have access to the production environment, and will they be able to test on that environment?* It's critical that the technical team be able to test its code in an environment that mirrors the production environment. I discuss this earlier in the chapter but it is important enough to mention it again.

Feasibility and Software Testing

Early in the design and specification phase, your technical team should be doing feasibility and software testing. A feasibility test is a test that explores a particular technical strategy to find out what the issues are in pursuing the strategy. For example, if your creative team wants to use pull-down menus in dynamic HTML, your technical team might do a feasibility test to see what kinds of obstacles they are likely to face. The reason for doing feasibility testing is to see early in the design phase what the problems might be in implementing a technical solution. This is a fairly simple example. Depending on the technical complexity of the Web site, many other sophisticated feasibility tests can occur.

Software testing is a kind of feasibility test. In software testing, the technical team tests all software that is to be used on the site, such as e-commerce server software, so that they can get up to speed with the features and the application programming interfaces (APIs). This should happen during the design phase.

Planning for Maintenance and Growth

It's important to begin a Web project with the end in mind. Who is going to inherit the site when your team is finished developing it? Will your team need to provide simple templates or is a content management system necessary to help the client's Web team maintain the site? Will the Web site be able to scale with growth? Both your technical and production teams need to think about maintenance in the beginning of the project when the requirements are being gathered. I talk about this more fully in the "Production Planning" section.

If a content management system needs to be implemented, your technical team should be the team to evaluate the different kinds of software and make a recommendation based on the client's existing technical infrastructure—both hardware and human resources. It's important that someone on the client's team take a part in this decision.

If the client is internal, then the same recommendation process needs to occur. Sometimes it's hard to get internal clients to support content management systems, especially when there are internal team members who can maintain the site. To persuade, you will need to show that investing in a content management system up front will save money. To confirm this, make sure you see how the system works and the amount of effort required to get it up and running and compare that information to the estimated maintenance effort required if your team coded the pages and searched for the image assets manually. Compare this in weekly increments. Good luck. I've found that internal clients are a lot harder to persuade than external ones!

Technical Specifications

The technical specification is a document that clearly details how a technical component will be built. It is different from the functional specification because it goes into very specific detail from an engineering standpoint. The users of the technical specification are other engineers who may be brought in to work on the project, as well as the client's technical team. This document tells them exactly what they are getting.

You don't always need a detailed technical specification, but it's a good idea to have one. The best reason to use the technical spec is to anticipate the need to bring an engineer in midway through the project. It should be written so that at any moment someone can be brought into the project and hit the ground running. Some other very good reasons to have such a document are to demonstrate to your client that you understand its technical environment and to ensure that once the project is finished it will be easily integrated into an existing environment. It's a good idea to get your client's technical team to sign off on the technical specification—that provides insurance that your team was exercising due diligence to ensure a smooth handover. It's a good way to communicate with your client's team. I've included a sample technical spec on the CD-ROM. Go to the /templates/chapter3/ folder.

Production Planning

Production planning covers two distinct areas: planning for the initial production of the site and planning for handoff to a client or another production team. Most of the planning before production, preproduction, is done to ensure that by the time a project is ready to move into the production phase, the production team is ready and completely informed about its scope and requirements.

Understanding End-User Requirements

After reading the creative brief, all team members should understand what the project objectives; we usually have a meeting specifically to discuss these objectives before gathering the requirements and certainly before going into the design phase. This ensures that the creative and technical teams understand their limitations when proposing features. However, the production team must understand end-user requirements in order to make sure that the site meets them. These requirements are usually the following:

- *Browser*   If your target audience is expected to have a certain version of a browser, the production team will make sure the site looks good on this browser.

- *Platform*   If your target audience is expected to own a certain computer platform (Windows or Macintosh), then your production team will make sure the site is optimized for that platform.

- *Connectivity*   If your target audience is expected to connect to the site using a certain speed of modem, then your production team will make sure the site downloads acceptably over a modem of that speed.

- *Plug-in*   If your target audience will need a plug-in to view a certain feature, such as a QuickTime movie, then your production team will make sure that users know this up front and will provide a method for getting the plug-in to the users.

- *Software Settings*   If your target audience needs additional software or has modified the software settings for particular browsers, then your production team also will need to alert the users to action they need take to get the optimal experience of your site.

Production Guide

As I said in the beginning of this section, you are planning not only for the implementation of the Web site, you might also be planning for handing the project off to your client's Web team or to a different Web team that might be responsible for maintaining and updating the site. I use a production guide to keep track of how the site was built, and then I hand this guide to my client to serve as documentation of the site, from how the

---

♦ **Knowing Your Users' Web Requirements**

It's impossible to know completely what your user's computer configuration is, but it's getting easier to detect certain settings through scripts that can "sniff" for certain settings. We usually sniff for browser, platform, and certain plug-ins that we use frequently, such as shockwave. We've developed a standard detection script for this. There are similar scripts in many places on the Web, such as *www.javascripts.com, www.webcoder.com,* and *www.shockwave.com.* I recommend that you assign a technical resource to build a script library of detection scripts—they come in handy and cut development time when you decide to use plug-ins and other media formats that are not natively supported by Netscape Navigator, Internet Explorer, or AOL's browser.

---

graphics were created to what the files were named and why. Here are some important facts to include in your production guide:

- ♦ *Directory structure*   A description of the file structure of the site. Be sure to include a summary of file locations.
- ♦ *File names*   A description of how files were named (i.e., the logic or method used to name them). A solid naming convention is important, especially for large sites. Files should be named in such a way that you can tell where the file lives and what it contains just by looking at the file name.
- ♦ *Coding and scripting notes*   if you are using any kind of Javascript or cgi-script, then it's important you describe what the script does and how to make modifications to it. As well, fully commented code will help the people who are maintaining the site to quickly see what to update.
- ♦ *Production art notes*   A description of how the images were saved. We usually tell our clients what settings to save GIFs and JPEGs. These numbers change, depending on the palette and the end-user requirements. We also provide Photoshop files with separate layers for text, so that clients can easily make new graphics if needed. See the /templates/chapter3/ folder on the CD-ROM for a sample graphic kit.

Production Infrastructure

Planning ahead and providing a good production infrastructure for your team is essential to a smooth production process.

Tracking Content

The production infrastructure is not only where the site gets built, but also where all the content of the site is kept in various stages of completion. The process of moving and tracking elements of the site such as copy, images, and other media is called asset tracking. It's important that someone (usually you or a production manager) is in charge of making sure all assets come in from the people who are supposed to provide them, and then go through a review phase before they get handed to coders to incorporate into the site. All assets should have sign-offs before they get incorporated. This step can be quite tedious, and that's why it's important for all members of the team to know where to look for assets so that they can review them, approve them, and forward them quickly.

The asset-tracking process should be a process that all team members feel comfortable with and it should evolve out of the best way for people to work together. At Red Sky, we have a folder structure in place and assets move through their various stages by way of these folders. When assets are ready to be integrated into the site, they get moved to the production folder, which contains folders for the different media types. This is a simple method of asset management but it works for small-scale Web projects (up to 40 pages or so). Figure 3.6 shows our production folder.

Development Site

The development site is the environment in which the site gets built. It's critical that this area be ready before the project moves into the production phase. Generally, the technical team sets up this area and provides you with the location of the development site, along with the access information for the production team. Some of the specific questions you might ask about the development site include:

- ◆ Where is the site? What is the IP address or URL?
- ◆ Does the team need a user name and password to access it?
- ◆ Do we need to use special software to access it?
- ◆ Is there appropriate security on it so that only the Web team can access and view it?
- ◆ Does it mirror the production (or live) Web environment?

When you know the answers to these questions, this information should go either on the project site or in the production guide, whichever makes the most sense for you and your team.

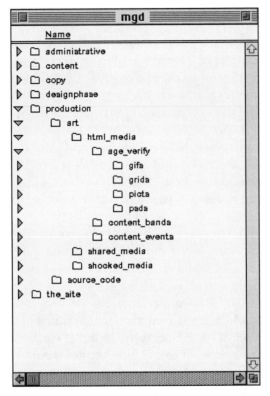

FIGURE 3.6   A sample of asset management using directories.

Planning for Change

No matter how much planning you do, changes will inevitably occur as a result of client or internal review of the site as it is getting built. While it often doesn't seem so, change is good. Let your team know that some degree of change will occur and to think about that in their planning phases. On the client's side, handling change can be a sensitive issue. It's important that you always go back to the original scope document and the supporting functional specification and make sure that you negotiate additional fees for changes that occur outside of the features outlined in these documents. At no point should you implement a change if it will compromise your delivery date (unless the client specifically approves this in writing). If a client wants a change and the delivery date is not moveable, then you will need to negotiate to implement the change at a later phase. You might want to draw up a service agreement with your client that states that your team will implement the change for an additional cost after the initial site is delivered. Remember, the reason for writing the scope document and functional specification is so that you and the client remain clear about the work and costs you've agreed upon. Clients need to know the costs of development, and they need to know when a perceived small change really is a large change with implicating costs.

This chapter's interview with Ken Norton, the vice president of Snap!, offers some insightful ways to deal with change on a Web project.

Reiteration

The planning process and design phases are iterative, and you will be reviewing your plan more than once with your stakeholders. It's important that you explain your development process thoroughly to your clients and prepare them for the reviews ahead. If they are aware of what is expected of them, including how important their prompt feedback is, then they will become willing participants in the project. It is critical that they understand that their actions, such as not giving prompt feedback, can push out a deadline on a project. Many clients don't realize this, and many project managers take this for granted. The result is that this muddled communication creates confusion between your client, you, and your team.

After a Web site goes live, a project manager's legal concerns involve contractual and on-line law.[3]

Getting clear sign-off on all aspects of the project (strategy, creative, and technical design) is also critical to success. Your client must be walked through each document and then should be presented with a sign-off form. This might sound too formal, especially if your client is your boss, but it really is a very critical step. At the end of the planning phase, there should be no doubt about what you are building. The only way to ensure this is to take the time and formally go over each piece, then sign off on it. You can also sign a document as a promise to build the site to the agreed-on specifications.

Effective Meetings and Reviews

You've got the green light to go, and you are now moving into production, where all your terrific planning can go out the door if you do not keep your team on track. The only way to do this is through a very clear and effective communication process, which includes regular meetings.

Nobody likes to go to a meeting that has no agenda. These kinds of meetings seem like wastes of time to programmers who have deadlines to

---

3. The myriad of legal options or scenarios are beyond the scope of this book, but you should protect yourself. For example, see Thomas J. Smedinghoff, *Online Law: The SPA's Legal Guide to Doing Business on the Internet*. Reading, MA: Addison Wesley Longman, 1996.

meet. Always have an agenda and send it out before the meeting, so that people know what to expect.

At these meetings, make sure you go over the schedule and determine if milestones will be hit on time. Ask your team for any issues or red flags that they see; this will help them anticipate risks as you move forward. Make sure people leave with clear action items. People should know what they are supposed to be doing and what to do next either by day or by week. Keep the meeting quick and focused, then follow up the meeting with a summary of points that were discussed.

People often ask me what the best tool is for keeping a project on track, and I always say the same thing: e-mail. E-mail is the best productivity tool because it provides a clear and undisputed communications path. I don't expect my entire team to be able to read a project schedule. I interpret the schedule for my team at our first meeting after the schedule has been determined. Then I send regular reminders to the team regarding their deliverables and who is depending on their deliverables to move forward.

Summary

You covered a lot of ground in this chapter. You learned about the different phases of a Web project and how to plan effectively during each one. To reiterate, it's always best to document the process carefully because it will save you headaches later when your clients (internal or external) want to change the features of the Web site. Your team members might complain about excessive documentation, but they will get used to it and come to value it as they become more experienced. In the next chapter, you'll learn all about communication and the role it plays in producing a Web project.

> TO-DO LIST
> - Determine the development phases of your project, and communicate these to the team and to the client.
> - Write the creative brief.
> - Write the functional specification.
> - Plan a weekly status meeting, and set routes with your client to communicate progress.
> - Ensure that the deliverables from each phase of planning are produced.
> - Create the project site.

Managing Change in the Web Development
Environment

Kenneth Norton
Vice President of Technology
Snap!

As vice president of technology at Snap!, Kenneth Norton is responsible
for the management and direction of the company's engineering department.
He has also been a leader in defining the site development process both
at Snap! and at CNET, where he spent two years as director of software
engineering.

Prior to joining CNET in the summer of 1996, he served as supervisor of
on-line services at Softbank Services Group (SSG), a high-technology out-
sourcing company. Mr. Norton began working the Web in the dark days of
1994, when he was developing on-line transaction processing software at SSG.

Mr. Norton sits on the Advisory Committee of the World Wide Web
Consortium (W3C) and is a member of the ACM and IEEE. He is a cum laude
graduate of Boston University. His professional interests include software engineering processes and practices, specifically requirements engineering and
change management as they apply to the rapid development of on-line
services.

What are the responsibilities of your job?

I oversee all of technology for Snap!, which includes software engineering,
Web site programming, software architecture, content aggregation (we have
96 content providers), the service group that provides tools for the content
group, QA, our internal support group both for the Web site and internal systems, and database engineering.

What prompted you to develop a talk on managing change?

I developed the seminar because I was tired of going to conferences and getting a "silver bullet," which was a talk about "this is the right (you fill in the
blank). I realized that 90 percent of the successes I've seen, heard about, and
read about has been about the process.

What is unique about Web development is its parallel development style
(simultaneous, few handoffs), which is also a factor of any kind of project, but
is really the way all Web projects are. In Web development, groups are mov-

ing in parallel (technology, design, writing, advanced programming) and you become more like an orchestra conductor than a project manager. And when all these things are happening in parallel, changes occur.

The watershed for me occurred when I stopped trying to fight change and learned to accept it. In my early career, I was always saying "How can I eliminate change?" I realized what I was doing was just delaying the change. Change is inevitable. Once I realized that change was going to happen and it was good, that it made a better product, then I began to look for ways to allow change to happen, to develop a process that supported change, that made us react to a very fast and changing industry.

A good example of how this process is working is Snap! If we had launched with what was spec'ed two years ago, it wouldn't have been as great, and we wouldn't have been so successful. Our ability to adapt to the industry and to relevant input makes us better. I asked myself "What do I have to do to minimize the impact of change and to harness it, to make sure it was a good thing?" It was difficult. At first I saw a lot of frustration and resistance, especially from the engineers who felt "I built this, and now they are going to throw this away" or "I built this, and now they want to change it again." I realized, while watching this go on, that it wasn't the change that was bad, but the process of reacting to change that was bad. The fact that it wasn't managed or communicated well, it wasn't a team effort. A lot of time it was change for change's sake. Then I looked at the some of the more successful changes.

How did you get your team to buy into allowing change throughout a project?

One of the things that I'm most adamant about is that the engineers must participate in every step of the process. I want to be pragmatic about it because I think it will positively affect the product and also because having them there helps morale around change. It helps everyone's morale if they participate, but ultimately because they're smart people and if you have them all in the room, great things can happen. So I was pretty adamant that they participate not only in requirements gathering but also in envisioning the product. And it works. I've seen engineers happily throw out their code and walk out of a meeting completely excited because they've participated in the process. Change is a cool thing, and it's healthy and it can make a good product better.

Why does change occur so often in Web projects?

Parallel development and miscommunication between teams. Often, I've heard the design team say "Oh, that was just the mock-up, that's not what we really wanted." Meanwhile, the engineering team took that mock-up to be an accurate representation of how the product would look. That's why it's important that everyone is involved in coming up with core functionality and signing off on the same specs.

Also, people perceive that it's easy to change things on the Web. It's not like the construction agency—nobody would take a look at the Sears Tower after it was just built and say "Hey, can you add a garage?"

But on the Web this does happen. That's the difference. People think it's easy to make a Web change primarily because of all the things that make the Web great: one-to-one communications, information on demand, instant results. This thinking leads to some of the less intelligent acts of change. I remember one example where someone recommended we launch with a major bug and then just fix it later. This totally offended my sensibilities. If you were shipping a million CDs, would you ship the first 150,000 with a major bug? Of course not. But that's exactly what you're doing when you go live with a major problem. Only you can't accurately measure the costs because you don't know how many people have been turned away or turned off by it.

Is the change management process the same for different types of teams (size, core functions)?

The process of managing change is different for different kinds of teams. If you have a team of three people and one person says "Hey, wouldn't it be great to . . . ?" and the dialogue is immediate and every member of the team is involved and buys into the change; it's very informal. In that situation, I can't imagine anyone saying "I need to write a specification" to implement changes for that kind of team. But there comes a point for larger teams where that kind of process is critical.

How does the engineering team handle changes now? Any lessons learned?

We used to work in a way, on very large sites, that a project would come in and we (engineering) would say "Tell us what you want." The business team would supply us with an objectives document and we would go off, build a specification, and give it back to the business team. And this type of process works great on huge, long-term projects, like when we were building download.com or Snap! with teams of 60 or more people. But that kind of process didn't have a good enough mechanism for handling change. The fundamental assumption with that kind of process is that there will not and should not be changes. But this is the Web. You just can't say "There will be no changes." You'd be shooting yourself in the foot if you did.

We try not to build software that does "not" specifically do something. If someone says the software should do "A," we don't assume it won't do "B" even if B is the polar opposite. We try to keep our options open.

I've found that once they buy into it, engineers actually love making changes. It gives them an opportunity to do more coding, which is what they love. However, there is a danger there and it needs to be managed very closely. They can get a little off-course because they are thinking "That's cool, I'll do that . . ." and what happens is that the code is totally useless in terms of the money and time spent.

How do you deal with changes that come from inside the development team?

We figure stuff out cross-functionally, where we all sit in a room and figure out how to implement the change. And we do this in the beginning too, when we determine the site requirements and write the initial specification. We're all contributing to the features, and so everyone buys in to that process. We don't say stuff like "You figure that out, you're the guy who designed the thing." Since we all participate, there are no conversations like that.

A good, high-performing team has a lot of trust in the team members. Teams need to trust that individual team members won't betray them, or make decisions that will make their lives miserable. A lot of the good that came out of developing our change process came from giving people a lot of visibility in the project. This also helps people feel more in control of changes, and it makes people more accountable as well as visible. Change for change's sake falls out pretty quickly in an environment like that.

In a team approach, good ideas are shared. It's important to keep teams together, to share the knowledge they learned on one project and apply it to the next. They gel and things work for them. I try not to break teams up that have gelled well.

We have change management meetings. We assess changes, talk about them, sit as a team, and try to figure out what's important and how to handle the change. Usually we come to a collective decision; sometimes it comes down to a vote. It's a democratic process, not by design, but by what works in our environment. In such an environment everyone is valuable and valued. That makes people want to stay around.

Who does your team consist of?

They are called feature teams, and they typically consist of a person from each of the following groups: on-line development, creative services, technical design, technology, and product management

Favorite tools?

StoryServer (by Vignette), which C I Net actually helped develop. We use our own version of StoryServer, specifically optimized for our needs. My most favorite tool is e-mail, however.

What tips would you give a Web project manager for managing change efficiently and professionally?

Hire people who get it—who get your business. I refuse to hire people who aren't interested in the business models. The greatest C/C++ programmer can come in here but if he's not interested or doesn't even know about the business, then I'm not interested—because he isn't interested in building a learning corporation.

Handling change is really a frame of mind.

CHAPTER 4

Communication Issues

IF YOU NEED . . .

♦ To understand what causes poor communication on a team, read the "Common Causes" section.

♦ To evaluate whether your team has communication problems, read "Evaluate the Way Your Team Communicates."

♦ Quick solutions, go to "Tools, Standards, and Methods."

♦ Tips on making meetings more productive, read "Leading Effective Meetings."

♦ Templates to help document communications on a project, check out this chapter's folder on the CD-ROM.

Whenever we finish a project, we always conduct a postmortem to hash out what we learned and what we could do better the next time around. And in almost every postmortem the issue of communication comes up. Often, when we trace issues like budget overages back to the source, we find that they point to a miscommunication of some sort.

Communication Breakdown: Why?

Good communication is critical to every project, but how easy is it to identify what "good communication" is? Even if you document every e-mail and hold prodigious meetings, you cannot be sure that what one person says, another person will understand. Good communication comes from learning, occurs over time, and must be practiced between people. You could have the world's best communication process, in which people meet daily and follow up each meeting with good notes that are dispersed to the whole team, and still have poor communication. For example, if Jennifer, an engineer, does not understand what Kevin, the animator, means by "low-res animation," there is a communication problem.

This chapter discusses how to identify communication issues and provides a framework for creating a team that understands what it means to have a good communications structure.

Common Causes

There are many causes of poor communication. Some are obvious, but most of the causes of poor communication on a team are not what you might expect. Here is a list of eleven of the leading causes of poor communication on a team. Do you recognize them? Any one of them could be the reason your projects keep spiraling out of control.

1. *People come from different disciplines.*   You know how it is when you get together with family? You all have a certain way of communicating—an understanding that is nonverbal, implied, and intuitive. It's the same with people who specialize in different disciplines, such as design, programming, and sales. People who come from these disciplines can understand each other but could have to work on communicating with people outside of their disciplines. It's important for you to be aware of this possibility and to encourage the team to work on ways of making communication clearer.

2. *Lack of a mutual understanding of terminology.*   One of the most common problems I've seen has to do with coming up with definitions for terms that are used loosely or differently. For example, "quality assurance," "functional specification," "broadband," "low resolution," and "concept" are all terms that might cause confusion among team members. Try to identify terminology that can be misinterpreted.

3. *Personalities.*   One of the more difficult communication problems to identify and treat is the issue of personalities. Sometimes, two people have a more difficult time communicating with each other than they do with other people.

4. *Hidden agendas.*   If people on a team have hidden agendas, it will be difficult to communicate with them because they will be led by their motivations. They will not be open to hearing suggestions, alternatives, and changes.

5. *Ineffective meetings.*   Meetings can be an incredible waste of time if they are not led well. It's not easy to lead an effective meeting; big personalities, lots of details, and conflicting agendas all lead to a sense of disorganization for the team. The result is a meeting that runs too long, and from which nobody comes away with a sense of what was discussed, and most important, what to do next. (See the end of the chapter for some guidelines on leading effective meetings.)

6. *Proximity.*   Members of your team might be in different cities, states, or even countries. This means that the meetings you have will be largely conference calls or videoconferences. Nuances in communication, such as facial expressions or colloquial speech, might be lost, which could make clear communication extremely difficult.

7. *Assumptions.*   Often, people make assumptions, and these assumptions can cloud their ability to communicate. For example, assumptions can cause problems when we get into production and the creative director begins to realize that she's made some assumptions about how the site will function, but she failed to write them into the functional specification.

8. *Poor infrastructure and support.*   This is one of the most overlooked causes of poor communication. Computer troubles, e-mail incompatibility, file format incompatibility, and other systems failures can contribute to a communication breakdown. When one occurs, consider how it will affect communication and have a contingency plan—such as calling an emergency meeting to make sure deadlines will not be missed.

9. *Being an expert.*   Beware of the team player who is an "expert" at something—often this person will not listen in meetings because he or she "knows what to do." Unfortunately what the expert may not know is what impact his or her piece of the site has on the other people who are working on it.

10. *Fear.*   I think that fear is probably the biggest barrier to good communication. When faced with a big, complex project, sometimes team members go into panic mode and they try to devise a game plan around their role. This can sometimes cause them to close down their creative minds, leading to narrow, poorly thought-out strategies. It also causes them to shut down their receptive minds during meetings.

11. *Lack of a good communications structure.*   A good communications structure is made up of communication systems that fit the way people work, that have the information that people need to get their jobs done. It does not have unnecessary information, is easy to use, and is usable (kind of like a good Web site!). It's usually made up of e-mail, e-mail conventions, telephone, and a project Web site, which we discussed in chapter 1. It also incorporates conventions that the team agrees on and that make sense.

Some of these causes of miscommunication are subtle, and so it's impossible to provide a series of detailed steps to correct the problem. Rather, just gaining an awareness of the causes can help you prepare for them by, for example, taking greater care in documenting meetings, defining terms, and taking other steps that make communications clearer. In this chapter you will learn what you need to learn about your different team members so that you can create a communications structure that works for your team.

Creating Effective Communication Systems

It's no secret that programmers and designers speak different languages. They have different ways of speaking, communicating, and thinking— perhaps. I know several designers who think like programmers and vice versa. The point is you cannot build a communications structure by trying to outline the differences in people. What you have to do is assume that people think and communicate differently, look for ways to standardize the terminology and process, and then create or establish tools that everyone can use.

Evaluate the Way Your Team Communicates

Here are six things to consider when evaluating your current communications structure:

1. What is your current communications structure? When news comes in that affects a project, who talks to whom? How can you leverage the existing structure? For those of you folks who grew up where it snowed, remember your school's telephone system of people who called people who called more people to announce that school was closed?

2. Do you often have trouble opening and reading file attachments from team members?

3. Is there a list of all team members' names, phone and pager numbers, and e-mail addresses on your project site?

The functional specification and schematics are documents that affect every team member. This is a good place to establish a common language to discuss functional elements of the site. You can read more about this later, under "Tools, Standards, and Methods," as well as in this chapter's interview.

4. Do people on your project team have lots of small, informal meetings that are undocumented?

5. Do you frequently go over budget on your projects?

6. Do you often find out things "through the grapevine"?

If you realize that you have answered "yes" to some or all of these questions, then you have weaknesses in your communications structure that you need to address. Your next step is to look for places where there are natural "checkpoints" for instilling good communications. For example, do you have weekly status meetings? If you do, start summarizing those meetings in e-mail. Be sure to end each a meeting with each team member reiterating his or her next step. Never leave a meeting with unasked or unanswered questions. What's worse: a stupid question or a stupid mistake?

Do You Need a Translator?

If you are faced with issues such as language barriers, you must have someone on the team (obviously) who can act as a translator. This means that the person understands each language well. You will experience this more and more if you are doing global Web sites. On a recent project we did for a banking company in Hong Kong, we found that even though the client's project manager could speak English, there were many instances where we could not effectively communicate with their technology team. In the end, we relied heavily on written communication following each conference call, and both project managers initialed each point discussed.

If you have a large technology team, your technical lead must be able to act as a translator of technical, creative, usability, and production requirements as they come in from the team. I'm not going to discuss what to do if you have a large technology team (three or more technical members) and no tech lead, because I strongly believe you need a lead—a single point of contact. The ability to communicate with the tech team and the rest of the team leads should be one of your major ways of evaluating your tech lead.

Tools, Standards, and Methods

Once you have taken a look at your communications structure, you can start to put some best practices into effect.

Chain of Communication

If there doesn't appear to be a consistent chain of communication in place, create one. Be logical; take into consideration the fact that news doesn't always come from the client alone. Figure 4.1 shows a common structure for communications on a project team.

The same people always talk to the same people. It's important to have one person who is the communications hub. In this case, the producer is the person who ensures that all members receive information. Here is how this structure would work over several kinds of events:

1. During a review with the account manager, the creative director, and the producer, the client requests a change. The producer communicates this change to the project team either by sending an e-mail to the entire team or by sending an e-mail to each of the respective team leaders, depending on the size of the team.

2. The MIS manager tells a programmer that the server the team is using is flaky and must be shut down. The programmer tells his team leader, who tells the producer. If the client has to know, the producer tells the account manager, who talks to the client. The producer communicates

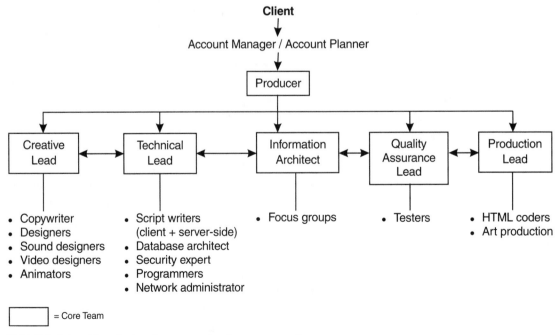

FIGURE 4.1   The chain of communication on a project team.

the news to the rest of the project team through either the team leaders or global e-mail.

3. The lead designer and the account manager come up with a great new feature, which isn't part of the project's scope. The account manager tells the producer, who communicates the idea to the other team leaders. If necessary, the other team leaders meet with their teams to discuss the new feature. If there is significant complexity, the entire team meets to discuss the feature to determine, within reason, the amount of effort and extra cost. Once the team comes up with a solution, the account manager communicates the idea to the client. (Note that all this communication occurs before the client is notified. Remember, this is an ideal scenario!)

The key to an effective communications chain is that all people know to whom to tell news and pass on information, and that one person is responsible for alerting the project team (the producer) and one person is responsible for alerting the client or stakeholder (the account person). Sometimes, the producer and the account person are the same person. If this is so, and that person is you, remember to get the team's input first and then communicate to the client. This will enable you to be prepared for the questions that will inevitably arise.

Symbology

Symbols are very powerful. When accepted by users, their appearance can make many people act in a known and consistent manner. For example, when drivers see a red light, they know to stop their cars. How can symbols benefit a Web team? Think about how often you've encountered a communication problem over how something is going to work on a Web site. For example, take the rollover. A rollover is a JavaScript event that makes something happen when a user rolls his or her mouse cursor over images or text. In this case, when a user rolls her mouse cursor over an image that is a link, what happens? Another image appears, indicating an "on" state. What if there were a symbol for rollovers on a page? If the functionality were standard, meaning that there is one possibility for the functionality of the thing, then a symbol would be useful because everyone on the team would understand what happens when a user rolls over it. This means that the design team would know to create two states for the image, on and off. It means that the programmer would know to use a rollover script. It means that the QA team would know what functionality to test for.

Where do these symbols belong? In the schematic documents that I discussed in chapter 3. These documents help your team build and test prototypes quickly. (See Figure 4.2.)

At Ikonic (now US/Web and CKS), two developers, a graphic designer and a programmer/usability specialist, pioneered the idea of using symbology to communicate functionality on a Web site to facilitate the design

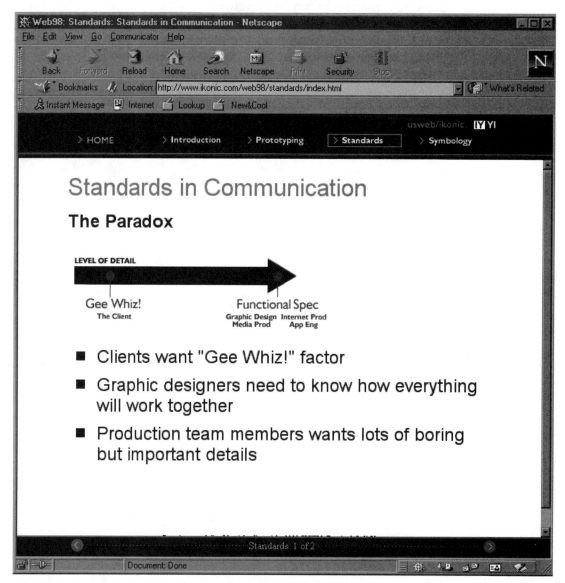

FIGURE 4.2   Schematics and symbols make cross-team communication easier.

and development process. Indi Young and Pete Howells, interviewed at the end of this chapter, developed a method based on establishing standards for communicating functional elements on a Web site. This methodology and its symbology can be studied at *http://www. threedollarbill.com/web98/*.

Style Guides

A style guide is important, but a good Web style guide is a hard commodity to find. Inconsistency is rampant on the Web. A style guide offers a consistent guide to word and acronym usage. For example, when do you capitalize "internet" or "web"? These questions, and more, should be addressed in your style guide. I recommend taking an established style guide, such as the *Chicago Manual of Style* or the *Associated Press Style Guide*, and creating an addendum that covers standard Web terms. The style guides cover more than 80 percent of the usage questions you might have, so there is no need to reinvent the wheel here. Every member of your team should have one of these guides.

Production Guides

In the previous chapter, I discussed the value of having a production guide and the contents of what that guide should contain. I've also included a sample production guide in the CD-ROM that accompanies this book; see the /templates/chapter3 folder..

From a communications point of view, the production guide is a valuable tool in case of the need to add or change production staff quickly. The guide gives new staff an overview of the production aspects of a project, such as server access information, directory structure, file-naming conventions, file formats, production art statistics, and file size limits. (See Figure 4.3.)

Infrastructure

Some of the worst communication takes place between computers. Nothing is more frustrating for a team member than to receive documents in a format his or her computer cannot read. It's critical to decide on hardware, software, and other platform-related standards before you start the project.

I recommend making HTML documents and posting them on your project site as often as possible—this eliminates many cross-platform issues. However, if you must use other programs, such as Excel or Word, make sure your team has access to these tools, or be sure to send hard copies along with soft copies. Sometimes low-tech is the best way to go.

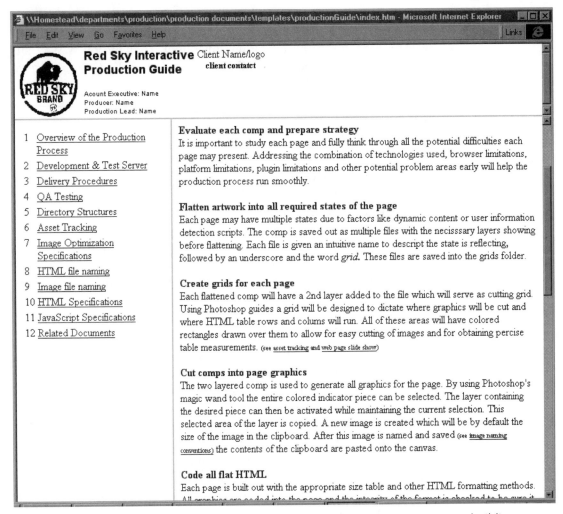

FIGURE 4.3   A production guide should incorporate all information pertaining to building the site.

Automating Communication

I haven't had much luck with automating communication on a project, since communication can be so critical. If you are curious, however, there are several systems you might want to check out.

Certain programs, like Team Manager by Microsoft, allows you to set up a system that alerts team members when people have achieved certain programming milestones. For example, once a person has finished a task, she sends an e-mail to the project manager, and the schedule is automatically updated with the new information. Personally, as a project manager, this feature would drive me crazy since I tend to be very controlling about who updates my schedule. But less controlling project managers or producers might find this useful. Appendix B is a resource guide for software that automates the scheduling and task management process. Be sure to look for features that enable teamwide communication.

The kind of automatic communication I like is still human: It occurs when teams are conditioned to communicate with team members in a timely, articulate manner, and to the people that the communication structure permits. If you can provide this kind of environment and encouragement, you've hit upon a huge success in your career as a producer or project manager.

Documenting Your Communication

I can't stress how important it is to keep a log of your communications throughout the life of your project. You know already that any communication with your client deserves to be documented, but communication with everyone is important. There is a lot you can learn from a project by rereading communications from the project.

I try to document my communication in two ways. The first is through my e-mail program. I use Microsoft Outlook, and I keep lots of notes about the communications that I've had. Other people keep a written journal of phone conversations in a spiral notebook. Either way is good, but try to be consistent.

The second method of documenting communication is through the project binder that I create for every project. This binder contains everything you could possibly want to know about a project, and I do this as part of the archiving process for the project. The binders give new producers insight about the way projects are managed. I keep all e-mail regarding the project in this binder, organized chronologically. I keep e-mail to the client separate, so I have quick access to it in case I need it.

Leading Effective Meetings

I've attended too many unfocused and unproductive meetings that waste time and frustrate team members. People often have meetings to help clear up confusion; but in an attempt to clear confusion, more confusion gets created because the meeting has no focus. In an effort to make meetings more productive, I went in search of some guidelines. Here is a meeting format that, so far, has worked to keep meeting time focused. People come away from meetings held in this format with a clear understanding of what occurred in the meeting and what to do next.

There are three important roles in a meeting:

1. The meeting leader calls the meeting.
2. The minute-taker takes notes during the meeting.
3. The timekeeper keeps track of time.

There are eight steps in the format of the meeting:

1. Establish who will be the minute-taker and who will be the time-keeper.
2. Reiterate the agenda on the blackboard or white board, or hand out copies. Ask if anyone has items to add to the agenda. Ask the time-keeper to assign times to each item.
3. Review the previous week's meeting. Follow up on the status of old action items.
4. For each agenda item, first define, then discuss:
   a. *Content*   What is the topic or problem to address?
   b. *Process*   How will the topic be discussed (e.g., brainstorming, go-around, presentation)?
   c. *Resolution*   Is a decision needed or are we just discussing? If a decision is necessary, define the kind of decision to be made (e.g., consensus, voting).
   d. *Action*   Record the actions decided on, the people responsible, and the date by which they have to accomplish the actions.
5. Summarize the meeting (minute-taker) and make sure everyone agrees on what happened.
6. Set roles and an agenda for the next meeting.
7. Evaluate the meeting.
8. *Close*   Formally end the meeting. I like to provide cookies and milk, but others clap or even sing a song.

It takes practice to lead an effective meeting. Try to stick to this format and you will see improvements in productivity and peoples' attitudes about meetings.

Summary

Miscommunication occurs on every project. In order to avoid or minimize the repercussions of miscommunication, you need to create an effective communications structure within your organization and your project team. This chapter provided you with suggestions for creating the systems necessary to enable better communication. It also gave you some common causes of miscommunication so that you can be aware of how miscommunications occur. While some of these causes do not have "out-of-the-box" solutions, it's important to be aware of them so that you can address them and temporarily build contingencies around them until you can resolve the issues—generally by trial and error of tactics described in the chapter.

To-Do List

♦ Evaluate your current communications structure. What can be improved?

♦ Add contact information such as phone numbers, pager numbers, and e-mail addresses to your project Web site.

♦ Make sure each team member knows the chain of communication for your project team.

♦ Evaluate whether you need an automated communications package, such as Microsoft team manager (though I still believe human communications are best).

♦ If you haven't started a system of documenting your communication, use the process binder.

Developing Standards of Communication
for Web Teams

Indi Young
President and CEO
Young Ideas

Pete Howells
Creative Director and Artist

Indi Young has been doing interaction design for more than ten years. Her interaction design background stems from software engineering, enabling tight collaboration with technical teams. The methodology that Indi applies is analytical, leading to designs that can be substantiated and that empower the user beyond the original task requirements. Indi introduces usability testing at points in development where the results can enhance design. She always works toward bringing genuine improvements to user productivity.

Working as both a graphic and user-interface (UI) designer, Peter Howells has developed interactive television shopping applications, electronic program guides for international digital satellite services, and large-scale, dynamic Web sites. As a director of interface design at USWeb/CKS, he works with clients to determine a project's features list, develops schematics and navigational flowcharts of the user's experience, and creates other information tools to guide the project from concept to implementation. Pete has worked on sites for Standard & Poor, Janus, ParentTime, Star TV, and Time Warner.

What motivated you to develop standards and symbology for Web UI?

PETE: Indi and I took a strong interest in developing standards and tools for user-interface design soon after we started working together. Her technical background and approach to UI interested me, especially since Ikonic's approach had developed from a design point of view.

Indi took most of the initiative in arranging our presentations. We wanted to validate some of our experiences in developing Web sites, a field where the concept of user-interface design and information architecture was starting to take shape separate from graphic design.

INDI: I was encouraged to do a presentation at a conference; and, while I was casting around for something to speak about, I had a conversation with a friend who is a computer science professor at Oregon Graduate Institute. He gave me this advice, "Talk about what you know. You'd be surprised that other people don't know the things you think are so simple." So, I thought about what I knew and seized upon this symbology that Pete and I were working on at Ikonic at the time. It was something I knew inside and out. Another friend asked me if I'd like to speak at Web98, so I asked Pete to join me in putting together a presentation.

The goal of our presentation about UI symbology was to spread two ideas: that user-interface design should be a separate step from graphic design or creative treatment, and that we needed to use some sort of language to communicate to the rest of the team what we were thinking as UI designers. We wanted to see if other members of our community would adopt our technique, and if so, how would they improve upon it? We intended to keep in touch with users of the symbology so that we could incorporate improvements to the symbols.

Does standardizing elements of Web UI make Web sites less interesting? Does it compromise creativity?

INDI: We are not standardizing elements of Web user interface. We are standardizing a way of communicating a UI design to the team that must implement it.

PETE: The standardization we are talking about is how we communicate the functionality of the site separate from how it looks, and this does not preclude developing new forms of interactivity. It just means creating language for communicating functionality so that you don't have to explain that this thing is a button and this thing is text. Instead, UI designers can focus on more interesting topics like what the page provides for the user. At no time have we implied that there should be standards for how buttons look on final Web sites or that creativity should be limited.

How are programmers used to communicating?

PETE: Programmers all learn some aspect of user-interface design in school, but they are generally given a pretty lean toolkit and their focus is not ensuring that users understand their interface, but that it function technically. User interface designers focus on making sure the collaboration between technical needs and graphic/creative needs leads to a usable/useful Web site.

INDI: The engineers I've worked with use a lot of diagrams and white boards. The diagrams can represent architectures, object models, windows, or whatever. Usually, engineers are involved in the requirements stage of software design, so they are also familiar with using words, tables, and lists to communicate their designs. Although every engineer has a valid background for creating a user interface, it takes someone who can truly adopt the user's perspective, and not get caught up in the technical challenges, to create an innovative interface.

How are designers used to communicating?

PETE: Designers obviously need to get the highest impact from their presentations to show creative vision. Because this aspect of the site is often the sexiest in the eyes of the client, these presentations can distract the client from the nuts and bolts, "how it works" aspect. In order for the client to feel comfortable with the UI, a clean approach to presenting information architecture and user-interface concepts, including standards, can streamline this approval process and help the client feel more involved and informed.

INDI: In my somewhat limited experience (only since mid-1996), I see graphic designers communicate with key screen images, storyboards, treatment write-ups, and mood descriptions. Often, the functionality of a user interface being discussed is shown in terms of fancy prototypes, and the discussion wanders away from the viability of the use of a piece of software and goes toward the graphic treatment. Everyone has opinions about graphics, and everyone has opinions about user interface. However, to discuss them both in the same session has proved inefficient. Thus, Pete and I developed the symbology to focus early discussions on functionality, rather than graphic design.

How do your schematics improve communication on a large Web team?

PETE: Schematics and prototypes help ensure that the design that is approved is the design that is implemented. On large-scale Web sites, there can often be a long time lag between schematic and prototype approval and final production and launch. With absolutely complete and clear schematics, quality of production can be checked from approval of graphic design through technical integration.

INDI: The symbology adds clarity to the schematics—specific messages to each team member: engineering, editorial, design, the client—about how the team is envisioning the design for the site. Any member of the team can sit down and read the schematics without a UI person present to explain the functionality. Our schematics are always accompanied by written descriptions of the interaction. This clarity allows large teams to operate across any distance and across any development time lag.

What are some typical miscommunications between client and Web team? Between programmers and designers?

PETE: Clients are often not interested in many of the tiny details of UI, like error messages or field sizes. If these details are not reviewed and approved early enough, the client may suddenly develop a strong opinion about them late in the process when it's too late to make changes. Effective and efficient communication of these issues as early in the process as possible will smooth out problems that could be large later on.

In my experience, there was a time when design was completely approved without even consulting technical, with a blanket assumption that anything that was designed was "doable." Considering the market today, including competitiveness and the size of budgets and time lines, that's just a laughable position. Sure, anything is doable given enough time and money, but it's far more advisable to represent to the client things that are practical, to control expectation. The UI designer can focus on defining the scope of the interface solutions and collaborate with technical and graphic designers to present the client with the functionality of the site before too much is invested in technical implementation or time-consuming creative development.

INDI: I wouldn't necessarily call this a miscommunication, but design is an iterative process. As the Web team starts to brainstorm solutions to the client's needs, the client learns more about technology and about other solutions that have been successful. Inevitably, the client changes the details of the initial request (often at the suggestion of the Web team). The faster the client learns in this process, the less redesign work the Web team must do. So having clear functionality laid out and discussed early in the process is an advantage.

Miscommunication between engineers and designers often appears more as misunderstanding of current technology. Sometimes, designers create something that is too difficult, time consuming, or broad bandwidth for engineers to implement for the Web. This happens in the other direction, too. Sometimes engineers want to try out some new technology on the Web and find a place to shoehorn it into the design. Either event is fertile ground for some passionate discussions, which are usually quickly dispelled. For the most part, engineers and designers enjoy working with and learning from one another.

How do you get your clients to buy into your process (cost, time involved)?

PETE: We are constantly evaluating the best approach to selling our clients on the value of our up-front work on information architecture and UI design. Once we do convince them that locking the UI early will save money, we still need to engage them with interesting presentations while getting them to review things that may be more mundane and practical. That's why I now advocate for prototyping instead of schematics whenever possible, because they are more interactive and require less of a leap to understand the user experience. These prototypes follow similar standards as schematics.

It's also helpful for clients to see creative "concepts" as early as possible to keep them engaged and excited about our creative solutions. These concepts are developed by the graphic designers' focus on the look and feel of the site while commenting as little as possible on the individual elements on the page, since those elements are still under development by the UI designer.

INDI: Actually, after describing the process, clients have little trouble seeing its merits. Lately, I haven't come across a client who was unwilling to engage in rigorous UI design up front. It doesn't even take two explanations to convince them. I have a more difficult time explaining the merit of task analysis, and often have that phase of design crushed into one day.

What tips can you give to Web teams that are just beginning to develop their communications structure?

PETE: In my experience, all creative groups go through no-process/process cycles, where there is constant trial and error to balance chaos (no process) and order (rigid process). Chaos makes projects very hard to deliver within time and budget while keeping the team sane, where absolute order can alienate the client and stifle creativity. I think a new group should, as much as possible, define roles, responsibilities, and deliverables on a project with an idea of what comes after what; but in the end, experience is what truly drives process.

INDI: A new team should be sure of their roles and be sure that everyone on the team understands and supports each role. (I have run across teams who ostracize the UI designer and throw away schematics. That's just a dysfunctional team—it could happen in a law firm as easily as in a Web design house.) Be sure each team member knows that this is a collaborative process—that design doesn't happen serially and get handed off from one person to another. Also, it's important for teams to adapt the process to themselves, rather than the other way around. The process is just a suggestion, not a "one-size-fits-all" solution.

CHAPTER 5

The Client

IF YOU NEED . . .

♦ To learn about legal documents, see the section "Communication throughout the Project."

♦ Sample documents like a contact report or non-disclosure agreement, go to the /templates/chapter5/ folder on the CD-ROM.

♦ Pointers on conducting reviews, see "Conducting Effective Reviews."

♦ To know how to build trust, read the whole chapter!

Client relationships take time to define, develop, and nurture. Additionally, you can't assume anything when you are contracted to build a Web site. The Web is an evolving medium, and you might find yourself having to understand where you stand with your client: Does he regard the Web as a productivity tool, as a marketing device, as the next cool thing? Do you have to work in tandem with an advertising agency? Does your client expect things from you that are impossible given their budget or time line?

The way you manage your client can be directly related to the success of your Web project. No matter how brilliant your execution is, your client will not realize it unless he has come to trust you. And your client will not trust you unless he is sure you fully understand what is critical to his success and, therefore, the project's success.

This chapter gives you some pointers to becoming an effective client manager. At the end of this chapter, you can read an interview with a successful client manager, Louis Malafarina, president and CEO of Ripple Effects Interactive. Louis offers some excellent tips and shares some good stories about working successfully with clients.

Definition of the Client

The client is the person who has contracted you to build a Web site. If your project is an internal project, then your client might be your marketing or IS department, your boss, or the CEO of your company. Even if your client is an internal client, the advice in this chapter will help you manage your project more efficiently because ultimately a client's satisfaction with regard to the work that you do depends largely on the way you communicate with your client.

Differences between Internal and External Clients

While many of the practices that this section describes will help you manage clients, there are still some important differences between internal and external clients.

In an internal situation, you will have to deal with internal politics because these politics can affect your career and certainly the success of your project. You'll have to be aware of who is supporting the project and for what reason. Departmental budgets, bonuses, and promotions tied to the success of your projects are factors that can affect your ability to get approval on different aspects of the project. You will probably find yourself getting very involved in the promotion of the site in order to build consensus and support. In fact, this is something you should plan on doing. You will probably need to build justification for the project's existence, especially if the project is your idea. Additionally, make sure you investigate the political risks for yourself and your stakeholders.

In an external situation, you do need to be aware of internal politics but you usually do not have to build consensus within the client's organization. Make sure your client has the authority to sign off on the Web site. If she doesn't this could mean many delays in your schedule.

The Client Education Process

No matter how obvious Web site development seems to you, you will need to educate your client about not only the Web site, but also your process in managing the project, critical factors that might affect the development of the site, and the assumptions you have about your client's participation.

Your Client's Point of View

For your clients, the Web site is just one aspect of their overall business so it's important for you to understand their position. Sometimes what you think is best, in terms of Web site strategy, may not be what the client thinks is best because she is looking at the bottom line. The better you are at understanding clients' business and objectives, the more successful you will be in providing a Web site that produces the results they need.

Your relationship with your client will benefit if you take the time to understand his overall business position, not just where the Web site is concerned. You need to feel the urgency your client feels; and, to do this, you must know what is at stake for your client. When you know this, you will be able to work well within your client's budget and strategy, and you will develop a rapport with your client that can come only from a genuine understanding of his position. Once you have done this, you are one step closer to communicating to the client what he needs to know about your process and needs for providing him with a Web site.

How do you come to understand your client's position? Here are two tips:

Get in the habit of sending your client appropriate industry information, especially if it pertains to her business. Always be sure to write a brief intro to what you send.

- ♦ *Research.*   Study your client's business, marketing brand, and competitors. Find out what your client's competitors are doing on the Web and in their other business functions.
- ♦ *Ask questions.*   What's at risk for your client? How do the Web site's objectives fit into the overall business objectives for the client? Does your client have a boss whose approval is critical? If so, make sure you understand that person's objectives as well.

Communicating Your Process to Your Client

It's important to take the time to communicate your work process to your client. Methodologies are very important. They show your client that you are professional, organized, and efficient.

I put an explanation of my work process both in the scope document (/templates/chapter1/ on the CD-ROM). Having an explanation of your work process in your business proposal might give you a competitive edge over other Web and new media companies. If you get the business, then you can reiterate your process in the scope document. However, you cannot rely on the written word to sink in without some reinforcement. At your very first meeting, it's important to reiterate the work process, including the critical milestones and assumptions you have for your client in order to meet your deadline. Specifically, you must communicate in the very beginning of your association your policies regarding changes in scope so that your client is not surprised when you tell her you will have to charge for changes.

Setting Clear Expectations

You know that if your client waits two weeks to give you approval on a concept or design execution that your deadline could be put in jeopardy, but your client may not know that. It's important to set clear expectations with your client and provide the rationale for these expectations. You need to flesh out what your client's and your expectations are for the following:

1. *Deliverables*   What will you be delivering to your client? What does your client need to deliver to you in order to move forward? Who on your client's team is delivering content to you? You don't want to be inundated with requests from all over the company. If your client is delivering assets to you (artwork, copy), you will need to specify the format in which you need to obtain these assets.

2. *Approvals*   How will approvals be handled? Do you need a 24-hour turnaround for approval? You approval should always be in writing, no matter how good a relationship you have with a client. This relationship could end abruptly over a dispute. Better to have a policy in place to handle approvals than to lose a client as a result of a dispute about what exactly was approved.

3. *Policies*   If you have policies, such as your change-order process or your approvals process, it's best to go over them verbally with your client. Your client should be able to ask questions about the policies. No matter how important a client is, try not to make exceptions in policies and pricing for a client. Doing so not only compromises your accounting of your business, it also makes you appear inconsistent to your co-workers, colleagues, and your clients.

Writing Contact Reports

You write a contact report each time you have a conversation with your client in which you discuss aspects of your project, issues raised, and changes. Send your client a copy and you keep a copy. It's a good way to document your project and to keep track of things you discuss informally with your client.

Getting "Buy-in"

While clients love the idea of having a process and method, sometimes they have a hard time paying for it. If your client resists paying the costs of development and production, then you need to educate your client with regard to the value of your process and the impact it has on your client's bottom line. Here are two important points to emphasize:

1. *Overall cost savings*   If you spend time up front evaluating exactly the functionality of the site, then you will uncover technical issues that might make the project unfeasible. Discovering this earlier rather than later will save the client money.

2. *Better results*   If you spend time in strategic planning and concept development to solve a business problem, then you will be closer to getting the results you want because you've spent the time developing and testing your idea. This is a common practice in advertising and software development, yet clients forget this when it comes to the Web. The perception of the Web as "easy" and "fast" makes clients uneasy when it comes to spending the time and money up front in proof-of-concept work.

We have an in-depth development and production process. It involves a design and specification phase, complete with black-and-white schematics of screen elements and functionality, a prototype application, significant documentation, and a full testing cycle that involves unit, integration, and regression testing (to learn more about it, read chapter 8, Quality Assurance for Web Projects). On paper, it looks as if our development costs are high, but in comparison to the trials and errors of developing a project without this process, the costs are insignificant. What's more, they can be justified easily. I've found that it's much harder to convince a client to invest in the design phase than it is to convince him to pay for the twelve iterations of the Web site that we had to produce before it was ready to go live. Try to illustrate to your client that this phase is like the foundation of a house and when the contractor and the client finally agree that the house will be rectangular, then everything falls into place. At the end of our development phase, we are confident we will be building the site that best meets the client's objectives; and it will function well, be usable and useful, and be bug-free. These are the very points we use to get buy-in of our process from our clients. If a client is not willing to buy into your process, you might consider resigning the business. Why? It could cost you money in the long run and might tell you something about how working with this particular client might be.

Explaining Technical Issues to Clients

If you are dealing with nontechnical clients, keep your language as simple as possible. Terms that you use every day, and that you hear people using every day, such as "site management" or "Web server" may not be familiar to your clients, so you need to define what you mean as you speak to your clients. However, if your client is technically savvy, don't try to oversimplify; you could appear condescending. Preface your discussions with something like, "You're very technical, but stop me if there is something you don't understand." Always wrap up conversations that deal with technical details with simple summaries and next steps. This will give you a chance to speak more simply and not insult the client.

I try to provide documentation of conversations with clients in a contact report, which is a summary of the conversation that lists important issues discussed. It's also a good place to define technical terms and communicate technical issues and the risks they might have. Figure 5.1 shows a contact report.

Building Communication into the Budget

It's a hard thing to track, but the costs of communicating with your client regularly can be significant, especially if you travel frequently to a client's place of business to communicate issues to other people in your client's organization, such as your client's Web team. Therefore you need to remember to build communication costs into the budget. I try to do this by estimating how much communication I'm likely to do per week. On most projects, I allocate two to three hours per week in communication costs for myself. However, if I know that the team will have to hand over the project to the client's Web team, then my estimates will be higher, or I might try to negotiate an hourly rate for maintenance and support (see "Giving the Project Back" later in the chapter).

You will also need to figure in communication costs for your whole team. This usually involves the costs of meetings, so try to set a regular

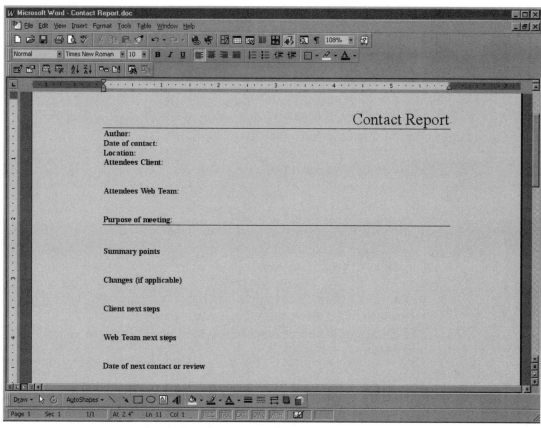

FIGURE 5.1   A contact report is written after meetings or discussions with clients.

meeting schedule. This way you have a good idea of what your team's communication costs will be.

Communication throughout the Project

In this section, you'll learn about the communication milestones as you progress from getting the business, to developing the concept, to executing the design, to deploying the site, and to wrapping up the project. As your relationship develops with your client, you will develop certain levels of familiarity; but it's important that you remain consistent in your approach to communication so that your client will come to trust you. As well, you want to look for consistency and follow-through from your client. This section will help you set up a situation that promotes consistency and effective communication methods throughout the project.

Legal Communications

This book isn't intended to be the ultimate reference for legalities concerning Web projects; however, I can provide some advice regarding important legal milestones to reach with your client.

Letter of Agreement

In the fast-paced world of the Web, source projects start before an actual contract is signed. I don't recommend this; however, should you find yourself in a situation where you trust your client and want to proceed on the project while the contract is still being written, then you can draft a letter of agreement that addresses the following points:

- You have been selected to provide this service for your client.
- You will begin work following receipt of a deposit.
- Include a brief description of the project with an outline of your process.

Non-Disclosure Agreement

A non-disclosure agreement (NDA) states that any information shared between the two parties remains confidential. This protects ideas, techniques, and methods that you bring to the table. Likewise, your client's trade secrets and other information must also remain confidential. You can find a copy of a Mutual Non-Disclosure Agreement (MNDA) on the CD-ROM in the /templates/chapter5/ folder.

Contracts

A contract is critical for the contractual Web developer or hired gun. An independent contractor agreement for the small Web company is on the CD-ROM. If you are a project manager for an internal Web effort or large Web company, contracts are most likely handled by your employer's legal department. It's important for you to understand the specifics of your contract, however, such as payment terms and deliverables; so try to participate in writing the contract or at least get a copy of it when it's been finalized.

Project Communications

Whenever I ask project managers what they could have done better with regard to a project, most say that they could have communicated better with the client. More cost overruns can be traced back to casual conversations about a Web site than to any other factor affecting cost. Therefore, it's critical to document every conversation you have with your client and make this information available to your whole team. This section focuses on specific methods for keeping communications clear between you and your client.

Assumptions

Every project has assumptions. All the deliverables that you determine in your scope document (see chapter 1) are made with certain assumptions. For example, if you need your client to provide you with copy about a product, then you might make the assumption that you can finish designing a product page on a certain date, assuming your client delivers you copy by a certain date and in a certain file format, such as Microsoft Word. If your client misses the deadline and faxes over some pages from a product brochure, then you will lose time due to the missed deadline and the time it will take to retype the copy.

Give your client your assumptions early on, when you deliver your scope document. Take the time to review the document, going over each assumption carefully to make sure your client understands what you expect. When you both have deadlines, you and your client can truly become a part of the same team. You client sees firsthand how his participation can affect the project's success.

Scope and Cost

The questions of scope, cost, and what can be done by the deadline are ongoing issues in project management; and it is no different for Web project management. In his excellent book on software project management, *Death March*, Edward Yourdon describes the common quandary that project managers face: complex projects with too-short deadlines.[1] On Web projects, when the scope can change as often as a new technology appears (about every two weeks), managing scope and cost can be 50 percent of your job.

---

1. Edward Yourdon, *Death March: The Complete Software Developer's Guide to Surviving "Mission Impossible" Projects.* Upper Saddle River, NJ: Prentice-Hall, 1997.

In most Web projects, you determine the scope of a project after a discovery phase in which you and your client discuss the project's objectives and requirements. Once the requirements are determined, you can enter the design phase with a sense of the project's scope. However, your client may not be on the same page as you, because most clients get an idea in their minds, and even though you go through the discovery phase together, you can come away with very different expectations. This is why a full explanation of scope, with the time and cost considerations clearly defined, is critical to getting your client on the same page as you as you move forward with the project.

The Iterative Approach: Compromise

Nearly every feature, screen, and element (image, text, animation, video, audio, JavaScript rollover) needs to be fleshed out in the design phase. We draw black-and-white schematics for each page on a Web site and try to nail down every single element, from introductory text to JavaScript rollover. It's not an easy task, since most design is iterative in terms of effects that are interactive, such as a rollover or popup window. However, we do as much as we can up front so that we can determine the exact scope of the project.

Often, the client wants more than what can be done by the deadline. In this case, we break the project up into phases. Phase I is always what can be done by the deadline. Phases II and III are usually what the client really wants to do. As long as you can determine the critical factors for success in the first phase, you client will most likely buy off on your iterative approach.

The Approvals Document

The approvals document is a document in which your client signs off on features that make up the Web site. Line items in an approvals document might be navigation, visual design, forms, data schema, network configuration, copy, site architecture, any relevant pseudocode, and success metrics. It's important to get sign-offs after each design milestone is hit. Figure 5.2 is a sample page based on the approvals document used by Aslan Computing when they were building the Quicken Financial Store.

Conducting Effective Reviews

Rarely will a client view your Web site design and exclaim, "I love it!" Even if your client does love your design, you need to do your job and explain to her how your design meets the objective of the project.

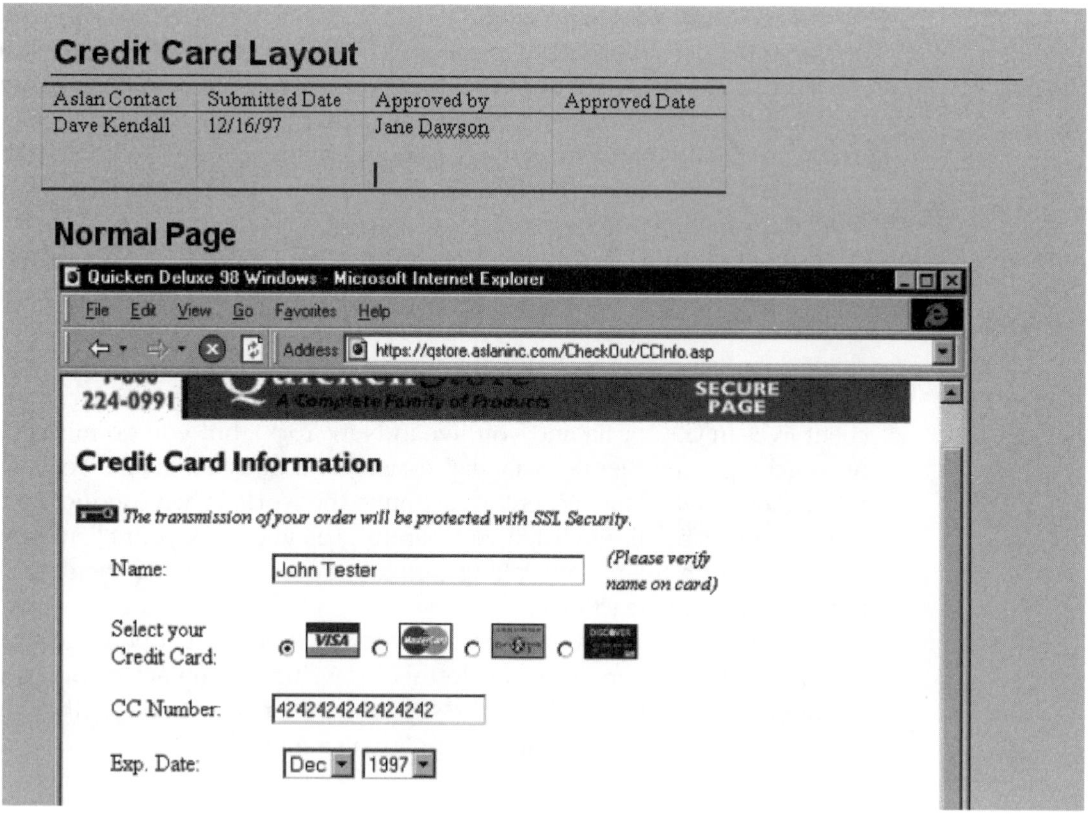

Credit Card Layout

Aslan Contact	Submitted Date	Approved by	Approved Date
Dave Kendall	12/16/97	Jane Dawson	

Normal Page

FIGURE 5.2   A sample page of an approvals document.

Conducting effective reviews is a skill that can be developed. It's interesting to watch experienced account managers present creative concepts to clients. They start by taking charge of the review quickly, before the client has a chance to react, and then they proceed to frame the concept around the objectives of the site. Experienced account managers own the authority of the design decisions and are very confident in explaining the reason for using a certain color or treatment. They also let the lead designer talk about the design if they are confident that the designer will be able to frame the concepts appropriately. If the designer can't to that, then the account manager or project manager must conduct the entire review.

Prepare for a client review by having an internal review first. Write down the important points to hit, and try to guess your client's reactions. A client might react to certain colors or treatments from a subjective point of view. If you expect this, then you can be ready to address the issue.

Always go back to the logic behind the decision, and the logic must always be traced back to an objective of the project. For example, if you choose a certain font and the client doesn't like it, you will need to provide a reason for using the font (readability, consistency), and you must be ready either to suggest an alternative or provide a strong rationale for using the font. If a client hates something, the best thing you can do is be prepared to offer several alternatives. Never argue with a client.

In the traditional world of client reviews, you would conduct the review in person. However, the Web has made it easier to conduct "virtual reviews" in which the client views your work on the "project site" (see chapter 2). Being able to conduct a virtual review is a good thing in that you don't have to travel (this is especially important if, for instance, your client lives in California and you live in New York), but you do miss out on watching your client's facial expressions and body language. You can intuit a lot by watching a client's reaction to the work. When conducting a virtual review, be sure to listen very carefully as you walk your client step by step through the review, taking care to hit every point and then pausing to listen to the reactions.

If your client approves a concept, your next step must be to get the sign-off on the design. You can do this by writing a contact report that has fields for signatures. Obtain the sign-off as soon as possible. Although your review might be "virtual," sign-off never should be.

Giving the Project Back

A time comes in every project when you have to give the project back to a client. This usually happens after the completion of the last agreed-on phase of work. At this point, you may consider an ongoing relationship with the client to do site maintenance, or you might need to give the project back to the client and provide either training or documentation on how to administer and maintain the site.

When to Hand the Project Back

It's important to hand the project back when it makes business sense to do so, when you have delivered the project up to the standards of your test plan (see chapter 7) and when your client is prepared to receive the project, though these things may not occur at the same time.

Sometimes clients are interested in keeping your team involved in the project to perform site maintenance functions such as adding a page here and there or putting up a link. In general, these kinds of ongoing relationships can be hard to manage, especially if your client does not have your team on a retainer. The best way to handle this kind of relationship is to negotiate a service agreement and charge for time and materials (T&M) for site maintenance. Do this only if you have the resources to provide this level of support. However, in time, clients must prepare to staff internally for site maintenance and Web administration. In fact, it doesn't make good business sense to outsource small changes if the Web site is a significant part of the business. If a Web site is used for brand awareness, customer service, or sales, then clients should hire a team of people who can maintain the site on a daily basis. You should help your clients make this decision by providing information about hiring or training people to perform these functions.

Success Metrics

Handing the project back doesn't mean an end to the communication with your client. You will add tremendous value to the project if your team is involved in the measurement of the success of the Web site. As we talked about in chapter 1, measuring Web site success if difficult, which is why it's so important to state the quantitative and qualitative measurements of success before you start the project. Provide your client with site traffic reports that are interpreted by you or someone who can provide analysis of where users stop on the site, where they spend the most time, and where they might not be able to get to. Two products that do this are Web Trends (*www.webtrends.com*) and I I Pro *(www.ipro.com)*.

Other metrics are harder to measure. Certainly "brand awareness" is such an amorphous metric that long-term sales trends might be the only true way to measure your site's success. Even then, unless consumers are responding to a direct promotion on the site, it will be hard to be sure that the site played a part in the increased sales.

A discussion of success metrics is one of the most important discussions you'll have with your client, internal or external. Make sure these metrics are viable and are in writing.

Handling Maintenance Requests

If you do decide to handle maintenance for your client, then as I said earlier, you should try to get paid for these requests based on time and materials. I caution against a retainer because it implies that you have a dedicated team for that account. Most Web companies cannot afford to keep a dedicated team on a project. New projects come up and resources get stretched. Even if a client offers a significant retainer, weigh the pros and cons. A retainer means that you must respond to the requests of the client in a timely manner. Little requests can accumulate and, if your people are spending time doing other project work, they can be forgotten.

However, if you work on a time-and-materials basis, then requests can come in and be prioritized by you. In this case, you must communicate to your client that requests will be prioritized and handled in a timely matter, when resources become available.

Summary

Developing skills in client management takes time. In this chapter, you learned that your relationship with your client can directly affect the Web project's success. A good business relationship is based on respect and trust. Getting to know your client's business, risks, and position in the organization is critical. It's also important to understand and outline success metrics with your client and to provide your client with information and the metrics he or she needs to prove success to executive management. Ensuring that you hand the project back in an appropriate and agreed-on manner is also important.

To-Do List

- Research your client's business. Who are the competitors? What are they doing on-line?

- Identify what's at stake for your client. Do you need to provide your client with information to justify the project? To measure success?

- Make sure your client fully understands scope and cost. Arrange a meeting to discuss this when you present the scope document and budget.

- Prepare legal documents. Download the sample contract and MNDA and tailor them to your business.

- Write contact reports and approvals document templates and be ready to use them as you progress through the design phase.

- Provide your client with regular communication via telephone, meetings, and e-mail. Follow each communication with a contact report.

- Provide your client with information about the industry. This will increase your client's perceived value of you and your team.

Effective Client Management

Louis Malafarina
CEO and President
Ripple Effects Interactive

Louis Malafarina has more than ten years' experience in client management and advertising. Prior to starting his own company, he was the director of client services at Red Sky Interactive, where he provided leadership and strategy for accounts such as Absolut, Shell Energy Services, and Lands' End. Before that, he was group account manager for Poppe Tyson.

What are the responsibilities of your job?

My job is ultimately to be the bridge between creative concepts that solve business problems and the client. I need to fully understand the clients' very core bottom line and the issues they face; and I must be able to communicate why the solutions that we propose can help them in supporting their bottom line. This combination of creative artistry, communication, and business strategy is very appealing to me.

Do clients have a hard time understanding the Web as an advertising communications medium?

Getting a consumer to act is really what we are trying to do; and getting a consumer to act really isn't anchored in advertising, it's anchored in business processes (marketing and sales, the retail network). When you move to interactive Web applications, what happens is not only is your communication method important but on top of that all the mechanisms to fulfill the call can be executed through the Web, through the interactive mechanisms. It's not just about the message anymore—it's about getting consumers to act as if they were in the marketplace, right there. Clients can still be focused on the Web as an extension of their communications campaign when, in reality, it is much more than that.

What are the biggest challenges for account managers of Web projects?

To be as technologically savvy as they are business savvy so they can understand and frame for their clients what the Web can do for them. I've found that clients have an instinctive understanding of what the Web can do for them; and so when you frame it for them, they are grateful. Clients who cannot understand the power of the technology and the medium end up falling back on the notion of using the Web solely for communications and end up missing the Web's potential completely. It's a challenge to reach this group of clients.

However, it's also a challenge to continue to convince your client to spend money on the Web because it's still so hard to measure a client's ROI on the Web. What you must do is build your client's trust in you and the medium, first by building up the message on the Web until it resonates, and then by adding and adding to that message with innovations (be they commerce or other) for incremental wins for your client. It's hard to convince a client to invest a million dollars on Web project. But you can convince them to invest a smaller amount and then build on this investment, going forward, with the appropriate strategic recommendations.

What are the biggest rewards of your job?

I love to be able to empower creative resources to come up with novel ways of communicating, in a way that will serve the client's objectives. Doing business creatively is fun. We are given business problems to solve and we get to solve them as creatively as we can. That's amazing. It is challenging on a completely different level (than traditional business problem solving). The average marketer will be worried about the size of the canopy, whether the product is on the second or third shelf, whether the retail organization is pocketing the discount or passing it the consumer. Those are not my worries. My worries are whether the consumers will understand and be stimulated by the message and act—immediately.

The people I work with is also a big reward. People in this industry have interesting and unique worlds. They tend to seek alternative lifestyles and are passionate and driven. They are devising new ways to emote and being a part of this culture is very rewarding. It would be nice to have the freedom that some of my colleagues have (in terms of style); but my job is to make the client feel comfortable, so I have to be careful.

What can damage a client relationship?

When the product you deliver does not get the expected business results. You have to understand business, your client's business, in order to make sure its Web strategy is in alignment with its overall business strategy.

Miscommunication and mismanagement will also damage a client relationship. One example of this might be an inability of the account manager to get a client to a necessary level of detail about the project. When a client cannot get past the concept stage, and is afraid to commit to precise features, you will get in trouble. Once a client wanted us to develop a CD-ROM for his company but would not commit to any design features. He wanted to develop the functionality only, but could not understand how inextricably related the concept (and therefore the design) was to the functionality of the CD-ROM. He was only interested in the conceptual framework of the functionality. He was afraid to be nailed down to anything and needed to have the security of being able to be noncommittal so if he ended up not liking what we proposed, he could throw out the ideas and start over, without acknowledging the consequences: time and money.

How do you prevent damage?

Don't get hung up on changes for changes' sake. Sometime changes are good, both for you and for your clients. Remember that changes mean two things: more time or more money. Try to come up with a solution that benefits your client and you.

I never say "no" to a client. I always talk in terms of money and time. I try as hard as I can to keep the client's options open as long as possible. I know very well that there is a point at which you cannot go further without nailing the client down—which I do.

You must have a contact report for every conversation you have with a client; and you must take the time to provide this report, because you need a way to be able to say, "Here's what we talked about today, and here's what we are going to do." Because you need a way to communicate to the client that, misunderstanding or not, this may cost time and money. Maybe you don't charge time and money this time around, but the cat is out of the bag, so to speak. So that the next time it happens, you have created a process to limit that kind of misunderstanding from happening again.

How do you deal with inflexible or overly controlling clients?

It depends on the client. It's hard, because I'm not just managing the client relationship, I'm also managing the morale of my team. If I allow a client to continue to change scope, regardless of how much money he or she spends on the account, I can run the risk of sacrificing my team's overall level of satisfaction with regard to its own work. In the long run, this can permanently damage a team because members begin to feel undervalued, and I don't want to do that. So I have to take each instance and ask, "Is this okay for the team, as well as the client?" At some point, I may have to fire a client if I believe we cannot provide service due to their needs or demands. I will choose to do that before sacrificing the productivity of our team. Hopefully, you don't get to that point. But sometimes you do.

Would you consider declining a job because of a client?

Sure. Especially if the project doesn't make sense for our business process and model, despite how much money the client was willing to spend. If I detect that the process the client wants does not fit how we need to work, then I will consider declining a job because we can end up with some big losses.

I'd also consider declining a job for a client who doesn't let us be the experts in the space that we occupy. When a client starts telling us how to work on a granular level, such as specifying which colors to use and why, it raises my suspicion that this client may not be a viable client.

What makes a great agency–client relationship?

Mutual respect and trust. Just like any good relationship.

CHAPTER 6

Multidepartmental and Large-Scale Sites

IF YOU NEED . . .

♦ Insight into high-level issues concerning development of a large-scale Web site, read "Up-Front Challenges."

♦ Discussion of architectural and production issues, read "Production Management."

♦ Information about publishing or content management tools before you purchase one, read "Publishing and Choosing the Right Tool."

♦ Tips on creating effective navigation systems, read "The Subsite: Risks and Rewards."

This chapter is about the challenges you will face and the team you need to develop a large-scale Web site or intranet.

Up-Front Challenges

Lisa Welchman was an experienced Web project manager, having built several complex Web sites and intranets for high-technology companies such as Whitetree, Inc., and NetFRAME Systems. She took a job with Cisco Systems as a production manager, feeling that her project management experience would put her in a good position to get Cisco's wily Web site on track.

"I was totally unprepared for the many issues involved in managing a Web site the size of Cisco's. And I wasn't even the only production manager."[1]

A large-scale or multidepartmental site holds challenges for even the most experienced project manager, who must fully understand them in order to lead a successful Web project. From communication issues to internal politics, from production issues to renegade Web sites, producing a large-scale Web site or intranet is a long-term project with many design, functional, and executional considerations. However, when planned and executed well, a large-scale Web site or intranet is an amazing business tool. This chapter introduces the issues you might face and the team you will need to deploy a multidepartment or large-scale Web site.

Do You Have an "Internet" Department?

Chances are that your company doesn't have a dedicated Internet department, and this is probably your biggest up-front challenge, if you have been chosen or have volunteered to create, revise, or maintain a large corporate Web site or intranet. At the end of 1998, few businesses had dedicated teams to handle their own corporate Web or intranet site. The reason is that the Web, as of 1999, is just now becoming part of the business cycle, now that the Web can provide interfaces among almost all business functions (sales, inventory, order tracking, customer service, accounts payable and receivable). Until recently, Web development efforts were driven by "ad-hoc coalitions"[2]—small groups that were thrown together to "get a Web site together." The problem with these coalitions (you are probably part of one) is that there is little executive support and strategy to address the critical question "What is our on-line objective?" as well as to provide the funding necessary to meet the objective. If your company doesn't have a dedicated department for on-line development, begin talking about it. A dedicated group will provide the authority, strategic vision, funding, and cohesion that a large-scale development effort needs.

Funding the Internet Effort

Most corporate Web efforts are funded via the budgets of several groups. In my experience, these groups are usually IS and Marketing, with other departments contributing to the corporate intranet. This lack of a clear

---

1. Lisa Welchman, personal communication,Spring 1998.
2. *Forrester's Interactive Technology Strategies,* June 1997.

funding path means that it's hard to plan for the long term because you don't know if budget managers will continue to fund the effort. As a project manager, it will be hard for you to develop a long-term project plan if you only have budgetary commitment for a single quarter, or even a single year.

Does Your Company Have an On-line Strategy?

We covered this in chapter 3, but it's worth repeating. It's critical on a large-scale development effort to make sure you have executive-level support. This support comes in the form of the strategic vision for the site, not a pat on the back. What you want from your executive management team is a statement of what the Web's role is within the company. Is the site to be used solely for marketing or will the Web interface with the rest of the existing systems such as inventory or customer service? This statement will help you develop measurable objectives so that you can benchmark the success of the site, which is something you must do in order to continue to get funding for the effort—in some cases, this will offer you job security as well.

Getting to Know Your Audience

A large-scale Web site or intranet usually has a diverse audience. In the case of Cisco Systems, there are different audiences for different sections of the site, from resellers to international business customers to individual network engineers seeking support. Most intranets are similar in that the many groups that make up the organization have information for different members of the organization's community.

As a project manager, your job is to plan a project that meets certain objectives; to do so, you must figure out how to reach a large part of your target audience. This section discusses issues you might face when trying to determine just who your audience is.

Balancing the Needs of Different Units

If you're hired to develop a large-scale Web site for an organization with several departments or business units, how do you represent each of those units? How can you be sure the site you build is the site that the end users need? Balancing the needs of different departments and business units is difficult and sensitive, especially if each unit is using its own budget to fund the overall Web site. There will be a lot of political land mines.

Before you start, you need to make sure you have a single point of contact for the entire project. This person should be a senior executive with decision-making power. If you don't have this person, you might find yourself dealing with managers from each of the business units or departments, each with his or her own agenda. Without someone to give the final word, you will spend a lot of time making decisions you shouldn't make.

The best way to balance the needs of different departments and business units is to make sure you first have an overall corporate objective, or mission statement, for the entire site. Having this statement will help you formulate your interview questions and help you prioritize the needs of the different units. If you don't have an overall corporate objective or mission for the Web site, you need to raise the issue with your client. The client might need the services of a senior strategic planner who can help them align their Web objectives with their corporate objectives.

Meeting the Needs of Different Audiences

What your clients believe their users need and what your team believes they need almost always will be different. In the case of the corporate intranet, it's important to conduct interviews with each department so that you can identify the key pieces of information that reach the greatest audience. This is sometimes referred to as the 80/20 rule. You want to identify the 20 percent of information that will reach 80 percent of your audience. No Web site can meet all the needs of all of its users, but providing a breadth of information and services that reaches the greatest number of users is the best strategy for a Web site with a large range of audiences.

Corporate Politics

It's important to know of any corporate politics that might affect the Web project. Being aware of the political landscape in your internal organization and your client's organization is very important, for obvious reasons. If your client is facing internal political struggles, the outcome could affect you either positively or negatively. Being aware and alert, yet objective and professional, is the way to handle corporate politics, especially when they are put directly in front of you. People you interview or meet with will most likely talk to you; do not offer advice and maintain a professional distance. Be pleasant but take note of the issues. Always try to identify how the political landscape could affect your project. Assess these issues as risks, and be sure to have a contingency plan.

Sitewide Branding

The issue of branding—putting the essence of the corporation or product on each page or within each section of the Web site—is a big issue, especially if the site has already been created and you are being hired to "fix" the branding problem. Most Web sites are branded with a logo placed strategically in the upper left or lower right corner of a Web page. This isn't the most creative placement, but it works. Users naturally look to the upper left corner first—making this a natural place for a branding treatment. However, this is a decision for your lead designer. Your job is to provide a strategy for ensuring that the large site is appropriately branded at the corporate level and that the different business units or departments get treatments that are secondary to the corporate branding.

If you are not working directly with the company's advertising manager or agency, a quick phone call to this person or team would be a good idea, both politically and procedurally. You can obtain specifications for logo use, trademark use, and other important global branding details. Be sure to capture this information in your production guide for the site (if you haven't read chapter 3 where production guides are explained, you might want to flip to that chapter).

Each department or business unit will naturally want to have its own personality. However, if each department or business unit receives different branding or treatment, the site will be in danger of becoming nonusable.

The critical team member for resolving issues of branding (which also relate to usability and navigation) is your information architect. The information architect will ensure that the visual design of the site allows users to know where they are in a site quickly, as well as whose site and section they are in. (This is discussed further later in this chapter in the section, "The Subsite: Risks and Rewards.")

Quality Issues

How do you ensure that your large-scale Web site or intranet is bug-free, has no spelling errors or broken links, and adheres to corporate standards with regard to logo usage, fonts, and other corporate identity elements? There are many quality issues for you to consider, from both a development and a maintenance point of view.

In a large-scale Web site, where there are multiple content authors, servers, and production systems, you will face big challenges in ensuring that all subsections of the site are up to an acceptable level of quality.

♦ Conducting Quality Reviews

A quality review might also involve the legal and regulatory groups in your company. It's important to develop a process whereby these groups are review the site regularly before it goes live, perhaps on a staging server. Make sure that your legal and regulatory groups re-view the content before it goes into produc-tion—this will save a lot of time if there are a lot of text changes. Copy changes generally take up to 40 percent of total bug-fixing time during the testing phase.

Quality level is something that you and your stakeholders need to agree on and document, and then you must provide guidelines for all prospective content authors and HTML programmers. These guidelines could range from display guidelines (how all pages should look), to file size guidelines, to copy guidelines (spelling, conventions, and type treat-ment). Until you have a standard, you will not be able to ensure the qual-ity of your site. (See chapter 7, "Quality Assurance and Testing," for more information.)

Another quality issue is that of configuration management. How do you ensure version control across your subsections? How do you catalog your site in such a way that you know what state it is in at all times? And, should this be a centralized effort with one quality control mechanism or decentralized effort with each subsection or subsite responsible for quality control? These issues are important to discuss before you begin your pro-ject. For a summary of tools that help in this process, see the section "Publishing and Choosing the Right Tool."

The main point is that in order to ensure quality, you must have a definition of quality. This is best done through thorough corporate guide-lines. Then, if you are dealing with multiple business units and depart-ments that are responsible for creating content, you must give them a standardized process and support for ensuring quality for their site. A centralized quality control department can help ensure that the sites com-ply with the regulations.

Making the Site Searchable

Large-scale Web sites should be searchable. Generally a large-scale Web site or intranet has too much content for just browsing. To make a site truly searchable, information must be tagged appropriately or identified based on what users would want to find. This means that before you implement a search engine, you have to take into consideration who your users are and what they would want to search for.

If finding information is a critical objective for your stakeholders, consider search engine software that permits searches based on word associations as well as definitions. Users think in associations, but search engine software often is rigid in returning information, mostly because they are programmed that way. To make a search engine return results that are more like a thesaurus than a dictionary takes a lot of human work. However, if you are creating a large site, you should consider putting in the effort to provide an effective search engine. A team member (usually an information architect or writer) should be dedicated to evaluating the needs of the users and developing the strategy for providing search functionality.

In evaluating a specific search package, consider the following:

♦ What kind of search do you need? Will a simple word search do, or do you need to search based on concept?

♦ What platform will your users use? Your search engine must be compatible with whatever platform your Web server is running.

♦ Does the search engine access files from the server's file system or via http? For a large-scale site, accessing files directly via the server's file system is a better option. Accessing files via http (like most Web crawlers) increases server load.

♦ What file types does the search engine index? If you have a lot of .pdf files, make sure your search engine will index the files.

♦ Does the search engine support hit highlighting? This is the ability of the software to highlight the searched-for word so you don't have to hunt for the reference in the file.

There are lots of good articles and books on setting up a search engine. For an evaluation of different tools, see Brenda Kienan and Daniel Taubin's article in *Web Review* (*http://webreview.com/wr/pub/97/11/21/webmaster/table.html*). Louis Rosenfeld and Peter Morville write about setting up an effective search engine.[3]

---

3. Louis Rosenfeld and Peter Morville, *Information Architecture for the World Wide Web.* Sebastopol, CA: O'Reilly and Associates, 1998.

Production Management

Overseeing production on a large-scale Web site is a tremendous challenge, especially because the Web team can consist of hundreds of people. You will need a core Web team, but you will also be including the content authors from every department, as well as an IS department and, perhaps, a marketing representative. Copy development, developing a usable, scalable design, and maintaining several servers are some of the challenges. As well, there might be content that changes daily or weekly, making content publishing difficult if it is not automated. In this section, I discuss the issues involved in managing the production of a large-scale intranet or Web site, some tools you might want to consider, and the team necessary to get the job done.

The Web Team

The roles for the Web team in a large-scale Web site or intranet are the same as you learned in chapter 2; however, there could be a lot more of them, and their roles could be more specialized. Here's a scenario.

Company X is an international company, with business offices in California, Minnesota, New York, and London. Their company intranet is the nexus of communication for company news and policies. Their Web team might consist of the following:

1. *A project manager*   This person is the Web site's executive officer. He or she handles all requests from internal clients, coordinates with consultants, and is accountable for the Web site.

2. *A design team (consultants)*   This contracted resource develops scalable information architecture and a design scheme so that Company X's team can produce templates and style guides for the different departments and business units.

3. *Information technology team*   This group is responsible for servers, security, and administration, as well as moving the Web site from a development environment to the live, or production, environment. This group could include a technical Web master who is dedicated to maintaining the servers that run the Web site. Additionally this person handles publishing from staging environments to production environments, troubleshoots the Web server, grants access to business partners and new employees, runs reports about Web-site usage and reports findings to the producer. There also might be an e-mail system administrator, a systems support person, a security specialist, and a database administrator.

4. *Departmental production managers*   Departmental production managers receive raw content from content providers and make the content into Web documents. Departmental production managers also post documents to the staging server, where they are tested.

5. *Quality assurance*   Depending on the site's needs, a QA group might be dedicated to the Web site, or be part of the department or business unit's production process. However, quality assurance standards must be followed and enforced by a centralized group, the department or business unit production manager, or the project manager.

6. *Content providers*   Content providers are employees of the company who provide raw content to production managers. Content providers come from all over the company.

Figure 6.1 shows how content should flow from content providers to department-level production managers, where it is staged on a server. An approvals process is necessary at the department level to ensure that

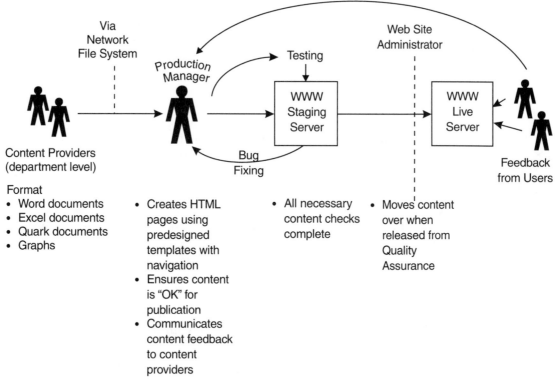

FIGURE 6.1   The flow of content from providers through production.

content is in line with corporate standards. Once content has passed through an approvals process at the department level, it can be published to the production site.

The Corporate Publishing Process

In the corporate publishing process, people who don't necessarily consider themselves Web developers or designers often create Web content. The corporate publishing process must include a way for content to be created, reviewed on-line, and published onto a live Web server in a systematic and efficient process that includes quality control. As well, corporate database systems such as accounting, inventory, and human resources might also need to become part of the content publishing process. Several tools purport to make this process easier; they are reviewed later in the section. However, long before you settle on a tool, you must understand the issues and be able to evaluate your client's needs. You may not need a sophisticated, dynamic publishing system if content changes once a year on your site. This section introduces you to some issues you might encounter in developing a publishing process.

My definition of a *publishing process* includes content creation, conversion into HTML or other Web-ready content (such as GIFs, JPGs, or multimedia files), quality assurance, version control, deployment, hardware, and software.

Web Servers

Looking for a good book on Web-site capacity planning? Menasce and Almeida have written an in-depth book that offers strategies to model, plan, and analyze Web server performance and needs.[4]

How many Web servers do you need if you have several business units or departments? The answer is complex. In reality, the Internet makes it possible for disparate groups to connect to a single server, so in theory you may only need one. Depending on the kind of content you serve (database content might require a separate server), you might need more than one. In-depth discussions of performance and scalability of Web servers are out of the scope of this book; however, as a project manager, you need to make sure a technical lead or systems administrator of the site is considering anticipated server load, security, administration, and Web server performance expectations.

The question to ask with regard to how may servers you need is the question of control. How important is it to your organization that Web site

---

4. Daniel A. Menasce and Virgilio A. F. Almeida, *Capacity Planning for Web Performance: Metrics, Models and Methods.* Upper Saddle River, NJ: Prentice-Hall, 1998. The book is pretty technical, but it does also offer a high-level view of the issues involved in capacity planning and analysis.

content adheres to corporate guidelines and is navigable? If it is very important (and it should be), then the Web servers should be centralized, meaning that the different groups throughout the organization do not control their own Web servers. I talk more about the issues relating to multiple Web servers without centralized control later in this chapter, in the section "The Subsites: Risks and Rewards."

Authoring Issues: Standards and Templates

Providing templates for departments, business units, and individual content providers is a very important part of creating a good publishing process. A template contains coded formats for all critical information such as navigation and branding, so content providers need only fill in the page with their own content (see the CD-ROM for examples of templates).

A production guide is also important; it should have information about file-naming conventions, text and link colors, background colors, word count per page, and other standards relating to production (see the /templates/chapter3/ folder on the CD-ROM for a template production guide). Approval and workflow checklists could also go in the production guide.

A style guide that instructs people on the use of corporate items such as logos and trademarks is also important. Legalese, acronymns, and other writing conventions should be part of this guide. Include guidelines that will ensure a consistent look and feel and navigation (if you employ contractors for special projects) in a style guide (or the production guide). Some style guides even include guidelines for using or evaluating new and emerging technologies. This document might already exist; but it will need to be modified for the Web, especially if logos are to be converted for use over the Web.

These documents are keys to quality assurance process. They provide a basis by which all content can be reviewed before it goes live. Your QA staff will make sure all Web content complies with your style guide and production guide.

Approvals

A content approval process is critical to the corporate publishing process. Does each unit have its own approvals process? Does a central Web team have final approvals? The answers will depend on your client. Your job is to evaluate the needs of the organization and make sure that if certain content needs certain approvals, a mechanism for obtaining approvals is built into the production process.

Right now, there aren't too many tools out there that make ap-provals an automatic thing, so I would think "low-tech." Certain written ap-provals might be necessary, and in some cases, a simple e-mail might do.

Publishing and Choosing the Right Tool

When you publish a site, you move it over to a place where the world can see it. There are tools that do this automatically, but it can be done manu-ally. There are two issues: what is the publishing process (meaning, how does content get created and published) and do you need a tool to expe-dite the process? You need to ask the following questions when creating a publishing process and choosing a tool:

- How often does content change?
- What kind of content gets published?
- Who is creating content?
- Are multiple team members working on the same content?
- Does content need to be approved each time it changes?
- What kind of Web server software does your company use?

Tools that enable approvals to occur automatically are still in their pre-teen stage. Most organizations rely on a quality assurance process to make sure there is some level of quality control based on agreed-on corporate standards. E-mail is still the best tool for corporate approvals to take place over the Web. Companies like Microsoft are trying to devise plug-ins to e-mail programs that enable approval.

In an article in *Internet World*,[5] Giga Information Group analyst Phil Costa cites three major problems that tool vendors are trying to solve: managing the development process by enabling workflow and version control, serving dynamic and personalized content to site visitors, and storing and integrating content (site assembly software like Wallop's BUILD-IT, which was acquired by IBM for use in its WebSphere product, and NetObjects's line of tools).

The vast majority of large-scale Web sites use their own production process, much like what is described in this chapter; but fewer and fewer are creating their own proprietary publishing tools. This is because the tools are getting better; and for large-scale sites with content that changes frequently, they are a necessity. These tools tend to be expensive; but im-plemented well, they can end up saving your company thousands of dol-

---

5. James Luh, "Large Sites Assess Tools for Managing Content,"*Internet World,* March 1, 1999.

lars in production costs. I review two tools below. Each has its strengths and weaknesses and should be used only after careful evaluation of your content management and publishing needs.

1. *Interwoven's TeamSite*   TeamSite is an application that encompasses Web content management, application development, and workflow for enterprise Web development. Some of the great features of TeamSite include robust change management, superior system performance, smart development, and a powerful solution for complex Web deployment. TeamSite is available for NT and UNIX servers. If workflow management and version control are your main problems to solve, TeamSite is probably the best choice. You can read more about TeamSite at *http:// www.interwoven.com.*

2. *Vignette's StoryServer*   StoryServer enables users to create, store, manage, and deliver content with flexibility and efficiency. Content assets are managed in either databases or flat files, depending on your needs. StoryServer supports multiple content authors and has workflow and notification services so that you can set up content approval processes, though not to the level of Interwoven's TeamSite. If serving dynamic and personalized content is your main problem to solve, StoryServer is probably your best choice. As well, content authors who do not know HTML can easily contribute content. StoryServer is available both on NT and UNIX systems. You can read more about StoryServer at *http://www. vignette.com.*

Centralizing Testing, Editing, and Approval Policies

A corporate unit that is dedicated to testing, editing, and approving content is becoming more important. As the Web becomes more and more of a tool for core business process and communications and less of a novelty (we're already there), then companies will begin to justify this unit.

The Subsite: Risks and Rewards

Jakob Nielson coined the term *subsite* to describe a small Web site within a larger site that has its own style and navigation. Subsites are very common, especially on intranets, and often get created by employees who learn how easy it is to make a simple Web page. Suddenly, everyone wants to put up a Web page. In 1995 and 1996 corporations were still trying to figure out exactly what the Web's role would be in their overall business model, and so they didn't pay too much attention to the many little Web sites that popped up on their network. However, these sites that start out useful can become detrimental to the overall usability of a Web site.

The subsite can actually be a very useful tool within a large Web site, especially when it contains information that pertains to a certain audience. For example, the Partners and Reseller subsite on the Cisco Web site (see Figure 6.2) offers content to a specific audience, Cisco's resellers and certified partners. It has its own style and navigation, and it also has Cisco's global navigation. Users know where they are and they know how to get back to Cisco's home page.

Allowing Creativity

I was developing an intranet for a pharmaceuticals company and was just beginning the interview process. I was very excited about meeting with the different departments and creating the Web site for them. When I met with each group to ask questions and assess their needs, they seemed suspicious and unwilling to talk. Later that day, I asked my client what was going on, and he told me that people were reacting to a memo he had sent out saying that his team was in charge of creating the intranet. Anyone else who wanted to participate could do so only by way of these interviews that I was conducting. No wonder they were so resistant.

The strategy for that particular site was to centralize Web publishing for the first phase. One unit, the IS department, was going to be in charge of the intranet. People could recommend content but they couldn't have access to the server, nor could they learn HTML and create their own pages. As a result, they were not interested in the site.

I asked my client if we could explore a strategy by which individual units could create their own pages using templates that I created. We came up with a design that would allow people to create Web pages and then found a tool (Microsoft FrontPage) that had version control and publication capabilities so that the IS department maintained control of the content that went live.

In order to get people excited about the site, we conducted two "how-to" workshops—one on creating HTML and one on creating Web graphics. This empowered the employees and excited them about the intranet.

It's very important to consider what it will take to get departments or business units to buy into the intranet or Web site. People want to participate and if they are not given the opportunity to create something as part of the greater Web team, they might not use the site or become demotivated—something that you never want to happen to good employees.

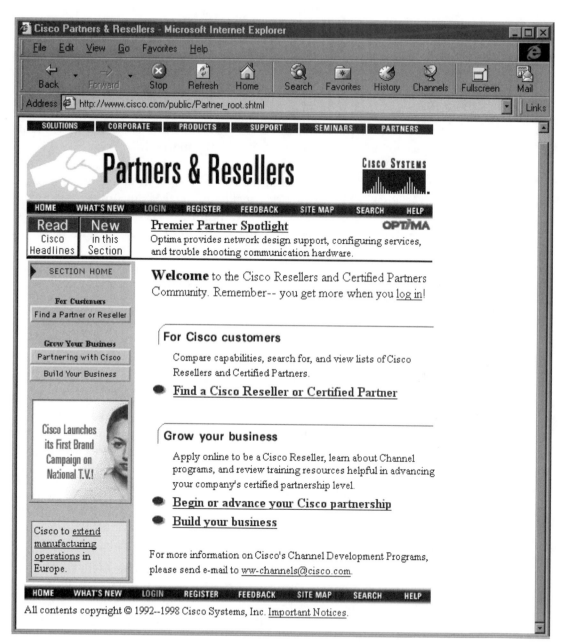

FIGURE 6.2   Cisco's Partners and Resellers Web site addresses a specific audience.

Having a streamlined publishing system makes it easy for people to contribute to the site.

Creating Cohesion

So now it's your job to develop a scalable architecture and design that will allow departments or business units to participate in creating Web content. This section gives you a few tips on what you can do.

As you begin to plan a large Web site or intranet, keep in mind that your team may have to design for subsites, so both global and sectional navigation should be primary considerations. Making this navigation a standard convention and then communicating it, via the production guidelines or style guidelines is critical to the success of the site. I recommend the following:

- Provide a clip-art library full of Web-ready graphics. Many companies sell clip-art for the Web.
- Budget for training employees who are interested in creating Web content.
- Create a publishing process that ensures version control and is a regular occurrence. People should know that on Friday at 5:00 P.M., all content on the staging server will be published.
- Set up a regular audit of your core Web team to discuss overall cohesion of the site. Make sure your network support person brings server logs to the meeting so you can see which pages get accessed the most and which pages might be too buried within the site.
- Always be ready for change.

Summary

This chapter introduced you to the many challenges you will face when producing a large-scale Web site comprised of multiple departments or business units. Such projects almost always have subterranean issues like corporate politics, and these kinds of issues can sink your project if you ignore them. A large-scale Web site is an expensive project to undertake, and the up-front investment in tools, hardware, and time will need to be benchmarked as the project gets deployed in order to justify the investment. You must spend the time to do the up-front planning (reread chapter 3!) or you will make some very costly mistakes. Your team must analyze the method of creating content and the needs of each unit in order to recommend and implement an effective site and system to support it.

To-Do List

- Write a mission statement for the Web site; consult your stakeholders and key personnel.
- Identify the core team and the extended team.
- Evaluate and audit the current site, if one exists.
- Conduct interviews.
- Identify the features of the site in the scope document.
- Determine development phases. What can be accomplished during the first phase?
- Create a contact list for all Web team members.
- Establish standards and create a production guide.
- Analyze production needs (use the production guide in this chapter's folder on the CD-ROM) and evaluate tools to facilitate production.
- Determine benchmarks.

Managing a Large-Scale Content Site

Janine Warner, On-line Managing Editor
Miami Herald Publishing Company

Janine Warner is the on-line managing editor for the Miami Herald Publishing Company, heading a team of more than a dozen developers who publish both the English and Spanish newspapers on the Internet every day. She is also responsible for developing partnerships with other organizations and serving as liaison with the newsroom, marketing, and business departments.

Ms. Warner is the author of six books on Web design, including *Dreamweaver for Dummies, Flash 3 Web Animation: f/x and design*, and *Conversion Techniques for Web Publishing*.[6] From 1994 to 1998, she ran Visiontec Communications, a Web design company that served such diverse clients as Levi Strauss & Co., AirTouch International, and the Pulitzer prize–winning newspaper, the *Point Reyes Light*. To learn more about her work, visit *www.visiontec.com*.

What are the responsibilities of your job?

I am responsible for the content sections on all ten Web sites hosted by the Miami Herald Publishing Company. Those sites include the *Miami Herald* and *El Nuevo Herald* newspapers, which are published daily in English and Spanish, as well as a travel site, entertainment site, community guide, teen site, three classified sites, and more. I manage fifteen producers and editors who maintain the content on these sites and develop new sections and products. I also act as liaison between on-line services and the two newsrooms, meeting regularly with editors and reporters. In addition, I work closely with the business and marketing managers to ensure that the content sections are well promoted and likely to attract advertising. I also seek out content partners and negotiate agreements with other Web sites and information sources that produce content we can use on our sites. In addition, I work closely with our technology manager to explore and integrate new technologies.

---

6. Janine Warner, *Dreamweaver for Dummies*. Foster City, CA: IDG Books Worldwide, 1998; Ken Milburn and Janine Warner, *Flash 3 Web Animation: f/x and design*. Scottsdale, AZ: The Coriolis Group, 1999; Janine Warner, Ken Milburn, and Jessica Burdman, *Converting Content for Web Publishing: Time-Saving Tools and Techniques*. Indianapolis: New Riders, 1996.

What are some of the greatest challenges of managing a site as large as the Miami Herald Web site?

Where do I start? Probably the biggest challenge is managing an entrepreneurial business within a large corporation. To stay competitive on-line you must be able to make changes quickly—not an easy task in a big, established company like the Herald, and often even more challenging when it requires the support of our parent company Knight-Ridder. Nonetheless, Knight-Ridder is one of the most progressive traditional media companies in the country, and we do benefit from the brand recognition and stability of being part of this company.

Staffing is another challenge. I am currently looking for a new on-line producer; and not only does that person have to understand journalism as well as technology, he or she has to be able to work in English as well as Spanish. There just aren't that many qualified people around yet.

Finally, technology is always a challenge. The software solutions are still evolving and none of them really solve our problems yet. Updating and integrating new technologies when you manage such a large, dynamic site isn't easy, either.

What is the goal of the Web site?

Making money is clearly the main goal in this corporation these days. Knight-Ridder has been willing to make a significant investment in the creation and development of the on-line departments, but they are demanding significant revenue growth in exchange. Serving readers better and attracting new readers to the papers is another goal.

Describe the members of your team.

Within the content team, most of us have a journalism background. My staff members are mostly former writers and editors who showed some interest in technology. Many of them taught themselves along the way; others were trained after they were hired. None of them have computer science degrees, and few have significant technical skills. We do have one person with a strong design background and some programming experience. The production team in on-line services is made up mostly of designers. We also have a technical staff with programmers and database developers. We also have advertising and business people.

How do they interact?

For the most part the different on-line departments—content, advertising, business, marketing, production, and technology—work very separately. The four top managers meet weekly to review projects and how they affect each other and every other week we have an implementation meeting where we bring together team members from different departments who are working on projects where their collective skills are needed. Otherwise, meetings are restricted to members of the same department. Within the content department, we have a daily meeting to discuss the news stories and how to lay out the papers and then meet on an as-needed basis to work on special projects.

What kinds of "best practices" have you developed?

Hire the best people you can and then give them tons of support and training. As I said earlier, one of my biggest challenges is staffing. One of our "best practices" has been to hire bilingual journalism students, train them in the technology skills they need on the job, and then keep them full-time after they graduate.

What do you think some issues will be in the future?

We have to figure out how to make our Web sites more than just newspapers on the Internet. There is so much more that we can offer to readers on-line than the newsroom can put in print. We need to make the sites more interactive, richer, and deeper. We're doing that in a variety of ways, from updating the sites more and more often to adding databases of information to supplement stories. For example, the real estate section will soon have a searchable database that provides access to information on housing prices, taxes, and much more. We're also working on more partnerships with other publications so that we can offer articles from more places. For example, in the Spanish site we are working on partnerships with newspapers throughout Latin America to provide breaking news from throughout the hemisphere.

What goes into starting a new section or Web site?

First someone comes up with an idea. For example, we are thinking about starting a health section on the site. Then, we have to determine if there is real advertising potential. If the business people like the idea, then we start looking at where the content will come from. We may talk to editors and reporters in the newsroom about writing new stories or we may just reassess how we can make better use of what they are already creating. We may also go through the archives of the paper to find articles that are still valuable and could fill out the section. Then we look at possible content partners. We may buy a drug database, for example, that we could add to the site so users can search for drug information. We may make a deal with a Web site that provides information about doctors and their medical and legal records. We may decide to integrate content from our yellow pages site so that users can search for a doctor's name and find contact information and a map. Then we start working on the technical and development plan. We determine who will design the new section and what underlying technologies it will require. Then we start building it. Then we test like crazy, put it on-line, and hope we haven't missed anything. Then we read your book and learn how to do it even better.

What makes your day?

When readers write in and tell us how the site has made a difference in their lives. I loved the mail we got during Hurricane Mitch. People wrote to us from all over the world, thanking us for keeping them informed about the storm, how people were doing, and where they could send help afterward.

I also love it when I get to promote one of my staff members. I can't say enough about training and developing good staff people. It makes all the difference in the success of our projects and my own satisfaction in my work. With such a small pool of qualified people out there to do this kind of work, and with such limits on our budget, we really have to make every person count.

Favorite tools?

Dreamweaver 2, Fireworks, Photoshop, and Outlook.

CHAPTER 7

Quality Assurance and Testing

IF YOU NEED . . .

- An explanation of quality assurance for Web projects, visit the section "What Is Unique about Testing Web Projects?" Also read "Quality Assurance: Some General Principles."

- Information about writing a test plan, read "A Successful Test Plan." Also, you can use some sample test plan templates on this book's CD-ROM.

- To learn about Web testing tools, visit the section "Web Site Load Testing."

These days, Web sites are complex. To ensure quality and get your site tested, fixed, retested, and fully documented before it is delivered to the client or customer, your Web team will need a QA manager or lead who has not only an understanding of Web testing but also some background in quality assurance standards and practices.

Quality Assurance: Some General Principles

What is quality assurance? How is it different from testing and how does testing a Web site contribute to its overall quality? What's unique about quality assurance and testing for the Web? What does the QA department need from you and the rest of the team to get its job done? This chapter tries to answer some part of all of these questions. I say "some part" because it would be fallacious for me to say that I could completely answer all of these questions. Quality assurance experts can't even agree on a single definition of *quality*.

Because quality assurance is such a vast field, applicable to many manufacturing industries, it would be impossible to cover it in just one chapter. Here I discuss a few principles, standards, methods, and tools that I've seen used. Also, because the Web industry continues to change so rapidly, I can't address all of the emerging technologies or the changing user expectations for the Web that might introduce unforeseen quality assurance issues.

The Quality Squeeze

In the fast-paced world of Web development, both cost and time impact the quality of a product. As a QA manager, I'm responsible for helping you to achieve a standard of quality that matches the objectives of your project and that is on time and on budget. The client or the strategy team wants you to deliver a product that meets the objectives of the scope document. With a scope document, a budget, and a schedule in hand, it is your job to deliver a quality Web site. Your scope document is transformed into a functional and technical specification; both of these documents are used to produce your Web site. I'll talk about the role of documentation and testing later in the chapter. If you match the objectives of the scope document, assuming the marketers and strategists have done lots of research about their target audience, then you have a good chance of delivering a quality Web site.

What Is Unique about Testing Web Sites?

The Web industry is in its adolescent phase, just barely becoming aware of itself. The challenge for quality assurance is to engineer standards, methods, and processes that meet the needs of a young industry. As a QA manager, I find myself striking a balance between innovation and process, trying to build and implement a process that respects and allows for innovation and meets the business needs of my employer. The interplay of Web site innovation, a young industry, and the company mission informs the way I define and implement quality processes and standards.

Quality as a Philosophy

Quality assurance is a philosophy, something that is woven into the mission statement of your company or your client or customer. Quality is also something that must be measured. I'd like to introduce two quality principles, two ways that I think of and measure quality when working on Web sites: product reliability and happy customers or clients. Both of these principles guide me through the development life cycle of a product.

The clients who purchase or the customers who use a Web site determine whether a Web site has quality. If the customer or the client doesn't like the end result of a Web site, even if it meets the specification and is reliable, then the Web site has failed the test of quality. If the client or customer is happy with the Web site you delivered but the product is not reliable, works on some browsers but not others, or crashes every time you resize a browser window, then you have also failed the test of quality. A Web site of quality is reliable and makes clients and users happy.

A QA manager/lead can help to ensure that these two things happen. Get your QA manager involved at the outset of your project. He or she can raise flags that will contribute to the success of a quality Web site, one that is delivered on time and on budget. I'll talk about how to do this a little later in the chapter. Check out this Web site for more general information about quality assurance: *http://www.asqc.org*.

Quality Assurance Begins at the Beginning

As a QA manager, I have one goal in mind when brought onto a project: gather information about the Web site so I can begin writing a test plan, which should be a live document. I look to the project manager to help me accomplish this task. With a solid test plan, I can identify ways to ensure some level of quality based on the project's various metrics and requirements.

With metrics, I can set benchmarks. For example, a benchmark might be that we want streaming media to download 5 seconds after the entire Web page appears. Without metrics to measure, or benchmarks to strive for, QA has no standard of quality to meet. We have nothing to compare to, nothing to help us define how we measure success. Metrics and requirements help QA to measure the success of a site (see Table 7.1).

Once the QA manager gets a sense of metrics and requirements, he or she can assess for risks and test types that will need to be conducted for the Web site. (More information about risks is in the section "Common Risks Associated with Testing" later in this chapter.) At Red Sky, we have a series of documents that describe all of the project metrics and requirements.

TABLE 7.1   Common Web Site Metrics and Requirements

Metrics	Requirements
Browser/operating system configuration	Database configuration for client/server applications or any cgi calls, often used with forms and ad banners. Database type and programming languages used on the server side are also included.
Hardware requirements	
Memory size requirements	
Response times expect for download and user interface	Network configuration
File and application size	Assets—audio, streaming media, moving or static images
Connection speed	Feature set
	Application types: scripts; scriplets, which could include Shockwave, JavaScript, Flash, Java

Note: You can review the series of documents about metrics and tailor them to your own use. They are located in the /templates/chapter7 folder on the CD-ROM that accompanies this book.

The Promised Environment

If you get your QA manager involved early in the project, he or she can be your technographics and metrics champion. Your QA manager must test your Web project in the promised environment. By "promised environment," I'm referring to the targeted technographics for your Web site, such as targeted browser, operating system, and other environment requirements.

Making technographic decisions up front and communicating them to your QA manager will not only improve the testing effort and the writing of a successful test plan but could also significantly increase or reduce testing time and cost.

Unfortunately, it has been my experience that technographics and other metrics either get buried or remain somewhat unknown throughout the life cycle of a project. Other Web team members are responsible for defining the metrics. The strategy team specifies scope, the producer specifies the functional requirements, and the tech lead specifies technical requirements, so testers can use those metrics to measure the success of the project.

Desktop, Client/Server, and Web Software Testing

To illustrate the differences between testing older, more established software and Web software, I think a discussion of desktop, client/server, and Web software and the environments they run on is appropriate. The amount of control over the environment on which the application runs decreases as you goes from desktop to client/server to Web software. This lack of control has the greatest impact on testing.

Desktop software runs on traditional personal computers and workstations, which means when you test, you focus on one application running in a very specific environment. Client/server applications run in a networked environment, and although you have two separate components to test, you still have control over the client part of the application. Web applications run in a networked environment, but you lose control over the client. Web applications are supposed to run on various browsers and platforms. Therefore, for testing you must set up an environment that simulates the various permutations of the targeted browser/operating system for that site.

Testing Approach: A Closer Look

Environment requirements shape the configuration that QA must set up to execute tests. Another significant difference between desktop, client/server and Web applications is that desktop and client/server applications tend to be written in one programming language. This is not to say that there aren't many layers of interactive complexity for these types of applications. The testing challenges remain, but the targeted environment is different.

Desktop software must be tested at the native operating system level. Web software in my experience does not get tested at the native operating system level; it gets tested higher up in the food chain, far away from the bowels of the operating system.

Instead, Web software must be tested for browser compatibility and operating system compatibility. But also, because so many various programming languages and scripts can live within a single Web page, the interaction of various applications must also be tested. External software, such as Shockwave and JavaScript and Java and Perl, along with network connection must work together to create the expected result. Although testing differences between desktop, client/server, and Web software applications exist, the principles of quality assurance and testing still apply for all three categories.

◆ **Desktop versus Web Software Testing: An Example**

I recently tested a very complex Java applet called Oxford Express. The applet ran on top of the virtual machine, which ran on top of the browser, which ran on top of the operating system. With a desktop application, I would want to test the Application Program Interface (API). The API provides services that a programmer makes calls to.

Those API calls should be tested to make sure that the application is doing what it is supposed to do, speaking to the API correctly. With this Java applet like Oxford Express, I never considered testing the API. With a Java applet I needed to make sure that it was speaking to the virtual machine API correctly. In order to do that, I would need to know the targeted environment, which would include the operating systems, browsers, and virtual machines, so that I could verify that the applet worked in its promised environment.

The Role of Testing in Quality Assurance

The terms *quality assurance* and *testing* are often used interchangeably. Because the QA group is responsible for testing your Web site, I can see why confusion about these terms might arise. Many programmers, producers, and project managers talk about "QA'ing" a Web site. I'm illustrating this point to clarify the difference between quality assurance and testing. Planning for the testing phase of your project and testing it will contribute to the quality of your Web site, but it will not ensure a quality product.

As a QA manager, I contribute to the quality of a Web site in a number of ways. The first way is by getting my hands on the scope document or project plan as soon as the project manager gets it. This way I can start thinking about the test plan and asking about metrics to measure the success of a project, for both technical and user-based requirements. I can start reviewing technographics to set up the appropriate testing environment based on the knowledge, which I've gained through testing before a project goes into production, of problem areas that continue to occur . The second way I contribute is by managing the testing effort; reporting and tracking problems; and, at the end of a project, providing a QA summary to the client and rest of the team. (More information about what to expect from a test plan and QA summary is covered later in the chapter.)

The Role of the Specification for Black-Box or Requirements-based Testing

"Testing against a spec is like walking on water: it helps if it is frozen."

—Source unknown

Before entering a discussion of what to expect from a test plan, I'd like to outline a brief description of black-box or requirements-based testing. The spec or requirement document (*requirement* is the layperson's term for *specification*) is what I use to verify that a Web site functions and looks the way it's supposed to.

Most of the Web testing that I have planned and executed has been requirements-based testing. Another form of testing, white-box or glass-box testing, is generally conducted by the programmer or coder. For Web sites, programmers use some type of HTML validator and also spend time executing and viewing JavaScript code in a browser. Debuggers are built into the director environment that Lingo coders use to white-box test the code they have written.

Testers: What They Do for You

As a QA manager who writes test plans for black-box testers, I'm interested in what a feature is supposed to do, not in how it was designed or written on the coding level. The spec is the document that tells me what is expected when I click on icon X or roll over graphic Y. A list of criteria for black-box testing follows:

♦ Testers don't not know the internals of the program, much like targeted user who doesn't know or care about the internals of a program.

♦ Testing is conducted based on the specifications. The QA lead or QA manager writes test cases based on functional specification.

♦ Testers execute every possible scenario. To verify that the Web site is reliable, representative tests are designed to imitate typical usage of Web site. *Representative* is testing jargon for creating tests that represent every possible scenario because it is mathematically impossible to execute every possible scenario.

♦ Tests incorporate valid and invalid inputs. I often design and execute these kinds of tests that make calls to a database on HTML forms. The focus of these tests is to enter valid or invalid data into text fields to check for error messages and recovery or other expected results.

Planning for the Testing Phase

"It's cheaper to
catch defects
upstream than
downstream."
–Source unknown

We've established that your QA manager needs to be involved in the project earlier as opposed to later. Even though testing your Web site occurs
in the final phase of your project, handing off rough functional and technical specifications and having him or her attend preliminary scheduling
and budgeting meetings will streamline the testing phase of your project.

As I mentioned, your QA manager can assess risks early in the project
and begin formulating a testing strategy and designing test types, both of
which will impact the testing schedule and therefore the overall quality of
the project. Oftentimes preliminary or feasibility tests can be executed in
order to avoid finding problems during the testing phase of the project,
when fixing problems can be very expensive both to the budget and the
schedule.

Common Risks Associated with Testing

Over the course of testing, documenting, and delivering Web projects, I've
noticed some areas that tend to pose risks to the testing phase of the projects. Here's a list of some risks:

- *Slipped schedule*   Either not enough time is scheduled for testing
  or the schedule slips and allotted testing time starts to shrink.
  Ultimately, this leads to less coverage of your Web site. *Coverage* is
  testing jargon for "getting to" as many parts of your Web site as possible. The more time testers have to execute their tests, the more bugs
  they can find, and so on.

- *Bug-fixing resources*   Web team members have to be allocated and
  scheduled for this part of the project. Often coders, production
  artists, animators, programmers, and artists are burned out when a
  project gets into the testing phase. If there is no one to fix bugs during testing, the delivery date could slip.

- *Metrics*   Testers can't measure something if they don't have a metric.
  Common metrics for Web sites include expected Java applet, Static
  Web page or Shockwave download times, minimum hard drive requirements to run an applet, expected response time for rollover
  behavior, file size limitations, data retrieval times, and expected
  streaming media time.

- *Outdated or irrelevant specifications and/or composites*   If the composites
  (comps) or specifications are not updated, testers will have inaccu-
  rate data to write test cases and to compare your Web site against.

◆ Preliminary or Feasibility Web Testing

I recently worked on a project in which the creative team decided, late in the development cycle, that they wanted to force a child window to refocus, to reappear, after users closed the child window and clicked on the link that was supposed reopen the child window. This feature was supposed to run in a cross-platform and cross-browser environment. Rather than implementing an untested feature directly into the project, QA was brought on to test functionality in the promised environment. No art was created for the test and no integration with the rest of the project was necessary. I tested the core functionality of the feature and, based on my results, was able to provide the programmer and project manager with bugs, which were fixed and retested. Once the feature passed certain tests in the promised environment, I was able to recommend that we go ahead with a full-scale implementation.

Had we not conducted preliminary testing of the feature in the promised environment, I might have found bugs during the testing phase of the project. Fixing and tracking bugs is very expensive during the testing phase of a project.

- *Untrained testers* Testing a Web site requires people who are not only the meticulous sort but also who are familiar with the Web site being tested. If you're low on personnel, make sure your QA manager writes test cases that anybody can sit down and execute. Bug reporting is also an important communication skill. Conventions for bug reporting should be made available to testers, so they know how to communicate problems they find to the rest of the team.

- *Changing or unclear technographics* Inadequate research or miscommunication with the client and with other team members about the targeted environment can be very costly to the testing phase.

- *Component, module, application, and system integration* Any time two distinct pieces of a Web site must come together, both technical and communication risks arise. For Web sites, at the application level, front-end to back-end database calls (coding integration) often present testing challenges. At the system level, Web hosting and site migration can also jeopardize the quality of the product and impact the testing schedule and strategy.

Web Site Evolution and Hosting

Earlier in the chapter, I tried to distinguish Web site testing from desktop and client/server software testing. Distribution of and access to a Web site present unique testing challenges for QA. Once again, the distribution and access environment differ significantly for desktop and client/server software and Web sites.

The term *Web site evolution* encapsulates the migration of a site over time. Version control and changes of both physical and virtual environments can have an enormous impact on the testing phase of a site. It might be a good idea to create a document the site evolution document. If your Web team isn't comfortable with this type of information being in a separate document, that's fine. Sometimes site evolution and hosting get covered in the technical specification. Regardless of where it happens, it is very important for testing that these issues are raised. The site evolution document tracks how and when the site migrates from development to staging to live locations. Internal and external site hosting is tracked, along with costs.

For each stage, the following details should be included: IP addresses, URLs, passwords, external hosting company/contact name, and costs; hardware, software configurations and types; and the number of servers as they increase/decrease over time. For example, at one point, AbsolutDJ lived on one NT box, with one type of mail server and one MS Access database; the site URL, server types and number, and database software changed over time. Later in the project, the mail server configuration changed, which introduced unforeseen bugs. This undocumented change was very costly because I had to re-execute a series of test cases. Planning for this change would have helped to negotiate up-front testing time and resources with the client and the rest of the Web team.

At the beginning of a project, all the details for site evolution tend to be unknown or sketchy, especially if the live environment, the final destination for the site, is at an external hosting company. If, like with many Web site projects, the application makes calls to the back-end and your site is being hosted at another company, then system integration problems will be introduced. I guarantee it. If your QA manager has access to details in the site evolution document, then she can include them in her test plan and also set up her environment to mirror the hosting company. Cost of setting up a mirrored environment during the testing phase can be assessed. If it's too costly to set up a mirrored environment in testing, at the very least, she can communicate those risks to the client. Because this part of Web site development is so challenging and unique to Web development and testing, it often gets ignored.

A Successful Test Plan

Most of this chapter has been about preparing for the writing and execution of a successful test plan. In this section I cover some key points for a typical Web site test plan, points that should help you understand what to expect from a test plan.

The Service Delivery Agreement

A test plan is a service delivery agreement. It's QA's way of communicating to you, the client, and the rest of team: this is what you can expect from us. All along I've been describing what QA needs to write the test plan. Once the test plan is done, QA has a chance to talk back to you. I won't cover all areas of a test plan; however, see Table 7.2 for some key points you should know about.

TABLE 7.2   Key Points of a Test Plan

Points to consider	Content
Introduction	Summarizes key features and expectations of Web site along with testing approach.
Scope	Includes a description of test types, such as load tests and functional tests, and details testing environment.
Bug categories and severity	Describes bug categories and bug types such as functional (JavaScript), usability (HTML font variations that impact readability), and creative bugs (palette bugs that indicate inconsistencies between a graphic displayed in Internet Explorer and in Netscape). Severity is also clearly defined, often in terms of a level 1, 2, or 3 bug. This is very important during the testing phase.
Configuration management	Version control system for the project and testing phase.
Risks and assumptions	This part should define a risk to the testing phase, such as criteria that could suspend testing. If testing gets suspended, then the testing schedule shrinks or increases. Assumptions for the testing phase might include something about both testing and bug-fixing resources. In other words, for the testing phase to be successful, X number of resources will need to be available.
Testing schedule and cycles	States when testing will be completed and the number of expected cycles. It also defines regression testing criteria.
Test resources	Specifies testers and bug fixers.
Test cases	A list of all test cases and test matrixes.
Bug report	A list of all the bugs; it is delivered at the end of the project.
QA summary	Observations, problems found, and recommendations handed off to client and project manager.

Test Types

You can find some sample test plans for you to use as templates on the CD-ROM in the /templates/ chapter7 folder.

Each test plan should, at the minimum, list all of the following test types. If any of the following test types is not executed, the test plan should state the reason.

- ◆ *Functional tests*   Verify functionality of features. For example, when I rollover X, then I should get Y. Do I?
- ◆ *Stress tests*   Find the maximum burden on system to show how it behaves. How long does your Web site take to download over a 28.8 kps modem on an older Pentium with the minimum physical RAM requirement installed on the system?
- ◆ *Load tests*   Iif a large number of users access the system, doing the same thing, you can check for data corruption and error recovery. If someone can't access your Web site, you can find out what happens. Is there an error message or does the system freeze?
- ◆ *Regression tests*   Ddefine how and what will be tested in the second and third phases of testing
- ◆ *Boundary analysis*   Tests the minimum and maximum working boundaries of a Web site. They should also go outside the defined boundaries. Often I try to test outside the boundaries of a Web site. If the spec says you can enter these kind of characters into a form, then I try to enter unspecified characters in a form field, like negative numbers or nonalphanumeric characters.

Web Site Load Testing

You've built a successful Web site, spent lots of money promoting it, launched it, but haven't load tested. More users than you planned for are accessing your site. How's your Web server holding up? Are users experiencing long download times or being told the server is down, please try again later?

Load testing for Web sites is, and will continue to become, more important as the Web grows. Load testing can be quite expensive and complex; third-party vendors offer software packages that can help with the load-testing effort. E-commerce or highly promotional sites, which might include a Webcast, are the kinds of sites that should be load tested. Both of these types of sites can have many concurrent users trying to access the site. Your QA manager can provide cost estimates along with strategy about how to include this type of testing for your Web site.

For more information on load testing, visit some Web loading software vendor's sites, such as RadView, *http://www.webload.com*. (See Figure 7.1.)

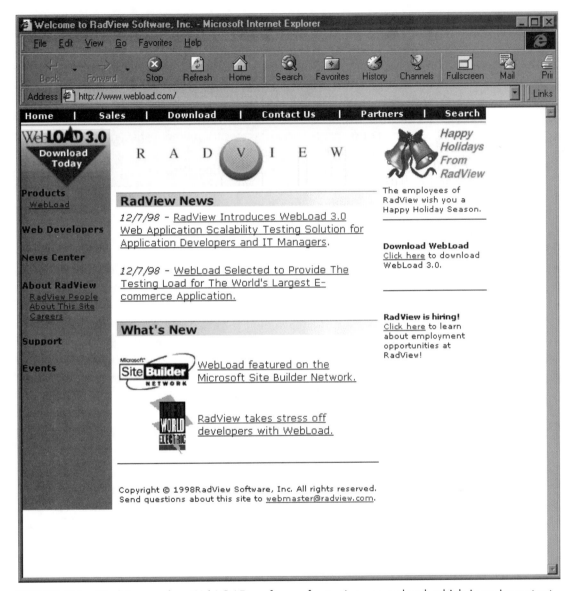

FIGURE 7.1 RadView makes WebLOAD, software for testing server load, which is an important part of quality assurance for Web sites.

Web Testing Tools

Each project has different testing needs. Automation can be the right solution for some projects but for smaller Web projects, automation isn't necessarily the answer. Setting up test scripts that work for the testing needs of your Web site can be very expensive. If you decide to automate, have your QA manager think through your testing objectives. The time you put into customizing scripts to meet your automated testing needs should cost less than the testing results you yield.

For more information on automation Web testing tools, visit these sites: *http://www.mercuryinteractive.com/* is Mercury Interactive—it's a great site for testing solutions for many business needs (see Figure 7.2); *http://www.segue.com/* is Segue Software (see Figure 7.3).

Here are four tools that I must have to get my job done:

1. *Bug-tracking system*   We use our own proprietary Bugbase, which we developed using Active Server pages. It's an excellent tool for helping us track, assign, and resolve bugs (see Figure 7.4).
2. *SiteSweeper*   I run SiteSweeper for most of my Web projects after I have finished executing manual tests. With big sites that have lots of links, it's very useful. It also measures file size, which can be useful when you're testing to make sure that your Web pages stay under a specified file size (*http://www.sitetech.com/*).
3. *System monitor for memory testing*   It comes with the Windows 95 CD. If I want to test minimum memory requirements, this tool helps track how virtual and physical RAM are swapping. I've used this tool mostly when testing Java applets.
4. *Soft Test*   This is a tool that helps to analyze system dependencies while reducing redundant tests. It helps with test case design so that all functions get covered (*http://www.softtest.com*).

QA and Testers Shake out the Bugs

Testers represent the users of your Web site. The only difference between a tester of your Web site before it is released and a client or customer user of your Web site is that tester can report problems to the Web team, who can fix or address them before the Web site is launched. Once a Web site is launched, problems that are found can be fixed but you might have already lost a sizeable chunk of your user base. It doesn't take much to drive users away from a Web site.

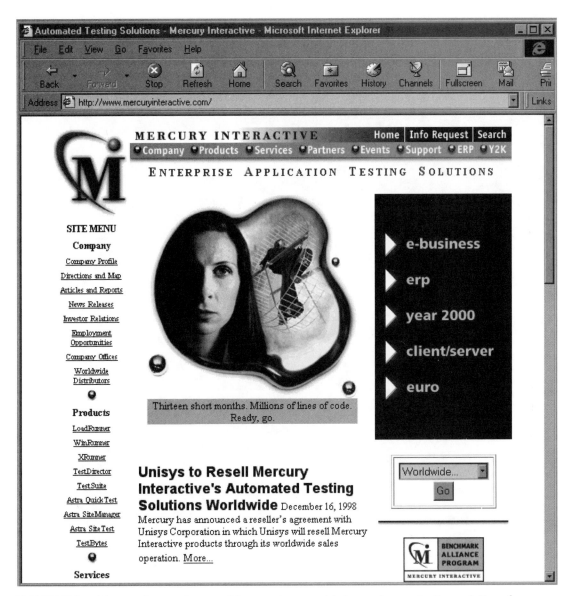

FIGURE 7.2 Mercury Interactive provides products and information on testing solutions for a large range of businesses, including e-commerce.

Treat your testers as if they were the client or end-users of your Web site. Because they represent the client/customer, you'll need to communicate the objectives of your Web site to them and give them enough time to execute the test plan your QA manager has spent so much time and effort developing. If you can't fix all the bugs your testers find, at least you've

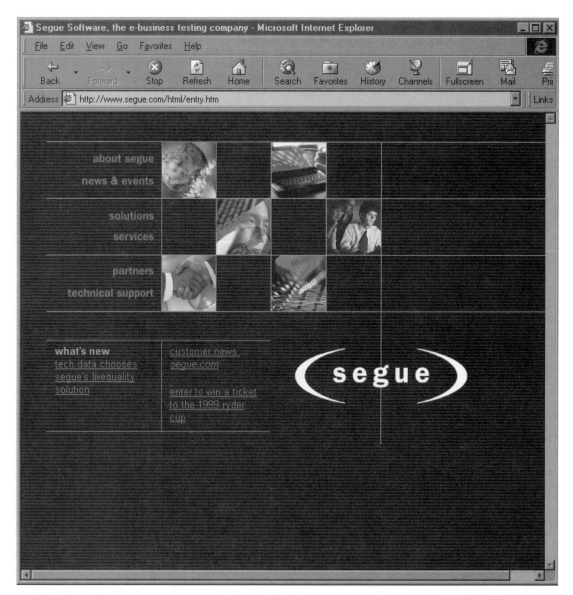

FIGURE 7.3   Segue Solutions' Silk Product package is one of the most widely used e-commerce testing packages.

documented the bugs and can communicate them to the client. If your schedule and budget don't allow more fixing and retesting, that's okay. You can use the bugs your testers find to communicate with the clients or marketers of your project. Let them make decisions about how to handle bugs, with their time and budget. If you don't empower your testers to

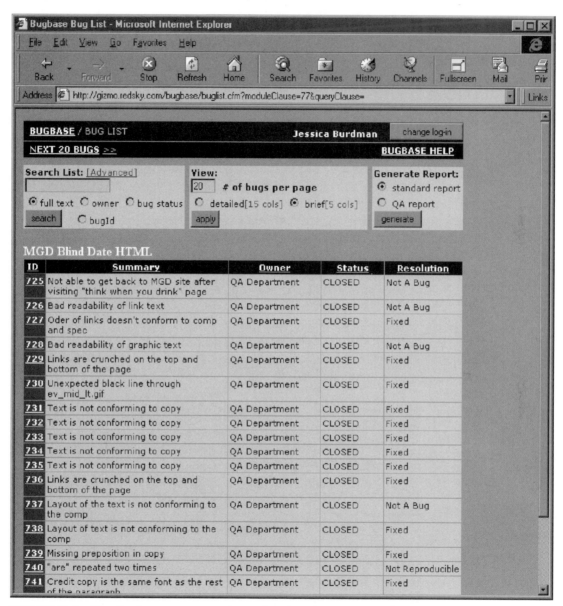

FIGURE 7.4   The Bugbase system tracks and assigns bugs on a Web site.

shake out the bugs first, you run the risk of delivering a Web site you know nothing about. It's better that you, not a client or customer, find the bugs. Clients don't like surprises, and customers can be warned about problems if you have to deliver with known bugs.

Summary

Quality assurance practioners need time and resources and structured information to test a Web application at the beginning of a project, as well as throughout the development cycle of a project, to ensure the release of a quality Web application for the targeted audience. This chapter provides you with some of the quality challenges that face this young, innovative, and rapidly growing industry. It also introduces some common metrics needed to measure the success of your Web application. Metrics that test engineers can use to write a Test Plan and test Web sites. The chapter also has an in-depth treatment of the unique testing challenges for Web sites, referencing documents and typical testing tools. Most important, you'll need a common language to speak to your QA team. After reading this chapter you should be able to communicate more effectively about ensuring quality. You'll have a basic understanding of testing terms and QA principles and standards.

To-Do List

♦ Have you scheduled enough time and resources for the testing phase of your Web site?

♦ Does your QA manager/lead have a copy of the project proposal and other preliminary documentation for your Web site?

♦ Have you defined metrics to measure the success of your Web site?

♦ Have you met with your QA manager and the rest of your team to clarify severity levels for the bugs that testers will find during the testing phase?

♦ Have you considered integration of different parts of your Web site and its effect on the testing phase of your Web site?

Quality Assurance for Web Applications

Sophie Jasson-Holt
Quality Assurance Manager
Red Sky Interactive

As the quality assurance manager for Red Sky Interactive, Sophie Jasson-Holt is responsible for managing a small group of dedicated testers, for engineering testing standards and practices that fit with the company business model, and for leading the company's growing quality assurance department.

Prior to joining Red Sky, Sophie worked as a technical writer, coder, and QA lead for Aslan, a small start-up software company. Sophie is the author of an award-winning book of poems entitled *Unfold the Chaparral*.[1] Her professional interests include learning PERL and keeping her eye out for better and cheaper load-testing solutions.

What are the responsibilities of your job?

I manage the testing phase for all projects at Red Sky, which includes writing test plans, scheduling testing resources, and managing Web application testers. Since I established a QA department at Red Sky in 1998, much of my work has included educating the rest of the company about the role of testing and QA and marrying software testing standards and methods to Red Sky's advertising business model. I'm also responsible for researching testing tools for the Web and for contributing the knowledge that I've learned from testing and finding bugs to improve the way Web teams build a new project.

What's the most common misconception about QA for Web sites?

That it's all about link verification, that a Web site isn't an application.

What is the most important service you provide to the Web team?

I try to prevent problems and to find problems before the customer or client finds them. I work very hard to make sure the Web application conforms to the specification. [If they don't, I] report those problems to the team and the client.

---

1. Sophie Jasson-Holt, *Unfold the Chaparral*. San Francisco: San Francisco State University Press, 1995.

Are there mistakes that you see over and over again on Web projects? What are they?

Yes. Web teams want to build beautiful sites with many cool features. What Web teams often overlook are metrics. The tough questions often get avoided, like, How big do we want this page to be? or, What kind of performance are we trying to achieve? Anything that can be measured gets overlooked, because I believe it's one of the biggest challenges that we face in this limited medium.

Are there any tools that make your job easier?

A stopwatch, a problem-reporting system (Bugbase), SiteSweeper to find broken links and report page and image size.

What does the future hold for the QA member of the Web team? How will your skills have to change?

QA members will have to become more proficient in software quality management and processes. Understanding Web applications and the environments they are developed for and distributed to will become increasingly important. Currently, I have to configure testing environments which mirror client systems; these always include browsers and operating systems. As broadband becomes a reality, I will have to learn about the new testing challenges for this technology. Most Web applications are connected to a database. For QA and testing, this means we have to understand how to design test cases that will unearth problems for these types of applications. Knowing more about databases, about how they're designed, the programming languages they're written in will help QA members to do a better job. QA members are generalists, people who know a little about a lot of things, but who ultimately must be specialists in quality standards, methods, and practices. The challenge for the QA member of a Web team will be to incorporate quality standards that currently exist into a young industry that is growing up very quickly.

CHAPTER 8

Technological Advances and the Impact on Web Teams

No one really knows the future, but it's not too difficult to take an educated guess about what the future might hold for Web teams and people looking to provide Web services to clients. People and organizations are beginning to figure out how the Web can improve their lives, their businesses, and their school systems. Demand for Internet access, information, entertainment, goods, and services will drive the development of new technologies that will, in turn, affect how Web sites and advertisements are built and managed. New developments will always affect how Web projects are managed and built—either for the better or for the worse. You will always need to be preparing to handle the change as is happens.

This chapter is about how technological change impacts Web teams. In this chapter, we discuss emerging technologies (as of 1999), their possible uses, and how Web teams might prepare to incorporate these technologies into the Web development process.

Emerging Technologies and Changing Needs

The Web has many audiences, all of whom come looking for information, goods, and services on demand. It's an active medium; users, for the most part, seek information at their own level of desire. This kind of information on demand has been the most prevalent kind of Web application. However, as people begin to use the Web for more and more consumer purposes, such as comparison shopping or advertising, the Web will become more like television or radio, where information is pushed toward the consumer through channels, stations, or other yet-to-be developed means.

The Web as Interactive Television

One of the biggest changes on the horizon is broadband Internet access. With broadband Internet access, the Web can provide richer types of media such as audio, video, and virtual reality. With cable companies getting into business of providing Internet access, we can expect to see the Web become more accessible from television sets and informational kiosks in the home or in stores and organizations, or even in cars or planes.

WebTV allows users to have both a TV interface and a Web interface simultaneously appear on screen. This user is still in control of this interface; however, in the coming years, content providers will begin to be able to push interactive content down to users, because they will be able to detect a user's preferences based on the Web sites he or she chooses. Users' experiences on-line will become personalized to their preferences.

For Web team members, this means that the requirements for providing this future content will change. Many Web sites offer resources for training and development, specifically for creating content for interactive television. Two sites are the WebTV Developer Resource site (*http:// developer.webtv.net*), seen in Figure 8.1, and the Microsoft Digital TV site (*http://www.microsoft.com/dtv/*). Both sites offer information about necessary skill sets, from art production to coding, and have libraries of pre-existing code to get started.

People with experience in television production, scriptwriting, sound design, and videography will all become part of the Web team that provides content for interactive television. NBC has launched several such experiences, including the 1998 U.S. Open Golf Tournament (*http://www. microsoft.com/dtv/creating/cr_usopen_01.asp*), which you can see in Figure 8.2.

The Web as Information Store

What if the Web became the central repository of information for national and international organizations like the postal service, libraries, and universities? Certainly the ability to search effectively for data is one of the key requirements for this kind of Web project. A Web team would necessarily have to include a librarian and perhaps a team of programmers to customize or create software that could search information accurately in

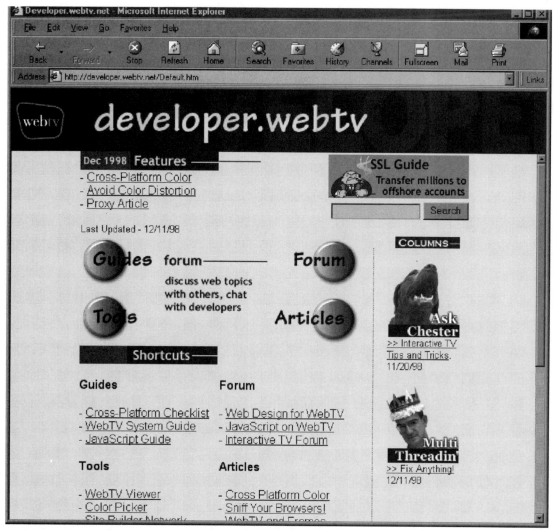

FIGURE 8.1 Developer sites help Web developers get up to speed in new technologies quickly.

both textual and binary formats. As well, significant usability testing is critical because these sites base their effectiveness on how well people can find information. If there are millions of records in a database, how does this data get displayed in a meaningful way to the user?

One site that is already seeking to become this kind of information store is the Internet Movie Database (*http://www.imdb.com*). This site may not seem complex to the average user; however, the database structure

◆ The End of the World Wide Wait: Broadband Internet Access

Broadband internet access is Internet access in which large chunks of information can be transmitted. The days of waiting for images to download will be over when broadband Internet access is a reality. You might be able to watch a movie over your computer, visit 3-D worlds, and create blueprints of your house using a tool created for on-line use in Hong Kong while hundreds of other people use it simultaneously.

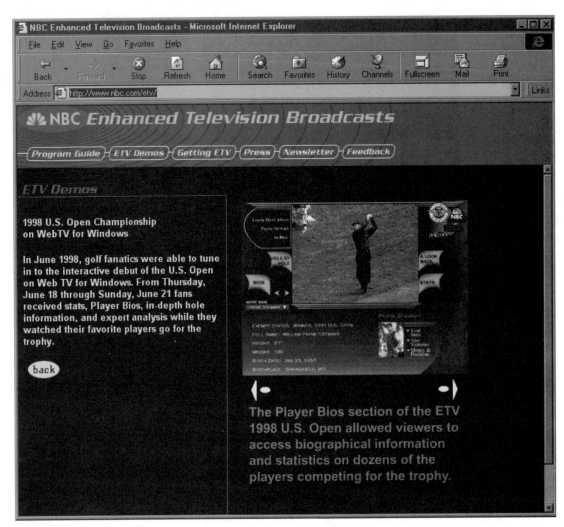

FIGURE 8.2   WebNetTV offers an interactive television experience.

behind this site took a long time to plan, design, test, and deploy. This site has some good features, but its interface is still evolving. With each iteration it gets better, easier to use and navigate. So it's important to note that it might be difficult to get these kinds of interfaces perfect the first time around.

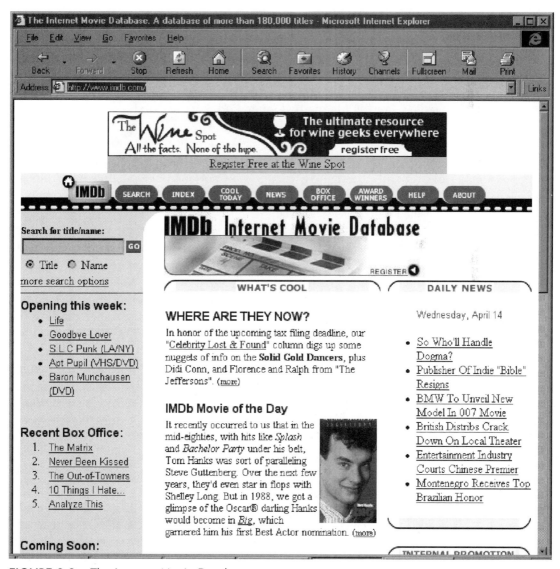

FIGURE 8.3   The Internet Movie Database.

The Web and Electronic Commerce

If every kitchen has a Web kiosk where consumers can log on to order groceries, find recipes, shop for merchandise, and interact with other users and the brands themselves, then what does that mean for consumer brands? Consumers risk being literally inundated with information and choices. Consumers will naturally choose brands they can interact with in a meaningful way.

For example, Red Sky Interactive recently launched a Web advertising campaign for Hugo Boss Fragrances in which consumers could click through the many gift selections that Hugo offers. For the consumer who was unsure about what to give, the advertisement provided a service so the giver could send an e-mail to the receiver to ask what he or she really wanted. For the tongue-tied giver, Red Sky provided a series of notes that the user could choose from—notes that were witty, charming or sentimental. Also, users could purchase right there, in the advertisement (see Figure 8.4). The result was an advertisement that gave the user something meaningful, entertained, and, most important, left a positive perception of the Hugo Boss brand, regardless of whether the consumer decided to purchase a Hugo Boss fragrance.

This means that companies who want to sell their products and increase brand awareness on-line will have to provide experiences for the consumer in order to do so. A simple banner advertisement will not be enough. The advertising space in the Web of the future is still undefined, but the team of the future needs to embrace whatever technology emerges and be able to build these interactive experiences by understanding the users' psychology and technoprofile. (For a discussion of technoprofiles, see the sidebar on page 160.)

On the technical side, Web teams that provide electronic-commerce (e-commerce) applications need to include a security expert, database programmers, and network engineers. Engineers and architects are working toward integrating the electronic transactions into the entire organization's business system, meaning that a Web transaction will be the first in a series of transaction that are automatic—ordering, shipping, updating inventory, invoicing, and replenishing inventory. Full integration with businesses' existing systems is the goal of electronic commerce.

Many vendors offer e-commerce solutions and packages. It's hard to wade through all the offerings and find a vendor you can trust, who is reputable, and who has a proven track record. Here are some tips to keep in mind when looking for an e-commerce partner:

FIGURE 8.4 The Hugo Boss gift campaign is an interactive advertisement.

1. Does the vendor have references and successful case studies? Ask to speak with contacts; ask them about the experience of working with the vendor.

2. Is the vendor using propriety software that has been reviewed and is reputable? Some vendors propose customized e-commerce packages. Generally, the customization should be with regard to the way the application talks to the front end (the user interface) and the existing legacy

◆ What Are Technoprofiles?

Technoprofiles (also called technographics) are a way of classifying users based on their technological configuration. It's a way of identifying users based on their computer platform, browser, connection speed, and other Internet software that they have downloaded or installed on their systems.

Web teams are and should be very concerned with discerning their intended audience's technoprofile. However, this information is not readily available. You might have to conduct focus groups, studies, or surveys to determine this data. If you do not take the time to do this, you risk developing applications that your users cannot use because they don't have the right software. As well, you could be selling your audience short by catering to older browsers if you continue to develop for older browsers.

system (such as an inventory database). Avoid vendors who want to sell a fully customized package.

3. Will the vendor work with your staff and provide specifications so your team can build the user interface? It's important that a representative be available and that the relationship is not an "install-and-run" relationship.

4. Understand what you are doing. There is a lot of information about e-commerce on-line. Read and understand the issues and the electronic-commerce cycle. Here are some good Web sites:

The Electronic Commerce Guide (a good place to start)
   http://e-comm.internet.com/

Netscape's Guide to Designing Commerce sites
   http://www.netscapeworld.com/netscapeworld/nw-04-1997/
   nw-04-techniques.html

Internet Commerce Site
   http://www2.metasys.co.jp/commerce/noframes2.html

The All E-Commerce Site
   http://www.allec.com/

Card Technology Site (a good place to learn about electronic payment technologies)
   http://cardtech.faulknergray.com/

Portable Web: Convenience and Access

The way in which people access the Web has a huge impact on Web site development and design. Monitor size, modem speed, and browser, al-

◆ Can Your Users Experience Your Site?

Detection scripts "sniff" your computer to determine your platform (OS), browser, and the existence of certain kinds of software, such as Macromedia Shockwave. Developers should use these scripts to deliver specific messages to the user, especially if the user does not have the browser or software required to use the site.

There is a lot of debate about whether developers should even develop sites that make users download new software. I choose not to enter that debate and instead give you some practical advice on how to make your site usable if you use technologies like Shockwave or RealAudio.

ready have a dramatic impact on the way Web teams develop Web sites and on the costs of Web site development. If you have a very diverse user audience, you are naturally going to want to provide the best experience for each user. Designing for every platform, browser, and monitor speed is not financially feasible, so the current solution is to study the technoprofiles of the target audience and design for that audience. If you use technologies that require certain plug-ins or software, most Web teams create detection scripts (see the sidebar above) to figure out what users have and then direct them to the software they need in order to get the most out of the site.

We all would like to see some standardization with regard to browsers and platforms so that our job as Web developer is easier, but that's not going to be the case. If anything, it will be harder and harder as people begin to access the Internet with their palm pilots, their television sets, their car dashboards, at kiosks in a library, or on kitchen countertops. The display screens for each of these devices will be radically different, as will the bandwidth that each device permits.

These innovations will have quite a significant impact on Web development and Web teams of the future. Developers will need to know much more about their audience, including and especially their audience's technoprofiles, if they want to make their Web sites useful and usable, and profitable.

Tools

Right now Web developers use certain tools to create Web content. Designers use Photoshop; animators use After Effects; programmers use many development tools; and HTML coders use many kinds of authoring tools to generate HTML. The tools will change according to the technology that is available for providing richer and richer Web experiences.

TABLE 8.1   XML Resources

XML Web sites	URLs
WebReference.com	*http://www.webreference.com/authoring/languages/xml*
WDVL XML Articles	*http://wdvl.com/*
WDVL XML Fact Page	*http://wdvl.com/*
XML DTDs and Valid XML Documents	*http://www.webreference.com/dlab/books/html/38-3.html*
Chrystal Software XML Page	*http://www.chrystal.com/xml/xml.htm*
Microsoft XML Page	*http://www.msdn.microsoft.com/xml/default.asp*
XML.Com	*http://www.xml.com/xml/pub*
The XML FAQ	*http://www.ucc.ie/xml/*
The W3C XML Page	*http://www.w3.org/XML/*

In the future, you can expect to see tools for authoring content for broadband spaces. These tools will be much like Macromedia's Director and other multimedia authoring tools. As well, XML will take a more prominent role in Web development, at the very least where database and commerce sites are concerned; tools for creating XML are already emerging (see Table 8.1 for a list of good XML sites to visit). Tools for graphic compression will also emerge, especially as new formats for graphics evolve—formats that enable graphics to scale automatically to the user's screen.

Preparing for Change

Technological change has many effects on Web teams. There is technological change in terms of how people create Web applications, as well as how the teams interact. For example, with wireless networks and the TCP/IP protocol, Web teams can and do work on the same project from many locations, making the Web team a virtual team. Communication is critical for virtual Web teams. Video conferencing and collaboration tools such as Microsoft's NetMeeting could become standard tools for communication. E-mail will continue to be the killer application for communication, but e-mail will grow to encompass visual messages as well as textual messages.

As technology changes, new tools will be created and new skills will be necessary. Web teams will begin incorporating specialized members in addition to the central core of team members (see chapter 2 for a refresher course on your core Web team). It will be critical to be able to communicate your team's development process to these new team members succinctly. These specialized team members will not always be a part of the central Web team, but will certainly be a part of the extended Web team, hired on a project-by-project basis (see Figure 8.5). Make sure your development process is clearly articulated on your project's Web site. Take the time to bring specialized members in for training and familiarization with team members, protocols, and processes.

Finding the right person for the job is always a challenge for the project manager however, this will begin to get easier. Networks of specialized developers are already forming. You will see more consulting groups form, offering specialized development skills such as 3-D design, sound engineering for the Web, and other to-be-developed skills. Partnerships

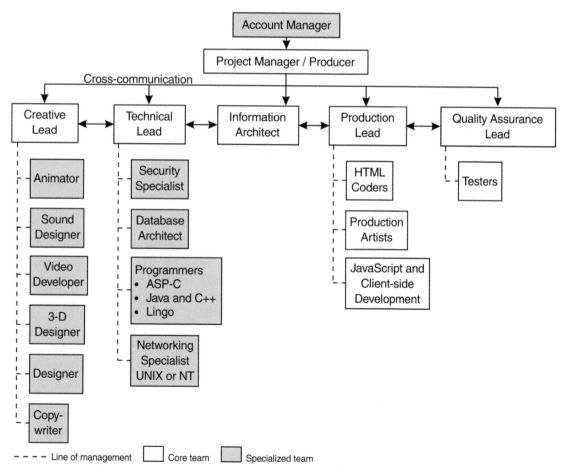

FIGURE 8.5 The appropriate core team members will manage specialized team members.

with these developers are critical to being able to deliver the kind of Web applications of the future.

Changes in the Process

When you develop static Web sites, the process is fairly straightforward. You can design a navigation system, and individual pages, that are finite and easy to test and troubleshoot. Programming these pages in HTML is very straightforward; and, even if you use a Perl script or JavaScript to process data or produce effects, you still are working with elements that remain the same after you create them.

Books by Weinschenk and colleagues and Cooper are good references for designing software interfaces.[1]

With Web data-driven sites, pages are created dynamically based on the user's input. The process for creating these kinds of Web sites is different, because you do not develop the many pages that get created. Instead, you develop templates and navigation systems that are scalable to accommodate the many pages that can be created based on your user's input. This means that your design, production, and testing cycles will be different from those for static Web site development. For instance, designers and engineers might have to collaborate to create iterations of templates depending on the kind of data that populates the templates. The logic used to create database interfaces will necessarily be used to create Web interfaces—the difference is that designers and production people must learn this method of interface development.

Broadband Internet access will bring about Web sites unlike any we've seen so far. Several agencies have prototyped these kinds of sites, such as TCI's @Home network, but I believe the broadband interactive space will be a much more immersive experience (see interview at the end of this chapter for a blue-sky description of the future). The people who will be creating these kinds of experiences could be filmmakers, storytellers (check out *http://www.bubbe.com*), or just imaginative people. It's hard to tell right now, but one thing is certain: The team will need to be comprised of businesspeople who understand the medium and can sell its values, a project manager who understands the project's complexity, creative people who can imagine what the space can do for users, information designers who understand what users want and need from the usability perspective, programmers who can build the functionality, production people who can bring the space together, and testers who can ensure a quality experience.

---

1. Susan Weinschenk, Sarah C. Yeo, Pamela Jamar, Theresa Hudson, Editors, *GUI Design Essentials for Windows 95, Windows 3.1, World Wide Web*. New York: John Wiley, 1997; Alan Cooper, *About Face: The Essentials of User Interface Design*. Foster City, CA: IDG Books Worldwide, 1995. Both books discuss the complexity of designing software interfaces in a concise, readable way— perfect for graphic designers and other nonprogrammers who need to learn or brush up on it.

Production Considerations

As I mentioned earlier, display devices will change, and there will be many more. The current method of creating and producing graphics for the Web in the .GIF or .JPG format will become unrealistic. Peoples' screens will be different, from 80 dpi for handheld devices to monitors at 300 dpi for television surfing. Developers will have to render their graphics using stylesheets in measurements other than pixels, and new formats for creating graphics must emerge—formats like vectors or something that can be resized dynamically.

Detection of users' platform, browser, and plug-in Internet software will become a critical piece of Web production. You will have to make hard calls based on real data gathered in the planning phase of your project. It will cost too much money to develop lowest-common-denominator Web sites, as is the current practice. The Web will become an integral part of life and to inhibit users from having the experience you want them to have (by catering to the lowest common denominator) will cost you in either direct sales or brand awareness.

The advent of new technologies should never mean that designing the user's experience should be sacrificed. In reality, technology should enhance the user's experience and should make the user's life easier, not harder. Getting the right software, which is currently a boon to the user experience, will no longer be an issue because the leading third-party developers will make deals to bundle their software with the leading browsers. Downloading software will become familiar to users because marketers will devise creative ways to introduce the user to the interfaces as part of integrated marketing plans. We see this already with Microsoft and the point-and-click motif in the "Where Do You Want To Go Today?" campaign. As well, the words "dot com" are becoming more and more widespread, as people pick up the language of the Web. The barriers to users getting what they want on-line are definitely coming down; but as new developments arise, so will new barriers. Be prepared.

Security on the Web

Security is and always will be important to consumers and to businesses that are selling products and services on-line. However, consumers will begin to accept certain levels of security (SSL) on the Web as increased good press and experiences spread by word of mouth or other channels. A Web developer's ability to gain consumers' trust is critical. Providing interfaces that walk users through the payment sequence and reinforce the security level is an important part of the design process.

At the time of this writing, LDAP (Lightweight Directory Access Protocol) is the latest recommended user-access control protocol. LDAP allows you to keep a central directory of users and their access rights. This is critical because you want people to be able to see your site, but this openness is exactly what makes it possible for people to break in and cause trouble. If a security engineer is not already part of your Web team, you will need to make this a reality. Big financial sites aren't the only sites being broken into these days. Visit *http://www.rootshell.com/*; this group keeps a bulletin of recent hackings and on-line fraud. The leading companies that provide firewall protection and other security products are provided in Table 8.2.

One of the more significant changes we will see is the emergence of SmartCards, which will replace the traditional logon/password method of authenticating users. In December of 1998, Microsoft announced its participation in the SmartCard market; it will be providing a SmartCard component of its Windows desktop.

Privacy

In addition to the myriad of security issues surrounding your Web site, you also have the to gain public's confidence if you want people to give you information, including their credit card numbers or other personal information. Consumers want to know what you are going to do with the information you obtain; so it's important that you have a privacy statement that is easy to see on the site. Figure 8.6 shows NASA's privacy statement.

Table 8.2 Leading Firewall and Security Vendors

Company	Product name	URL
Cisco Systems	Cisco Security System	*www.cisco.com/warp/public/cc/cisco/ mkt/security/index.shtml*
Sun Microsystems	SunScreen	*www.sun.com/security.*
Network Associates	Gauntlet and CyberCop	*www.nai.com/products/security/ security2.asp*
Microsoft Corporation	Security Advisor	*www.microsoft.com/security/default.asp*
Netscape Communications	Netscape Security Services	*home.netscape.com/directorysecurity/ index.html*

FIGURE 8.6   A privacy statement helps a Web site gain consumer confidence by telling users what you intend to do with their personal information.

Summary

I hope this chapter excited you about all the new technologies and opportunities for you and your team. Most people are so busy working on current projects that they don't have the time to surf around, read articles, and keep up to date on emerging technologies. It's important that you make some time to at least read the major trade zines (see Table 8.3 for some resources). If any of them offer an e-mail headline list, sign up for it. That way the headlines can come to you and you can decide whether you want to read the whole article. Each innovation is going to present a challenge to the team—and an opportunity to learn and improve.

TABLE 8.3   Recommended Reading for Web Professionals

Forrester Research
http://www.forrester.com
  An excellent source on trends and insights, based on solid research.

The Harvard Business Review
http://www.hbsp.harvard.edu/products/hbr/index.html
  On-line or on paper, this publication is critical reading for people who need to stay on top of the industry and business issues in general.

CyberAtlas.Com
http://www.cyberatlas.com
  An excellent Web marketing site.

Web Review
http://www.webreview.com
  This site has terrific articles on Web tools and usage.

Web Developer
http://www.developer.com/
  This is my favorite site for finding new tools and learning about new technologies.

To-Do List

- Formulate a plan for your future team.
- Keep a spreadsheet of your current team and their skill sets. Include all contractors, rates, and skills.
- Evaluate the kind of sites you've been creating, or would like to create, and begin thinking about the specialized team members you might need.
- Bring people in for informational interviews.
- Establish relationships with vendors with whom you might work.
- Attend industry events and stay on the high-tech watch, but also read magazines (see Table 8.3) that predict trends in the on-line space.

Web Sites of the Future

Tim Smith, CEO, and
Joel Hladecek, Chief Creative Officer
Red Sky Interactive

This interview was conducted in early 1999 in the office of Tim Smith. It is meant to be a blue-sky view of what the Web might be like in the future; it is not a prediction. It is purely an exercise in imagination and speculation.

Tim Smith, founder and CEO of Red Sky Interactive, played his first computer game (Adventure) on an IBM 360 mainframe sometime around 1977. He has been a hopeless early-adopter of new technologies ever since and takes great pride in the fact that his Osborne can still boot CP/M and run VisiCalc. While earning his business degree from the University of California at Berkeley, Tim wrote articles on artificial intelligence and software development. After Berkeley Business School, Ernst & Young consulting hired Tim to help run their Advanced Technologies group in San Jose, putting him inside many of the largest technology firms in Silicon Valley.

Suffering what he refers to as an "early mid-life crisis," Tim left Ernst & Young in 1991 to travel for a year with a handful of books. He returned with a ponytail and an idea of what the successful new media company would look like. Two years later, Red Sky Interactive was founded with the simple charter to design and produce the most creative, and effective, interactive communications in the industry for the best companies in the world.

Since graduating from the California College of Arts and Crafts in Oakland with a BFA in Film, Joel Hladecek has created numerous award-winning digital movies, special venue films, animations, and special effects. After working on several personal projects, Joel was recruited by Matte World in Novato, California, as their motion-control camera operator and as a special-effects supervisor; he worked on numerous feature film projects for more than five years.

Joel draws heavily on his extensive theme park experience when developing creative concepts for Red Sky Interactive. Joel says, " Designing for multimedia is a lot like developing a theme park attraction; the reality you must create cannot be linear like a narrative film. The viewer must be immersed and have the freedom to move around in an interactive project as they would in an amusement park."

There's a lot of speculation about where the Web is going—toward PC/TV convergence, or to virtual reality, or to something else altogether. As two people in the new media industry who are very interested in giving consumers what they want, where do you see the Web evolving?

JOEL: The theory that informs much of our expectations regarding the long-term future of the medium is that gross technical advancement, in any new media, gradually tends to flow toward a re-creation of real-life experience. Historically, we've seen this law play itself out in all traditional media. It's why we all see color as an improvement over black and white or stereo an improvement over mono. It's closer to what is real, so we automatically classify that as a technical improvement. Naturally, technical improvements in all media also have a tendency to top out over time as we reach the limits of the technology. Advancements become more and more incremental. You see this clearly in film today. After the development of color, a lot of effort went into improving film grain; it's still getting incrementally finer and finer. Look at audio—from surround sound to THX. Curved TV screen to flat screen. Sure, it's a little better, but what it takes to jump from the plateau, from the point of technical fine-tuning, is a whole new additional capability, a giant step. What we did with the traditional broadcast of moving image and sound was add interactivity to the picture. So taxing was this interactivity that it forced us to adopt a much more rudimentary form of moving-image and sound transmission. You saw this difference when comparing the aesthetic differences of television and CD-ROM technology. A trade off, but we inherently saw the value of the added capability. And then again, we went on-line; yet another big capability leap. Now we're all networked, but that added another whole new set of technical limitations. This left us with the dumbed-down visual and audible aesthetics of today's Web page. Based on our theory, the technologists have their work cut out for them, and you can bet they see it. They'll work to improve the transmission of moving image, sound, and feedback across the interactive network. Bandwidth and processor speeds are some of the culprits here. They'll soon work to improve the the way we interface with the medium, so we'll likely say good-bye to the keyboard and mouse. Technologists will make improvements in this medium into the future until, with it, we can recreate real-life experience. Keep in mind, the power of this medium is that it is not restricted to passivity of television, so our ideas surrounding the nature of the TV living room will have to undergo some fundamental changes if we are to see this medium firmly establish itself there.

Are we talking about the Star Trek holodeck here?

JOEL: Yes, if you extend this law way out there, you are certainly talking about a holodeck of sorts. A medium that stimulates all five senses, that is fully and fluidly interactive—totally believable and yet completely artificial. But don't get me wrong, there is little true value in rote re-creation of real life.

People often mistake my message here. The value in having the capability to recreate reality only lies in the power it gives us to abstract that reality to our whim.

It used to be called virtual reality, but I don't like that term anymore for two reasons: one, because it implies a synthetic, yet rote, duplication of the real world, which as I've said, isn't what the point of it is. And two, because the term is popularly linked to the current state of the technology—even the dictionary defines *virtual reality* as the use of the goggles and gloves. That makes about as much sense to me as saying that literature is the use of a pencil. Just as the holodeck cannot manifest with current technology, nor can the interactive experiences that will be created as soon as one year from now be created with the technology of today. The technology, the tools, are changing so very rapidly. In the quest for a more universal name, I've been calling the medium "perceptual reality." This puts the emphasis on the illusion, the artifact, the moment of perceived reality that the user experiences through stimulation of the user's senses, its reaction to their action, and their resulting willingness to suspend disbelief, regardless of the technology used to create it.

Divorced from specific tools and technologies, the number of possible forms that perceptual reality (P.R.) can take explodes.

Forms of P.R., it occurred to me, as pieces of work unlocked from the tools and platforms used to create them, have existed for all human history. Further, there are at least three general strata of P.R. that I could identify.

The first (and likely the oldest), being the most restrictive in terms of allowing for manual abstraction of reality, I call "contextual P.R." I say the most restrictive because, strictly defined, this form does not allow for an alteration of sensorial, real-world experience at all. A contextual P.R. is an alternate explanation or fictional story which affects the conscious understanding of the user's reality. One which, but for the observational limitations of the user, cannot be immediately disproved. It's a story that must clearly coexist with the user's real-world experiences. The clearest example I can think of would simply be a believable lie. For example, if I told you that I'm wearing a pair of red socks. That doesn't make for very compelling P.R., but short of lifting my pant leg, that's your reality. Of course I would never make such a fashion faux pas, unless I was also wearing a red tie! A more dramatic example is Orson Welles's "War of the Worlds." On the night of that radio broadcast hundreds of people believed that they lived on a planet that was being invaded by Martians, and they acted accordingly. For them, for a period of time, it was reality. Eventually, these people discovered that it had not happened at all, but what of those stories that can not be disproved as easily? Gravity is a "force," right? Well, actually there are little invisible beings infesting the entire universe that like to push everything down, so fear the day they grow weary.

It could be argued that many of the world's religions are a form of contextual P.R. In each case, these stories build a context or belief through which we live and shape our personal experiences, and to that degree they affect our perception of reality.

The second strata of perceptual reality I call "physical P.R." Here, there is an attempt to literally reshape the world around the user through sheer construction—actually building an alternate reality. With physical P.R. the storytellers have a bit more freedom to abstract perceptual experience (thereby assisting the suspension of disbelief) than they did with contextual P.R. Take, for example, any of the simulation style rides in theme parks. There are certain aspects of reality that can be manipulated here, but even this does not allow for full abstraction of real-world experience. While most of the users' senses (sight, hearing, feeling, smell) can be tricked into believing the story, there are still aspects of reality which cannot be altered. There is a physical distance separating the user from the constructed environment—even if it's only from the eye to the screen, or the ear to the speaker. The user is still a human being, can look down and see her legs, and was just in a theme park and is now with twelve other people who still have their Mickey Mouse hats on—that's just the reality of the moment. Now if you, as the creator of a physical P.R. story, choose to ignore that reality, that contradiction working against the users' ability to suspend disbelief, then you distance yourself from making that experience as powerful as possible. However, if you embrace that and admit: *We're not trying to convince you that you are in another world. You are in a theme park, you are getting on a ride*—this *ride, and whoops, this ride breaks and you're out of control and in danger,* and if this is all part of the story, then you can overcome those contradictions.

You're talking about both contextual perceptual reality and physical perceptual reality then.

JOEL: Yes, you've combined contextual and physical perceptual reality to make something that's much stronger. You've filled the holes with contextual P.R. that your construction, or physical P.R., couldn't.

Finally, the third strata I call "illusory P.R." This is where the storyteller has complete control of the user's perceptual reality. There is no distance between the senses of the user and the illusion. All senses can be tricked thoroughly and convincingly. Here, a reality may be that the user is not human, or that the world is not 3-D, the imagination becomes the only limitation. There is no reliance on, or restriction of, the realities in the physical world, and no opportunity for real-world experience to inject itself and break the fully fabricated reality of the storyteller's story. This is the holodeck, and it's what virtual reality pioneers talked about.

How do these types of perceptual realities affect the work you do?

JOEL: Wow, reality check, right? It informs us to a degree and gives us some insight into where the technology and medium is going. Until we have the capabilities of illusory P.R., we will continue to perceive weaknesses in our technologies, and technologists will continue to make "improvements." But not every technical development is going to stick to the growth of this thing. The right timing and order is also critical. In this industry we see all sorts of false, or poorly timed, innovations. Push technology, for example; I already have TV, thanks. Before any of the VRML, Quicktime VR brand of technologies are going to be popular on the Web, we have to first solve some of the bandwidth and processor issues. Then take the example of the 3-D movies with the polarized glasses. Why didn't that technology stick around? That got us closer to a realistic experience, didn't it? Actually I don't think so. In part, the problem with the effect was that it required the user to work for it—unlike real-life three-dimensional perception. Eyestrain was a huge complaint in the feature film attempts. Also, the 3-D effect was limited by the edges of the screen, which significantly degraded its effectiveness. That is why we see that technology most often used for short (to reduce eyestrain), large-format (IMAX, dome screens, etc., to involve peripheral vision), novelty experiences.

Right now, one of the more powerful attributes of the Web is that it is an information-on-demand medium, meaning that users can go after what they want and turn away what they don't. Yet in many discussions about broadband Web development, you hear talk about passive, immersive user experiences, which really is the opposite of what the Web is now. How do you see this dichotomy resolving?

JOEL: I think that users, being human, will want both, and both or any combination will be available. If the user wants to have a passive experience, then the user will be able to have it. As the medium matures, and developers begin to discover the power of letting the user drive, we will see richer experience environments that will allow the user to involve herself actively or passively to the level that interests her. More like real life.

I'm going to use an analogy. Imagine that our story is the "Poseidon Adventure" and you're a character on the ship. As the creator of the story, I create a host of characters and tools, and decide when the ship is going to tip over. You should be able to sit back and watch the story unfold. The ship tips over; there's a lot of panic. If you sit back in the background and not do anything, the characters in the story (and this is the challenge for the creators) ought to begin to form themselves and the story should play itself out. But if you want to participate, be the hero, then the characters should respond, changing their behavior to follow you if your argument is compelling. And anytime during the story, you should be able to back off and not participate, and some other character will rise to the challenge. Regardless, the story should continue—because that's what would happen in real life.

You can bring this example back to even the most basic Web site. It should allow for all the different psychologies that users enter the site with—all ought to be considered and addressed. This is daunting if we're trying to build every avenue by hand, but less so if we build a system or environment that involves some form of simple artificial intelligence that responds real-time to actions and requests. Take for example most automated tellers. You know the first menu that asks you to type your code and hit "enter" in both English and Spanish? It doesn't ask which language, because it can be inferred based on your actions. Likewise, at the very least, if I'm coming into a site and I know what I want, I should be able to find it easily. If I'm coming in and I don't know what I want, clear choices, descriptions, and messages ought to be presented to me.

Let's take a 90-degree turn here and juxtapose what you're saying about giving users what they want with one of the biggest problems we face, which is how do we identify who users are in order to deliver these experiences? I'm talking about the many modes of access users have and will have. They might be accessing the Web from their kitchen kiosk, through their car dashboard, or from a very powerful computer system. It looks to me as if it might be getting harder and harder to actually deliver these kinds of experiences. Should more effort be put into figuring out who users really are technographically? How does what you predict map to the different modes of access? Or does it? Perhaps what you're saying is pervasive and beyond the Web. I'm talking about the Web today, with the TCP/IP protocol, and so on, as the way we access the Web.

TIM: We've been talking a lot lately about a systemic approach to interactive rather than just talking about Web sites. Web sites aren't new—the model we are working in, which is the central repository of information and satellite smart or dumb terminal goes back decades; so from a systemic perspective, it is not new. And in the future, as you said, we are going to have very thin clients and not just the consumer PCs that double as game machines, but also devices from Braun sitting in the kitchen that are connected by a yet-to-be-developed protocol.

We've always believed in the death of the browser—that it would be reincarnated in the OS itself, which is the promise of Java and Microsoft's Active Desktop. If you look at it as a systemic issue in that in the future we will be able to touch and respond to people through a much wider variety of portals than a Web has, that you do have to get into the psychology of what you're offering and how it can benefit people—you have an amazing landscape of experiences—everything from a watch running a Java VM, to the smart devices in kitchens, to the server in the basement that controls four dumb PC terminals in the home, running homework to entertainment.

We don't believe (here at Red Sky) in the common definition of convergence, where there is a mythical melding of passive and active experience.

Reading e-mail from your TV on your living room couch is just as awkward as watching a feature-length film on a PC screen. Fundamentally, these are very flawed concepts.

This book is about the "new Web team"—the groups of people who are collaborating in the interactive space. Whom do you predict to be the players in this space in the future?

TIM: There are no masters in this field right now, which is kind of awkward. It just hasn't been here long enough. The best artists out there are the ones who have mastered the technology of their art, the craft of their art, and as Joel says, they've gone beyond a virtual-reality capturing of reality into an abstraction. Take Ansel Adams, a master of the technical aspects of his craft, who in fact captured reality but took it so far beyond reality that it became pure magic. Likewise, in our space, people and teams will have to conceptually create things that are very attractive because ultimately it has to be extraordinarily attractive, more so than any other mass medium has had to be. The master teams will be those teams that can understand, over time, what a mind-boggling array of distribution technology exists, and if that isn't hard enough, to abstract this information into a cohesive story. They are the directors and artists of the future—those people who can do that.

There is another good reason why the leaders of other mass media are not necessarily going to be the masters of this one. You would think that a Steven Spielberg might have a leg up in this space to entertain or move people because of his success in the other broadband (but linear) space. However, that's not the case, because these masters will bring all of their biases from those previous media into this space and you end up with streaming broadband video. It takes a far different thinker to come up with the conceptual approach that will work effectively. The fundamental reason why the old masters and the advertising agencies that are in power now will not necessarily be the masters of this new medium is that the related technology media are not going to stabilize anytime soon—unlike print, television, and radio, which stabilized quickly into a common way of delivering something with very little innovation necessary.

From the creative perspective, what do you think is going to change with regard to the people who are responsible for conceptualizing and designing these new experiences?

JOEL: In the short-term, from a creative perspective, you currently have graphic designers leading the conceptual and design effort. The people who stay focused on the graphic design issues alone will not be successful. If they don't grow to embrace issues of performance, storytelling, and human experience, they won't have a place in the conceptual design. I think (and I'm not biased) that the best designers of interactive experiences will be people who design physical environments, and, ideally, entertaining ones. Those people are the ones who are best positioned to grokking [understanding] what this medium is about and creating what Tim would call "true-use" work.

CHAPTER 9

The Evolving Team

This industry is moving fast. There are a lot of opportunities out there. Many people are doing freelance work, but as this book explains, the days of the jack-of-all-trades Webmaster are over. However, good people will continue to go to the best opportunities. It's going to be hard to keep good people if they perceive that the grass is always greener somewhere else. If you are like many project managers, you probably do not manage the resources on your team from a functional perspective. Rather, you might work together on certain projects, disband and reform months later on another project. Even if this is true, it is within your best interest to do what you can to keep good people available to you. To do this, you must provide good working experiences and opportunities for the growth and evolution of your team.

Where Do You Go from Here?

This chapter is intended to help you stay abreast of changes and therefore opportunities, and to give you some tips on nurturing your team members so they stay happy, motivated, and sane.

Stay Up to Date

If you are aware of new and exciting technologies, then you can share them with your team members and keep them excited about the work they are doing. Most people in this industry are in it because it's new, challenging, and (let's face it) well paying. However, when people work a long time on a project, especially if they are not freelancers, they don't have the opportunity to surf around, read industry magazines, or attend meetings. They begin to get out of touch with what's going on. As a project manager, you should make time to stay on top of industry news and bring information to the attention of your team.

Attend a Conference

I attend a Web conference at least once a year. Whenever I get back, I have a new perspective and a fresh attitude. I bring back scores of new software, and I send a detailed report out to my team discussing what I've seen. I encourage you to do this and, if financially possible, send as many people from your team as you can.

Go to User Group Meetings

I live in the Bay Area, where there is a Web Developer's User Group every night of the week. If you live here, in New York, Portland, Seattle, London, Hong Kong, or Tokyo, you should be able to find a user group meeting; if you can't, start one! Chances are you know enough people who either are doing Web development or want to, and each of you has something to share. It's amazing how energized you and your team will be from a weekly or monthly group meeting at which topics of Web development are shared.

Stay on Top of New Technologies

When you read an article, write a short summary and distribute it to your team. Try to initiate weekly informal coffee breaks where you can talk about what's new in the industry. Encourage the team to share knowledge whenever possible. Make time in your hectic schedule to download and test new software and to make some evaluations about when and if you will use it. Simply playing with software doesn't cut it—you need to weigh the pros and cons and think critically about the feasibility of implementing the technology. This is an excellent way to create good communication and cohesion on your team.

The Care and Grooming of Your Team

Taking care of your team takes a lot of work and some investment in training and education. Team members must be kept challenged and excited about their work. To do this, you need to provide opportunities for your team to grow.

Changing Skill Sets

As I discussed in the previous chapter, new technologies will change and have an impact on your Web team. It's important for you and your team members to be aware of the impact these technologies have on Web teams, and your team should be given the opportunity to grow into new roles.

HTML Developers Become Extinct

Like it or not, the days of coding static HTML will soon be over. Sure, static HTML pages will still need to be created, but the majority of Web pages will be much more dynamic and will require more sophisticated programming. HTML coders will need to evolve into scripting programmers; they will need to understand the Document Object Model (DOM) in order to create the kinds of experiences that will soon be prevalent on the Web.

Programmers Face Increasing Demands

The ability to communicate with the Web server, databases, and existing business systems (such as inventory) is already a very desired ability. Application developers, server-side programmers, database developers, CGI programmers all will continue to be in high demand.

More Creative and Technical Staff Members Needed

The bar will continue to be raised in terms of the user experience; and therefore the best creative and technical staff members will always be in high demand. A team member's ability to truly understand the medium and develop interfaces and applications that exemplify the true use of the medium is tantamount to being successful. People who study the medium and who strive to exploit its features in the most creative ways will be the people who will stand apart. It will be hard to find these people unless you are also aware and abreast of what people are doing and what is possible to do. Don't be complacent. Get out there and investigate and learn.

Detecting Weakness in a Team

As a project manager, you probably are aware that you need to do a significant amount of risk assessment in order to project accurately how long a project will take to complete, the likely cost, and to what level a contingency plan needs to be put in place just in case your "plan A" falls through. You can apply this same level of thinking to the team's development. How do you know when there are weaknesses on the team? The easiest way to detect an overall weakness is if the team consistently misses deadlines or produces work that is not acceptable to the client or stakeholder, or to you. However, this kind of team weakness is easy to spot—but not easy to treat, because you have to understand exactly why and with whom the weakness occurs.

One of the best ways to detect weaknesses is to listen to what the team members say. They know better than anyone where the weak links are. Ask them for their opinions and conduct anonymous peer reviews.

Make sure you review all work created, including time sheets of your team. Time sheets say a lot about people. It might take Sue twice as long to do a task as Janet. Maybe Sue needs a private office. Maybe she needs a training session. Maybe she needs to be on projects with less critical deadlines. Pay attention to the surroundings of the team and make sure they work in suitable environments for their jobs. Programmers need quiet space and few interruptions. Designers need big monitors and a collaborative space (some do, some don't). Do what you can to improve their workspace. You will see improvements in the quality of work.

The best way to detect a weakness on the team is to be close to the team and the work. If you sit in your office all day long waiting for status reports and sending out task lists, you will not be able to detect anything. Get out every day and interact with the team members. Understand what their days are like and you'll see how productive they are—you can then effect some change to make them even more productive.

Training

Most people love the opportunity to learn on the job. If your company does not have an educational reimbursement policy, you should strongly suggest it. It benefits both the employee and the company.

I try to give my team members a lot of feedback on what kinds of classes I think they should be taking. I often suggest courses and keep many school catalogs in my office. I try to take a class every semester, especially in disciplines other than project management. Project managers should strive to understand every role on their teams. Individual team members should take classes that interest them and that are relevant to the work they do, and the work that they will probably do in the future.

In-house training and mentoring is also a great way to share knowledge and improve the team's performance. Assign mentors to new team members and have new team members spend time with each functional group (let the programmers see what the QA staff does all day, for instance). Formal in-house training programs are great—suggest it at a company meeting or draft a memo. Many companies have formal mentor programs for new employees (see *www.fastcompany.com* for excellent articles on this topic). These programs get employees up and running quickly, and it provides them with someone they can go to consistently for leadership and advice.

User Groups (UseNet)

User groups are a great way to learn and to stay connected in the Web community. Make sure your team knows how to access user groups. For those of you who have not used UseNet (the network that serves user groups), you will first need to download a Newsreader. Newsreaders usually come with Internet Explorer and Netscape Navigator, but they aren't necessarily the best newsreader. Most newsreader software is shareware, meaning the cost is free or minimal. A great place to download shareware (you probably know this, but for those of you who don't) is WinFiles, a resource for Windows 95 and 98 users (*http://www.winfiles.com/apps/98/news.html*).

Classes

Depending on where you live, you may have access to a community college or university that offers classes in Internet technologies. If you do, then encourage your team to take classes in subjects that interest them. It doesn't have to be related directly to their job functions; it's important to provide team members with opportunities to grow into roles that are outside of their current jobs. Several producers with whom I work have taken classes in Java programming and database design and it has helped them manage the more technical projects we've produced.

There are many technology education centers (sometimes called ATECs) that offer classes, often in more traditional networking and software development tracks. However, more and more are offering Internet classes. Check your local phone directory under computer learning centers. Also, Microsoft and Netscape have links off their Web site for specific centers that specialize in their particular software applications.

If you don't have a college or learning center nearby, encourage people to sign up for on-line classes, such as the ones offered at Ziff-Davis University (ZDU). Table 9.1 lists several Web sites that offer in-depth help and tutorials.

TABLE 9.1   On-line Resources

Type	Web Site and URL	Comments
On-line Courses	Ziff-Davis University *http://www.zdu.com/*	Offers many classes in Web development, has a great library and discussion boards
Developer Resources	Developer.com *http://www.developer.com/*	A great site for finding out about new tools, downloading them, and trying them out
	Web Developer *http://www.webdeveloper.com/*	Always has great articles and tips
	Web Monkey *http://www.hotwired.com/ webmonkey/*	Produced by HotWired; has great tutorials by leading developers in the Web industry
	Sun Microsystems' Java Technology site *http://java.sun.com*	Java technology galore; has the most exhaustive resources for Java language programmers
	Project Cool's Developer Zone *http://www.projectcool.com/ developer/*	A Bay Area group; always seems to find the best sites to analyze and review
	Microsoft's Site Builder Network *http://www.microsoft.com/ sitebuilder/*	An excellent site for people who focus on developing for Internet Explorer
	Netscape's Developer Network *http://developer.netscape.com/*	The 'DevEdge' site; incredibly well-organized and cross-referenced; full-text access to many Java and JavaScript books
	UpdateStage.Com: A Resource for Macromedia Director Developers *http://www.updatestage.com/*	The bible of Director developers; includes bugs, quirks, hacks, and examples; independently maintained; archives go back about two years
	O'Reilly FTP Archives *ftp://ftp.ora.com/pub/ examples/nutshell/*	Examples and source code for most O'Reilly Nutshell books
	JavaScripts.com *http://www.javascripts.com*	Lots of good, tested, stock scripts to use or modify

Type	Web Site and URL	Comments
Industry Information	The Association of Internet Professionals *http://www.association.org*	The premier professional association for those involved in the creation, maintenance, facilitation, or distribution of Internet-related content
	EMarketer *http://www.emarketer.com/*	A great source for on-line advertising and marketing information, including ad revenues
	CyberAtlas *http://cyberatlas.internet.com/*	Net population, demographics, frequented sites (and more)
Surveys	NUA Internet surveys *http://www.nua.ie/surveys/index.cgi* GVU's WWW user surveys *http://www.gvu.gatech.edu/user_surveys/*	International information about the Internet and attitudes about the Web (and more)
Browsers	Browserwatch *http://www.browserwatch.com* A CNET Topic Center *http://www.browsers.com*	General information about browsers

Books

There are so many good books that it's impossible to recommend any (except the excellent selections offered by Addison-Wesley at *http://www.awl.com/cseng*). If you have the budget to do so, give your team a yearly allowance for books. I often ask team members to review books for the rest of the team—this helps other team members, too.

Heading toward Efficiency

I attended a fabulous seminar sponsored by the American Management Association called "Managing Project Managers," which is what I do. In the seminar, the instructor reminded us that a successful team always goes through the four phases of team dynamics: forming, storming, norming, and performing. In the forming phase, team members are trying to figure out how they work together and this phase is one of confusion, where team members reinforce their own opinions and importance on the team. In the storming phase, the team goes through conflict with each other, largely due to a lack of familiarity and process. Finally, in the norming phase, the team is starting to "find their groove" and the team members are creating processes that make the workload seem more fluid. A performing team can come together quickly and immediately know what to do because they feel comfortable in their roles and they know how and what each member of the team does.

Summary

The care and grooming of your team should be a priority in your busy life, because everything depends on a good, productive, and balanced team. People perform to the level that you expect them to perform; if you don't believe in people you will never be able to motivate them. Look beyond the surface to the realities of the workplace and the work conditions. Start there if you want to make improvements in your team's productivity.

It's important to create standards and processes with your team that they buy into and help create. The high-performing Web team of the future will be able to come together quickly and produce great sites, on time and on budget, because there are standards, systems, and processes in place that are familiar to them. This book provides a framework for you to establish these kinds of processes and environments. Ultimately, your team members will feel saner, and they will become more productive, motivated, and enthusiastic. But this won't happen by chance. You will have to make it happen.

To-Do List

♦ Write a skills analysis of your team. What are people's strengths and weaknesses? Given the current state of technologies, what can people start learning or reading about?

♦ Take a look at your team's surroundings. Do they have optimal work conditions? Are their computers fast enough? Do they have quiet if they need it? Are they frequently interrupted? How do they feel about their space? Decide what you can do about it and then do it.

♦ When was the last time you read an article or attended a conference? Make sure you are up to date on industry developments.

♦ Does your team have in-house training? A mentoring program? Why not write up an initiative to start one?

♦ Start a library and collect relevant books and magazines. Make these available to the team.

♦ Ask a team member out to coffee and discuss a trend or technology.

CHAPTER 10

Case Studies

No amount of reading can teach you what you will learn from experience. These case studies were selected because together they show how diverse a Web project can be and therefore how different the Web team and development process must be. These case studies are not meant to be an exhaustive representation of how to build a Web site. What they do provide is a look at five different Web teams and the objectives, processes, successes, and failures each encountered, plus some valuable lessons to think about if you find yourself in a similar situation.

CASE STUDY   Absolut DJ: The Consultancy Team

Introduction

Absolut Vodka knows the value of a brand on the Internet. With the debut of the first two Absolut sites, Absolut Kelly and Absolut Panushka, Absolut branded itself on the Web by continuing its support of well-known visionary artists, as represented in its long-time advertising campaign. With Web technologies continually improving and more people downloading plug-ins, the ability for a more interactive user experience unveiled itself, thus allowing an enhanced Absolut-branded experience. A third site for Absolut was soon in discussion; but first, Absolut began a review of Web development consultants that would allow the third installation of *www.absolutvodka.com* to reach new levels of interactivity, while supporting their previous effort to build an on-line brand.

The consultancy team is a common Web team these days. It is usually comprised of members from a client's Web team and members of special professional service teams. In this case, the team was led by Absolut's long-time advertising agency, TBWA Chiat/Day, who upheld the brand. Red Sky Interactive (RSI) was recruited to lead the on-line creative development and implementation. Acknowledging a need for strong back end, Red Sky recruited Servinet to join the team and recommend, support and manage the back-end systems.

Objectives and Metrics

The following objectives were set for the new Absolut site:

- ◆ Broaden the reach and appeal of the "visionary" concept
- ◆ Increase user interactivity
- ◆ Continue to support the Internet culture and community
- ◆ Maintain a high level of creativity that is consistent with the Absolut brand

Because the objectives of the site were considered rather subjective, it was hard to map out metrics by which to judge the success of the site. TBWA and Red Sky brainstormed and decided to create a contest where users would create their own compositions and post them on the Absolut site. The server logs would be analyzed using Webtrends software (*www.webtrends.com*) so that TBWA could see an increase in traffic and time spent on the composition page.

The Consultancy Team

The Absolut Web development team was led by TBWA Chiat/Day and included a Web design consultant, Red Sky Interactive, and a back-end specialist, Servinet.

TBWA Chiat/Day

TBWA Chiat/Day in New York led the *www.absolutvodka.com* project with its long-standing experience with the Absolut brand. It served to uphold the Absolut brand while keeping the primary client, the Absolut Company in Sweden, involved in the project and aware of progress.

Red Sky Interactive

Red Sky Interactive's role was to lead the interactive design and strategy for the new site. This included creative concept and content development, site design, production, and implementation. The team at Red Sky included an account manager, a producer, a creative director, a designer, a technical lead, a

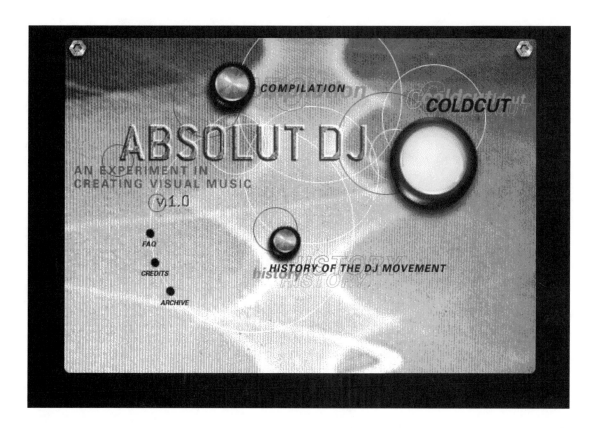

production lead, an HTML programmer, a production artist, a copywriter, a QA lead, and testers.

Servinet

A network engineer and security specialist were recruited from Servinet.

Background and Planning

Red Sky, in conjunction with TBWA Chiat/Day, conceived a highly interactive Web site that centered on a visionary icon—the DJ. The Absolut DJ concept changed the historical focus of the campaign from a single visionary to an icon that is leading an innovative and exciting genre of music in today's musical environment. The Absolut DJ allowed users, from New York to London to Tokyo, to associate themselves with a visionary icon. The Absolut DJ concept crossed cultural and geographical barriers by introducing an icon that is asso-

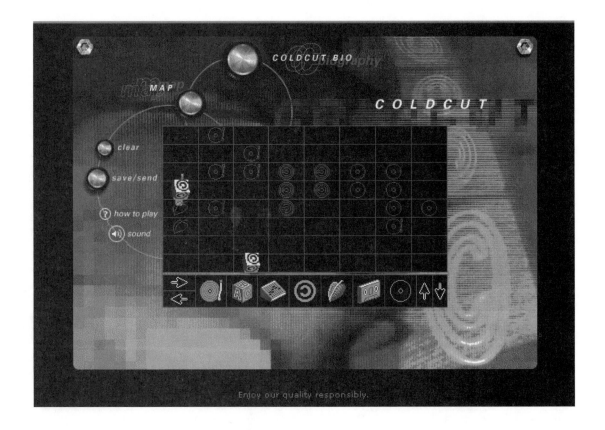

ciated with people all over the globe. This concept achieved the objective of expanding the reach of the Absolut campaign, which in the past had focused on one single artist that may or may not be well recognized internationally.

The site also increased user interactivity by allowing each user to be a "DJ." A user can mix sound clips from the interactive mixing board (based on each DJ's unique style) and form his or her own visual musical composition. After creating a composition, users can send this composition to a friend and the two can share their experience on the site. This save/send function allowed the site traffic to grow from a grassroots level as users began to email compositions to their friends. Friends would click on a link in the email and visit the site to experience the composition.

The third partner, Servinet, which provided the back-end hardware and support to run the site at its optimal performance, managed this back-end systems support. Servinet ensured a smooth user experience and provided a Web-farm event hosting solution at site launch in order to accommodate the growth of the site dynamically.

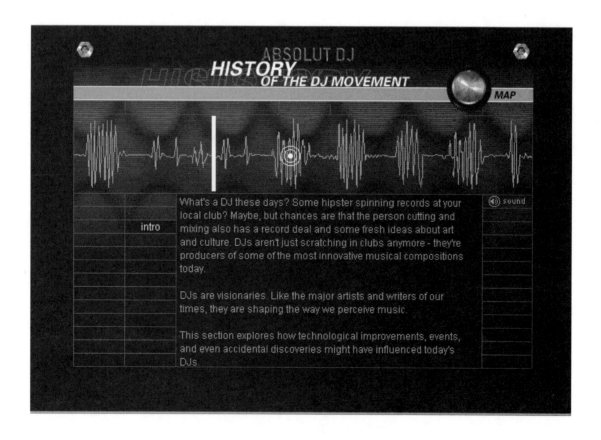

The Process

After creating the Absolut DJ idea, the Red Sky team developed a prototype as proof of concept for TBWA. The concept was received with excited approval. The TBWA group then presented it to the Swedish client, the Absolut Company. For seamless coordination considering the time differences between San Francisco, New York, and Stockholm, the RSI project site (called the "client support system") was used extensively as a tool to update the project status, creative reviews, and new iterations of the prototype.

Since the TBWA team is the long-time advertising agency of record for the Absolut Company, TBWA was empowered by the Swedish client to run with the idea and the client allowed the Red Sky/TBWA team to move rapidly into the production phase. This included recruitment of the DJs, writing a functional specification for the site, and getting started with the actual development of the site. The Red Sky team created an artist draft list, made calls to agents around the world, and finally, flew to New York, London, and Tokyo to capture from selected Absolut DJs—DJ Spooky, Coldcut, and United Future Organization.

Although most of the code from the Absolut prototype was thrown out in production, the prototype served three very important tasks: (1) it got the concept approved by the client, (2) it enabled the technical team to uncover technical issues early on, and (3) it was used as a selling tool during recruitment meetings with prospective artists. The prototype established the level of expectation with the client and the artists. This moved the schedule rapidly in the design phase of the project. In addition, the impact of the Shockwave prototype and the resulting user experience caused the client to make a very important decision that would shape the scope of the project. There would be no non-Shockwave alternative pages for users without Shockwave. Users either would need to get Shockwave or they would need to visit the older Absolut sites. This was part of the strategy to push users to upgrade their systems and the resulting experience would have been very difficult to achieve without a Shockwave experience.

Once the prototype was approved and the artist recruitment begun, the production team began to prep for production and started on a functional specification document for the site. The creative team worked closely with the engineering and production teams to define the actual parameters to be considered for the production to run seamlessly.

At the San Francisco offices of Red Sky, the team worked with the content, held creative reviews with the client, and started the production, copywriting, and content development of the site. As the production team worked on the first artist module, other RSI team members flew to Tokyo to collect content from the second artist. When content was retrieved from the second artist, the production team finished the first module and proceeded to the second module. This staggered type of production worked well, allowing the RSI team to make an aggressive launch date because as one module went into production, another module was being designed, and a third artist was being recruited.

To ensure a quality product and efficiency, the team staged the site and unit tested it in an environment that mirrored the final server's hardware configurations.

Lessons Learned

Acknowledging the strengths of the consultancy teams, there were lessons learned that can be applied when working with consultancy teams.

Communications

Red Sky and Servinet offices are based in San Francisco and the TBWA Chiat/Day offices are in New York. Coordinating teams on two coasts required an updated and efficient extranet that facilitated communications among the groups. The extranet was also the staging site before launch, and was a central communications portal for all team members, including the client in Stockholm.

The teams agreed on syntax so that all team members were speaking of the same thing. The most costly and frustrating problems may arise from the use of syntax.

Teams derived of specialists often bring their knowledge to the table, but they also must be able to explain things in very simple terms to the other team members, especially to the client, if processes or technology are not understood.

Creative Process

Creative development is a chaotic process. And a good creative process allows the teams to understand the idea and provide input. This requires creative directors to work in harmony with the engineers to develop ideas, and discuss technical limitations, and create prototypes of the idea. The best thing the team did early in the Absolut project was to develop a rapid prototype to sell the idea—all the way to Sweden.

When a consultancy is hired by an advertising agency to work on a project, a clear delineation of roles, from a creative standpoint, must be made and adhered to. It is very important to understand who has final creative approval and who leads the creative process. It is very difficult, costly, and inefficient when groups battle for creative power. In the Absolut project, roles were determined clearly, and this led to a great working relationship.

Synergistic Promotions

The Absolut site launch was supported by a promotional event in New York City, which included a global Webcast. The promotions surrounding the Web site needed to be synergistic in concept and design and also supported by the back end. Because the team was not sure of server load at the site launch, a Web farm was built to accommodate the "unknown" factor; it also provided the team with a policy for site performance. This is a great example of a consultancy team using the expertise of its members to develop off-line promotions, host a Webcast event, and support the event with a Web farm.

Unit Testing and More Testing

Never underestimate the power of testing. The Absolut DJ site is a beautiful weave of technology that is seamless to the user. Because this is a Shockwave-only site, complex detection scripts were used to provide the user with the best path to the site. In addition, the unit testing the coding, scripting, emailing functions, and detection engineering uncovered bugs that could be fixed early on, making the final integration of the site smoother than it would have been if the team had had to fix all the bugs at the final integration testing phase.

Power of Ten

Consultant teams bring to the table ideas that are developed from years of independent work for a diverse group of clients. The creative, engineering, and development expertise from consultancy teams provide more effective and efficient Web development in this era of interactive design than a single Webmaster or one internal development group. The forging of ideas among a group of specialists allows the power of the group to develop a far greater product.

The Results

The Absolut DJ site launched with great success and server hits have climbed 60 percent in over two months. The average user session time is rising toward 7 minutes as users are exploring and interacting with the DJ modules. The site launch event, a Webcast performance from London, went off without problems and the Web farm handled the load perfectly. Overall, the Absolut DJ site is an example of a great consultancy team formed of many specialties. The site continues to gain popularity. Site hits are reaching nearly 1 million, only two months after the initial launch.

CASE STUDY   The E-Commerce Team

Introduction

Intuit's QuickenStore (*http://www.quickenstore.com/*) is a Web success story. The demand for purchasing the popular tax software, Quicken and TurboTax, had grown exponentially in 1997. The customer demand began to exceed the capacity of the existing technical architecture. Intuit decided that to be able to meet the demands for the upcoming tax season, the current system needed to be re-architected. Additionally, multiple-item orders were handled awkwardly from the viewpoints of internal management and customers.

Objectives and Metrics

Servinet Consulting Group was hired to increase the capacity, efficiency, and accessibility of the site. Specific objectives included:

- Implementation of a scalable solution that could handle the anticipated load of the 1998 tax season.
- Development of a standard commerce platform and centralized point of purchase environment.
- Development of a sophisticated tracking system to monitor site traffic, identify consumer purchases and customer sources, and determine associated marketing campaign impact.
- The site's success was to be measured by how well the new server architecture managed the load of the 1998 tax season.

The Team

Servinet's responsibilities included technical design and architecture, network infrastructure and security, commerce development and system load testing. Members of the Servinet team included a program manager, a project manager, a technical lead, a commerce application developer, a C++ programmer, an NT Network engineer and a QA manager.

Intuit's responsibilities included creative, navigation design, and copy development. Members of the team included a marketing manager, an Internet project manager, a designer, an engineer, and an HTML coder

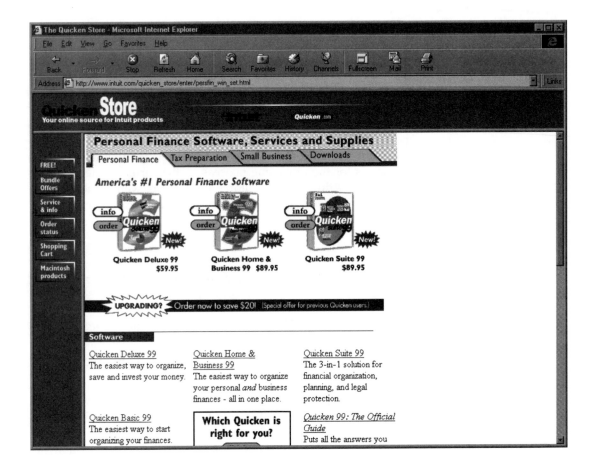

The Solution

Servinet developed a scalable, powerful, multitier architecture for centralizing point-of-purchase and providing "shopping cart" functionality using a Microsoft Commerce Server Environment. Portions of the existing QuickenStore, including product pages, were integrated into the new and improved site in order to minimize site disruption and maximize dollars invested. Additionally, the initial stages of the tracking system were implemented to track customer purchases and marketing campaign sources.

The Process

Implementing an e-commerce solution for a Web site that is as demanding as Intuit's has many risks and obstacles. In order to investigate these risks and obstacles appropriately, the account manager negotiated a significantly long design phase for the project.

The project manger had to keep the project on schedule and ensure that the scope of the project did not grow. He identified the tasks of the project so that he could build a schedule and a budget for the project. Then he identified and recruited the appropriate resources. Following initial client meetings, he wrote the discovery document, a milestone-based approach for deliverables. Fearing multiple scope changes, he implemented a change control process to handle the many changes that sprung up during the design and implementation phases. The aggressive schedule and complexity of the project meant that any miscommunication could mean serious oversights, and so he held weekly full-team meetings to keep the project on schedule and to keep all members communicating, because the team was working in different locations.

During the design phase, the network engineer designed a server architecture that could handle the expected load and spec'ed hardware and software. This phase took weeks, proving that the extended design phase was a good negotiation. During this time, the network engineer researched and spec'ed the security plan and created development, testing, and live environments. He also implemented load and stress testing and helped the project manager and QA manager design the test plan.

During the design phase, the application developer was creating the data model that would become the shopping cart application. He also coded the rough HTML template pages, as well as the sophisticated application itself. He also managed a junior application developer and communicated with Intuit's creative team so that he could integrate their graphic and text assets seamlessly. Together, the application developer and the Intuit team developed a file-naming convention so that the application development team could use placeholder artwork so that asset creation did not hold up too many programming tasks.

Based on the technical design of the project, the QA manager wrote a test plan and then developed appropriate testing suites to test the shopping cart application. The network engineer conducted significant load-testing cases using WebLoad software to make sure the new architecture could handle the expected load.

After the design phase was complete, the project entered the production and implementation phase. During this phase, the actual application was built, graphical assets were integrated, and the servers were deployed. Finally, the project went into the testing phase, where bugs were reported and fixed. The project went live on March 13, 1998, and despite superstitious warnings, was a great success.

Key Obstacles

No project is without risks and obstacles. This project, because of its technical complexity and serious risks, especially legal and technical risks, provides an excellent study of valuable lessons learned.

♦ *Identifying bare minimum objectives to draft discovery document*   The tendency for the client is to "blue-sky" the project; however, Servinet wanted to be sure the most important objectives drove the project.

♦ *A junior programmer didn't meet deliverables*   To solve the problem, no high-risk tasks were given to this programmer.

♦ *Integrating with the legacy back end*   The front-end Web application and server needed to tie into back-end legacy systems, on different platforms.

♦ *Understanding the business process*   The team needed to fully understand the back-end payment-processing system and how an order gets fulfilled. This knowledge was critical to the project, but understanding it from a technical point of view was very challenging.

♦ *Late delivery of assets*   The design team missed their deadlines and delivered much of their assets late. As a result, the application developer had to redo a lot of the code when assets got integrated.

♦ *Miscommunication of roles*   Servinet's network engineer set up a network architecture for download servers, but Intuit's technical team had a different view of how download servers should be set up—on a different platform from Servinet's architecture. The groups were not brought together to discuss who would be responsible for this task, so Intuit's team did not follow the architecture. This caused a lot of problems.

♦ *Changing requirements*   Some aspects of the scope changed during the life of the project.

♦ *Client tardiness*   The client was slow to deliver on their deliverables, assets, and approvals. This put the launch date at risk.

♦ *Choosing the right load-testing tools*   Servinet chose WebLoad to conduct load testing, though at the time, there was no reference material for what they were doing, Microsoft did not support WebLoad, and we didn't have access to other support. WebLoad was so new that a revision was written for Servinet's use.

♦ *Communication of security risks*   Internal groups (Intuit) wanted things done a certain way, and we had to communicate the complex security issues and how to implement appropriate security.

♦ *Implementing security*   Security was a huge obstacle. Servinet was prepared to make compromises in the user experience to ensure security. They took great pains to make the consumer feel comfortable with doing business over the Web.

Results

With Servinet's expert assistance, Intuit, a highly visible and enormously successful company, migrated from a Unix system to an NT-based solution in order to strengthen and enhance its Quickenstore site. Furthermore, the collaboration fully integrated the digital delivery of goods during the height of the 1998 tax season. The site was able to scale to anticipated capacity, handling the 20,000 purchases per day during the two weeks prior to April 15th. Total revenue generated over that two-week period was estimated to have exceeded the previous year's revenue by more than 100 percent.

Oxford Express: A Shopping Utility
for Lands' End

Introduction

As interactive agency of record for Lands' End, one of Red Sky Interactive's tasks was to develop the "catalog of the future." Lands' End already had an e-commerce Web site, but they wanted to know the best way to market their products in the interactive space. They also wanted some insight into what an electronic catalog might look like two to three years in the future.

Objectives and Metrics

Lands' End overall Internet objective is to be one of the top five retailers on the Internet and to promote Lands' End as a leader in the e-commerce space. Several interactive initiatives were conceived to support this goal, one of which was a highly interactive catalog or shopping experience. Specific objectives for the success of this initiative included:

- Develop an application that enabled an easy and convenient method of browsing, customizing, and purchasing their most popular item: the Oxford shirt.
- The application must be fast. Users must not be held up by slow Internet connections.
- The application must be accurate. Inventory had to be up to date at all times and users must have access to the latest inventory.
- The application must be interactive and highly creative. Experiences with the Land's End Adventure Site showed that users stayed longer on pages with interactive content.
- Success would be judged by monitoring usage of Oxford Express.

The Team

The large team was made of specialists. At Red Sky, the team consisted of an account manager and producer, a technical lead, a creative director, a QA lead, an information architect, a Java programmer, a Perl programmer, a JavaScript/HTML coder, a production artist, and several testers. A special 3-D-rendering group, ModaCad, was brought in to render the thousands of shirt images. Berbee Information Systems handled all back-end integration.

Background and Planning

Red Sky first considered a virtual salesman that would mimic the work of the customer service representatives at Lands' End. After some investigation, Red Sky abandoned this approach. The artificial intelligence approach was deemed too complicated technically. Gathering the information from the customer service representatives was a formidable task as well. Instead, Red Sky decided to build a more traditional but carefully designed parametric search interface.

At first, a CD was the target interactive medium. The team thought the entire catalog could be on CD and updates to the product line could be obtained through an Internet connection. The CD could deliver "high-impact" media (video, animation, etc.) while the Internet could deliver smaller updates. But this medium was also abandoned. Creating a CD for the entire catalog was too much production work for testing a new concept. In addition, the connected CD approach was really a temporary solution to on-line development. In the near future, high-bandwidth connections to the Internet would be commonplace, eliminating the need for a connected CD.

A Better Way to Buy a Shirt   Instead of trying to produce an electronic catalog of all products in the print catalog, Red Sky focused on one particular product. After discussions with Lands' End, the team decided to focus on the Oxford shirt. There were a number of reasons to do so. The Oxford shirt is considered a core product of Lands' End. The product is difficult to present in print due to the number of variations (collar, fabric, color, size, etc.). Early attempts to present the Oxford shirt on-line by the internal Web team forced Lands' End to reduce the product offering. Because Oxford shirts are always in style, the applet would be useful for a long time. Finally, Lands' End is proud of this classic well-made shirt, so the applet was an opportunity to put it on a pedestal—to celebrate the Oxford shirt.

Since the traditional HTML and CGI model was considered too restrictive to present the shirt effectively, Red Sky decided to produce a Java applet. Java enabled the user to download the initial data necessary to choose from the thousands of product offerings in a single download, so that the applet did not have to make return trips to the server during a user session. The applet was named Oxford Express because of the speed and ease that it afforded the consumer in finding the perfect shirt.

The Process

During this project, refinements in process were made as new team members were added. The producer relied heavily on the project's extranet to keep all members of the project team up to date with consumer findings, design approvals, and technical specifications.

Analyze the Product

The Red Sky team spent a great deal of time studying the database of shirts and their interrelationships before any coding or creative concepting was begun. In addition, they talked with users (shoppers and friends) about what they wanted in a shirt and asked experts (Lands' End employees, salespeople in stores) how shoppers behaved. The final decision was to create a parametric search that made use of rollovers for "look-ahead" functionality.

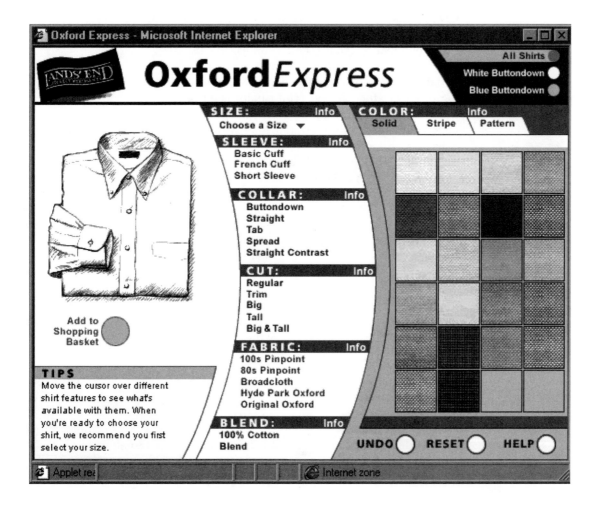

Determine the Look and Feel

To the designer, the most important interface element was the ability to view all possible features at one time. The final design consisted of three display areas: a shirt display, a feature list, and a color display. As the user selects color

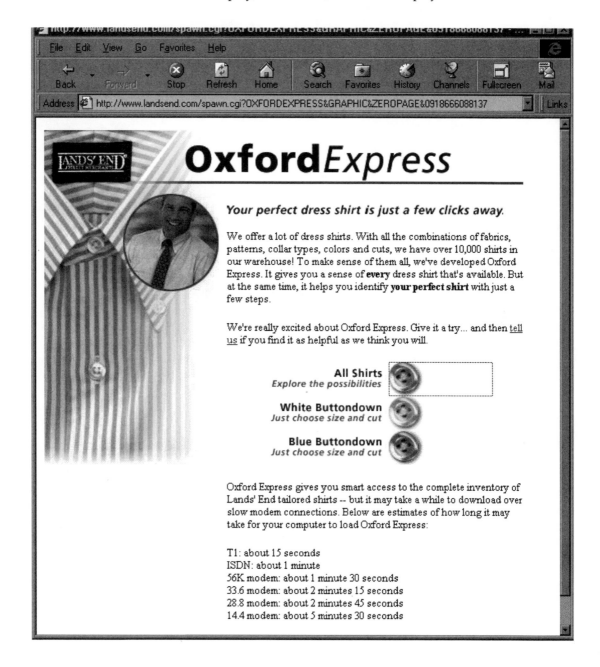

or feature, the other areas are refreshed with available choices. For example, a choice of button-down collar would cause the shirt to display a button-down shirt and the color display to list only the available colors for that shirt.

Build the Prototype

Since Java development is time-intensive, Red Sky prototyped the applet using Director. This made it possible to go through several iterations of the user interface in a relatively short period of time. Both the design and the user interface were changed considerably with each revision.

Usability Testing

Another factor in the development of prototype revisions was usability testing. Red Sky wanted to create a simple and intuitive interface that gave the user the feeling of the entire universe of shirts. Three rounds of usability testing were performed. The first tested the concept. The second tested the user's interpretation of the concept and shopping tasks. The third tested task completion and other elements of the interface.

Build the Application

Once the client had approved the look and feel, Red Sky proceeded to develop the applet based on the prototype and the technical specifications. In addition to the Java applet itself, several scripts were created to interface with the applet. A "crunch" script was developed to compress the product data on a daily basis, based on the most up-to-date product listings from Lands' End. In addition, scripts were developed to allow the applet to check inventory in real time and to place the selected shirt into the Lands' End shopping basket.

Test and Deploy

As with any software development effort, testing was crucial to the success of this project. If the applet did not work reliably, users would be discouraged from using it and the entire point of the effort—to develop a better way to buy a shirt—would be lost. In particular, testing across browsers (Netscape, Internet Explorer) and across operating systems (Mac and PC) was time consuming. Once it passed system tests at Red Sky, the applet was staged on a server at Lands' End. The back-end "crunch" script was tested with the legacy system. Once the back-end integration passed testing, the entire system was tested. Only after the entire system had passed testing was the applet moved to the live server. Both Red Sky and Lands' End participated in the testing process.

Obstacles Overcome

Insufficient Information in the Beginning

The biggest challenge to RSI at the start of the project was understanding the nature of the raw data. Several departments and a third-party vendor needed to be interviewed. It took a fair amount of investigative work by Red Sky before the true nature of the data was revealed.

Integrating with the Back End

The Lands' End IT group was very busy maintaining the current site as well as moving forward with other internal Web site projects. The physical distance between Red Sky (California) and Lands' End (Wisconsin) made coordinating this project difficult. Red Sky's extranet system was extremely helpful in transferring information and keeping the client up to date on development.

Applet Concept Matures

As the applet was being built and used by both the Red Sky and Lands' End teams, several improvements to the original spec were imagined. The commitment on both ends to making Oxford Express a truly next-generation shopping utility intensified production and stretched resources in order to meet the completion date.

Devising New Data Models

Oxford Express presented shirts in a way never before attempted. This meant that Red Sky Interactive had to invent new ways to handle the data about raw shirts and create scripts that spoke to the legacy inventory system in new ways.

Browser Compatibility

The original spec called for support of 2.0 and better browsers. By the end of the project, the specification was changed to 3.0 and better browsers. Differences between the JVM, documented and undocumented, caused far more compatibility problems across browsers than had been anticipated.

Currently the applet only runs on 4.0 browsers. Java Virtual Machines that run on 3.0 browsers were not originally built to handle the memory requirements needed to run a Java applet like the Oxford Express Applet. Attempting to support 3.0 browsers resulted in a better application. The Java programmer and QA group spent many hours coding and testing the applet on 3.0 browsers. To overcome the 3.0 memory problem, the programmer built the architecture for the distribution of data in such a way that it would download incrementally. This incremental distribution did not help to overcome the 3.0

problem but it improved the performance significantly, decreasing the amount of time it takes to download the applet on 4.0 browsers. A perceived failure was turned into a success.

Results

Oxford Express went live on the Lands' End site in late November 1998. From the Lands' End perspective, this applet behaved exactly as a sales associate. Lands' End was impressed with the speed of the applet, not only the download time (given a selection of 17,000 shirts) but also the interaction time once the applet was running. Although Lands' End does not, by policy, reveal sales figures, the company told Red Sky they were pleased with the results.

CASE STUDY   The Miami Herald Publishing Company

Introduction

The Miami Herald's Web team not only must meet the demands of daily on-line publishing; it must also publish in two languages: English and Spanish. This team was chosen to illustrate what a difficult task it is to keep a large publishing site current with innovations in technology. When you absolutely must publish every twenty-four hours, it's difficult to reengineer your publishing methods. The *Herald* and *el Nuevo Herald* Web team's biggest challenge is getting those stories on-line every day. Improvements in process happen slowly; but they do happen.

Objective

As a traditional print publishing company, the Miami Herald was faced with the challenge of producing Web sites that complement its print products and would help it stay competitive in the changing landscape of advertising and news. To meet these goals, the *Herald* produces ten Web sites, each designed to meet a different need in the marketplace. The flagship site, the Miami Herald Online (*http://www.herald.com*) began in 1995 and was followed several months later by the Spanish newspaper, el Nuevo Herald Digital (*http://www. elherald.com*). The other sites were designed to attract new readers to the *Herald* and to add value for readers of the newspapers. Those sites include:

- A travel site (*www.cometothesun.com*),
- An entertainment site (*www.justgo.com/southflorida*),
- Classified sites (*www.carhunter.net, www.homehunter.net* and *www.jobhunter.net*), and
- A site for teens (*www.herald.com/underground*), and more.

New projects are always in development, and the company expects to add more Spanish products to meet the needs of the rapidly growing Spanish-speaking population on the Web.

The Team

The *Herald*'s many Web sites are developed and maintained by a diverse team of editors, designers, and programmers capable of working in English and Spanish. Since the department was created three years ago, the staff has grown from two to more than thirty. The on-line services department is divided into five areas: technology, production, content, marketing, and business. The technology staff is responsible for selecting and implementing new technologies and for maintaining and updating current systems. The production staff creates ad-related content, such as ad banners, and often full Web sites for advertisers. The content staff is responsible for all of the content sections of the sites. This includes determining the placement of stories on the site, moving breaking news to the site, and working with the newsrooms to implement new sections as they are created. For the purposes of this case study, the following sections will focus on the content team and the production of the two main news sites, *www.herald.com* and *www.elherald.com*.

The Solution

When the *Herald* started publishing on-line there were no off-the-shelf systems capable of handling the envisioned large, complex site. Instead, a complex CGI program was created to convert articles created in the newsroom computer system into HTML and move them to specified locations on the Web sites. Each article is assigned a "map" word, such as Cuba, which is used by the system to direct it to a particular page in the site, such as the Cuba page in the

news section at *www.herald.com.* The same program, written by a programmer
in the Knight-Ridder New Media Center in San Jose, is used by most of the
Web sites in the Knight-Ridder chain.

The content staff still manually designs many stories. This is done so that
the on-line department can make the final decision about which stories will
appear on each of the section fronts. This is also the only way to integrate photos into the designs because the images created for the paper are sent through
a different system than the stories and there is currently no automated way to
match stories with photos.

Key Obstacles

Human error, mistakes made by editors in the newsroom, is probably the
biggest problem. The automated system works fine when editors in the newsroom properly label and format articles. Unfortunately, the editors are not always consistent in their efforts and the on-line staff are forced to manually edit
stories, headlines, and bylines that were not formatted properly during the automated process.

Another problem is that stories and images are not kept together as they
move through the current system in the newsroom. Most images are created
and edited on Macintosh computers and most articles are written and edited
in a PC-based system in the newsroom. The images and articles are then
matched up in the paste-up room (yes, they still manually paste up the newspaper). As a result, there is no effective way to publish photos with stories that
are automatically sent to the site. Even when pages are built manually, this is
a time-consuming process because an on-line editor or producer must move
to a different computer, look for the photo that goes with the story—a process
that first requires identifying the story and then finding the caption that goes
with it—and then he or she must move that photo to another system to build
it into the site.

The on-line staff's best hope is that the newsroom is in the process of moving to a system of pagination. Although things may get worse before they get
better—because now some articles come through one system and some come
through another—once the entire paper is paginated, the human error factor
will be reduced significantly because people will not be able to count on a
human in the paste-up room to fix things and because stories and images will
all be processed by the same system.

Results

A typical day in the on-line department looks like this: Two part-time employees come in very early in the morning to "clean up" the site. Their task
is to find all the of human errors that cause missing headlines, bylines, and

articles that are sent to the wrong section of the site or didn't reach the site at all. In the early dawn, long before the site's peak traffic hours (between about 9:00 A.M. and 11:00 A.M.), these employees look for all of the places the automated system failed.

At about 7:30 A.M. the day news editor arrives and starts updating the site with breaking news. It's her job to watch the wire-service feeds and even keep an eye on the television, manually sending articles to the site as she receives them. Throughout the day, she continues to watch for breaking news and to update the site.

At about 3:30 P.M. the night editors arrive and head to the news meetings at each of the papers, one in English, the other in Spanish. At the news meetings, editors from the newsroom decide where the main stories of the day will appear in the paper, what will make the front page, and the cover of each section. They also review photos and graphics that will illustrate the stories.

When those meetings are complete, the Spanish and English on-line news editors return to the Internet department to hold their own news meeting and discuss how to use the stories from each of the newspapers. Often, what appears on the front of the print edition of the *Herald* is not what appears on the front of the Web site. They differ for many reasons. There is a broader, more diverse audience on the Web that views our pages from many countries. The issue of timeliness requires that stories on the Web be more up to date. If, for example, the stock market sets a record at the end of the day, it will probably be on the front page of the business section the next morning in the newspaper. However, in the business section on the Web site, that story would look terribly out of date the next day when reports of the stock markets' renewed activity are already on many other Web sites.

The night staff continues to update the site with breaking news as it builds the section fronts for the main sections of both sites—news, sports, business, living, and so on. They also look for ways to supplement those stories by linking to related Web sites, adding animated graphics, sound clips, and other multimedia features. They usually finish with the main stories in the daily paper at about 1:00 A.M. and then leave the rest to the automated process to pick up over night. From about 2:00 A.M. to 4:00 A.M. the automated process converts every story published in both newspapers and directs it to the Web sites.

At about 5:30 A.M. the morning crew returns to clean up the site and the process repeats.

The *Herald* on-line department is now working to replace the proprietary system currently in use with a database system, such as StoryServer or Open Pages. Such a system should make this a more efficient process and free some staff time to do more supplementing and enhancing of news coverage and spend less time simply moving print stories to the Web.

CASE STUDY   When the Process Fails

Introduction

This fictional case study is not intended to illustrate in great detail the technical challenges of a project. Technical failures are the easiest to pinpoint because if the software is not working, you can see it immediately. If you do, you have time to communicate this to your client and negotiate a change in budget or time line. What this case study really illustrates is that how complex and hard-to-pinpoint issues like client and team expectations can drive a project to fail.

Objective

TrainRight is a small, well-funded company that provides on-line training resources to both the consumer and the corporate markets. They differentiate themselves from other on-line training facilities in that they have a roster of well-known teachers, specialists, and visionaries who provide material and give personalized responses to the participants. TrainRight had launched a large public relations and marketing effort to announce its services on-line when a large software company, Commerce Systems (fictional name), agreed to fund a large portion of TrainRight's Web site to promote the use of its electronic-commerce software.

The objective of the project was to create a fully functioning Web site that had the following features:

- Original content from well-known specialists
- On-line, interactive training modules
- A payment system for purchasing subscription or single-use sessions
- A community system for members to interact and share knowledge
- A personalized journal where members can keep their homework

Additionally, TrainRight wanted to ensure that the Web site was sophisticated, with a dazzling and edgy look and feel, and effective navigation.

Commerce Systems brought in a development partner, Internet Muscle Systems, to manage the project, do the Web development, and integrate the commerce system. Internet Muscle Systems subcontracted the creative work to a third shop, Invision.

The Team

The team consisted of a project lead (TrainRight), an account manager (Internet Muscle Systems), a producer (Internet Muscle Systems), an art director (Invision), a writer/content developer, an information architect (Invision), a technical lead/program manager (Internet Muscle Systems), a director programmer (TrainRight), a script programmer (Internet Muscle Systems), an HTML coder (Internet Muscle Systems), a production artist (Invision), and a quality assurance lead/tester (Internet Muscle Systems).

Background

The first vendor brought in by Commerce Systems was fired by TrainRight because its estimates were too high and the first round of creative composites were weak, according to TrainRight. Commerce Systems then called in another vendor, a systems integration shop called Internet Muscle Systems(IMS).

The executives at TrainRight were under the gun. They had pressure from the specialist with whom they had contracted and their funding partners were scrutinizing their every move.

The team at IMS was experienced in Web development, with a solid history in networking and software development. IMS brought in a third vendor, Invision, to do the interface and graphic design. This was the first time these two groups had worked together.

The development time, by the time all contracts were signed, was twelve weeks. The first mistake the team from IMS and Invision made was assuming that they could negotiate a longer time line. They could not. The team from TrainRight had made too many promises. Also, they had a budget that IMS's team thought was too low, but Commerce Systems made a verbal agreement to absorb the majority of the costs.

The Process

The account manager and producer divided the project into distinct development efforts that could be completed in parallel, after an initial design and specification phase was complete. Because of the time line, only the schematics were to be completed by the design phase. The team decided that if the schematics were complete, the interface and programming teams would have enough information to start the parallel tasks of developing creative composities and writing the scripts to hook into the commerce system and the member database. During this time, the writer would be working with several visionaries to finish the training modules.

TrainRight had a great director programmer on staff, and he wanted to be involved. To maximize development effort and to save some money, IMS decided to use him to develop the on-line training modules with TrainRight's course creator. This was beneficial because the two had worked together on other projects. However, this programmer was not a video engineer and could not handle digitizing the video that came in from the content providers. The producer had to scramble to find someone to digitize and deliver the files, causing the schedule for the modules to slip. This slippage eventually caused the whole schedule to slip because a critical unit test of the module was missed. As a result, there were software bugs in the module that did not get found until the first round of integration testing. Fixing these bugs late in the schedule caused further slippage.

When the technical spec was written, the producer called a full-team meeting to discuss it with all parties. After a two-hour meeting, everyone walked away believing he or she understood the overall functionality of the site and how it would be implemented. A big mistake was that each person did not specifically articulate his or her responsibility. There were hooks that needed to be made within the training modules that weren't, and scripts were written in the wrong version of Perl because those specifications were left out.

Of all the teams, the network and programming teams were the most successful. They were able to configure the server, perform load-balancing tests, and implement the commerce system on schedule. During the implementation, a bug in the commerce system was found, and Commerce Systems wrote a patch specifically for TrainRight in the nick of time.

Because the schematics were finished first, the script programmer and the HTML programmer were able to develop the scripts to carry input from the users to both the membership and payment systems. However, since TrainRight's Director programmer was handling the modules, the IMS team thought he was also handling user input. This wasn't the case. A major miscommunication occurred, especially since the team missed a critical status meeting. Two weeks passed before the producer and technical lead (who was also leading another project) realized that no one was writing the programming necessary to take critical information from the training modules.

During this time, another major slippage was occurring. The interface team was in conflict with the client. Two design reviews had gone by without sign-off. To the creative team, the clients seemed impossible to please. To the clients, the creative team seemed to have its own agenda. The producer was beginning to panic, as the schedule was slipping and the client would not move the delivery date.

After the second design review the producer told the account manager that unless the delivery date was pushed back or the scope was cut significantly, they would fail to deliver this project on time. The account manager and the producer flew across the country to meet with the clients, and were able to negotiate a small change in scope (not all the modules would have to be completed and several information sections could be dropped). They were able to get another week of time, but the producer was skeptical. The account manager and producer began to have communication trouble; the account manager was pushing the producer to push the team.

After the third round of design concepts, the client signed off, but this momentary win was offset by a major setback. Commerce Systems pulled out of the project after the executive who championed the TrainRight site was fired. IMS was close to abandoning the project for fear that it would not get paid, but TrainRight wrote a letter of intent along with large check. IMS, a small and privately funded company, chose to stay on the project. This choice was the biggest mistake they made.

Although the clients signed off on the visual composites, they continued to be dissatisfied with the creative team, and each review was more and more heated. Finally, at the client's insistence, Invision resigned the business and IMS was left to finish the site with two HTML programmers and a production artist.

In the end, IMS delivered a functioning site, but with only a fraction of the original features. The technical architecture was solid, but the interface and the content were never fully developed. TrainRight defaulted on payments to IMS and Invision, causing both businesses to go into bankruptcy. This happened because the people who were funding TrainRight rescinded their financing when Commerce Systems pulled out of the project. TrainRight didn't divulge this to IMS at the time.

Key Obstacles and Project Risks

Identifying these risks earlier in the project would have helped the project team. Although the team held regular "red flag" meetings, some risks just can't be identified. It's best to have contingencies like extra money in the budget or time in the schedule built in so that obstacles like these do not cripple the project.

- The biggest risk and most key obstacle was TrainRight's reluctance to compromise in scope or time line.
- The team was comprised of members from four organizations. They were not able to get through the forming stages to become a high-performing team.
- The producer and technical lead missed several clues that the project was slipping, most notably, that the task of integrating the training modules with the rest of the application was glossed over.
- The commerce software had a bug that required a custom software patch to be written by the vendor. Fortunately, the vendor was compliant.
- The orginal content was not written at the time that the site was being designed. All the content milestones were missed.
- Creative composites weren't signed off until the third round. The original schedule allowed for two rounds, and all three rounds took longer than scheduled.
- In order to provide the client with two design options per round, a contract designer was hired. This was an unbudgeted expense.

- In order to digitize video from the content providers, a video production person was contracted. This was an unbudgeted expense that could have been charged back, but due to political conflict between the account manager and producer, was never charged back.
- As a result of schedule slippage, critical rounds of unit testing were not completed. This resulted in a longer bug-fixing phase at the end of the project, and major bugs that could have been identified early in the project were not identified.

Lessons Learned

This case study is loosely based on one of my first multiteam commerce projects. I think about this project whenever we kick a project off, whenever I am drafting a schedule or summarizing production needs. I am always reminded of how the relationships are—between client and project team, among team members, with third-party suppliers. The most valuable lessons I learned were that there are projects you just shouldn't take on and that it is sometimes wise to resign from a project after it is underway. This was one of those projects; the risks really outweighted everything else. Other lessons include:

- Make sure, after each meeting, that each team member articulates his or her responsibilities and next steps. It may sound like overkill, but over-communicating is better than undercommunicating.
- At no time can the three aspects of project management (scope, time, quality) be fixed. If your client insists they are, then this is a project that you should turn down.
- Do not let the egos bully you. In this case, a high-powered art director acted like a prima donna, which ultimately cost the project significantly.
- Do not ignore internal team strife.

Conclusion

Everyone needs a good failure in order to truly learn something. This project was one of the most educational experiences of my life; certainly in my career as a Web project manager. It was during this project that I learned that commerce was going to truly change Web development and that, to be a good producer, I would need to understand the complex development cycles required to integrate a commerce system. I also learned that it's easy to blame others; but in doing so you never really learn about yourself. The greatest accomplishments of a producer or project manager are to take responsibility appropriately, admit oversights and weaknesses, and never make the same mistake twice.

APPENDIX A

CD-ROM Index

This is an index of the templates and documents located on the CD-ROM that accompanies this book. All of these documents are located in the /templates directory, under the chapters specified here.

Templates

Chapter 1

Budget Tracking Sheet

Estimating Worksheet

Project Template

Rate Sheet and Ballpark Pricing

Sample Budgets

   Intranet

   E-Commerce

Scope/Objectives Document

Strategic Brief

Chapter 3

Asset Management Sheet

Creative Brief

End-User Requirements

Functional Specification

Production Guide
Technical Brief

Chapter 5

Approvals Document
Contact Report
Independent Contractor Form
Mutual Non-Disclosure Agreement

Chapter 6

Style Guide/Production Guide

Chapter 7

Budget Report
Quality Assurance Summary
Test Plan

Appendix B

Web Team Resource Guide

To do any job well, you need the right tools. When the job is building a Web site, the tools you need come in the form of software and hardware. This resource guide is designed to help you choose from the best-of-breed tools out there. My Web team and I have tested each one of these tools (hardware and software) and each comes recommended. We believe that the Web team of the future will use most of these tools on a regular basis. Most of the software is available on the CD-ROM for demonstration purposes only.

Project Management Tools

Milestones, Etc. 5.0

www.kidasa.com

Designed for project supervisors, team leaders, coordinators, planners, engineers, managers, or anyone who spends time scheduling projects, Milestones, Etc. requires no formal training to operate and cuts scheduling time to mere minutes.

Project KickStart v2.02 for Win 95/NT

www.experienceware.com
www.projectkickstart.com

Project KickStart is a powerful, but easy-to-use planning tool that helps you brainstorm, plan, and schedule any project.

MS Project 98 for W95/NT–Full Version

www.microsoft.com

Effective project management is at the core of every successful business. Whether you're overseeing simple, short-term projects or managing complex multiproject schedules, you can stay in complete control with Microsoft Project 98.

Web Design Programs

Over the last few years, Web design programs have evolved from buggy, unreliable programs that were difficult for even the experts to sophisticated, stable applications that make Web design easy for everyone. If you're new to Web design, you should definitely start with a graphical (WYSIWYG) editor. If you've been using an HTML text editor or if you're not happy with your Web design program, read the following descriptions and see what's new on the market.

Microsoft FrontPage 98

www.microsoft.com

One of the more sophisticated and complete Web design programs on the market, Microsoft FrontPage 98 bundles everything you need to create your Web site in one, competitively priced package.

Macromedia Dreamweaver 2.0

www.macromedia.com

One of the newer editors on the market, Macromedia Dreamweaver 2.0 came out fighting with a powerful WYSIWYG editor that supports the latest HTML tags, such as Cascading Style Sheets and Dynamic HTML. The price tag and feature set make it clear that this is a professional tool.

GoLive CyberStudio 3.0

www.adobe.com/prodindex/golive/main.html

Making a splash on the Macintosh, GoLive CyberStudio 3.0 has raised the bar for Web design programs on the Macintosh. The company wins kudos for its loyalty to Macintosh, but in this cross-platform world, it's usually best to provide the same tools for both operating systems. Nonetheless, CyberStudio is an excellent program, combining precise design control with the ability to edit the HTML code by hand in its built-in text editor.

Symantec Visual Page 2.0

www.symantec.com

Available for both Mac and Windows, Symantec Visual Page quickly beat out many other HTML tools designed for those who are new to the Web, such as Adobe PageMill and Claris Home Page. Why is Visual Page better? It's priced competitively, and it provides a more robust HTML editing environment that is more accurate and more respectful of HTML code created in other programs. Yet it's easy to learn and has a friendly, intuitive interface.

SoftQuad HoTMetaL PRO 5.0

www.softquad.com

HoTMetaL PRO has led the way with great features, support for the latest HTML tags, and the ability to convert word-processing files to HTML. Overall, this HTML editor has shown great potential, but I know few Web designers who use it because many people have found the interface clunky and difficult to use. If you've been turned off by HoTMetaL PRO in the past, the enhancements in HoTMetaL 5.0 should make you look again at this Web design tool. That is, unless you use a Macintosh (the upgrade is only available for the PC). SoftQuad took care of one of my biggest complaints when it added a built-in text editor in version 5.0.

Claris Home Page 3.0

www.claris.com

Claris Home Page is an easy-to-use Web design program with the advantages of being cross-platform, relatively inexpensive, and user friendly. However, one drawback of Home Page is that it does not include image-editing capabilities or site management features.

NetObjects Fusion 2.0

www.netobjects.com

NetObjects Fusion is an innovative program designed to push the limits of HTML and provide precise design control. But in its effort to reign in the wild Web, it overlooked one of the fundamental differences between the Web and print. You can't really get the kind of control on the Web that you can get in print because you can't guarantee the operating system, screen size, font size, and many other variables of the viewer. Many designers are delighted when they first see Fusion and discover that it provides the design control they've been wanting. Unfortunately, when those same designs are viewed on different computers, which use different font sizes, screen sizes, or other variations, those beautiful designs can fall apart. Fusion provides rigid alignment control to achieve precise design, but as a result it lacks flexibility and often does not adapt its designs well when viewed on other computers.

HTML Text Editors

If you insist on working in the HTML code manually, you should at least get an HTML text editor to help you. Of the many programs available, the best ones support the latest HTML tags and let you add tags or combinations of tags. These programs work by inserting HTML tags, such as <B> for Bold, around text you highlight in the editor. You still have to look at the HTML and try to imagine what it will look like in the browser, but at least you don't have to manually type all of the HTML tags. The following are some of the best HTML text editors available today.

BBEdit 4.5 by Bare Bones Software

www.barebones.com
BBEdit is by far the most popular HTML text editor for the Macintosh. In addition to supporting HTML 3.0 and 4.0 tags, BBEdit includes such powerful features as multiple page search and replace, Grepp searching (a complex system of search and replace that enables the automation of many tedious tasks), and a range of third-party plug-ins that add functionality. BBEdit is now bundled with Macromedia Dreamweaver.

HomeSite 3.0 by Allaire

www.allaire.com
Joining forces with Macromedia, HomeSite 3.0 is now bundled with Dreamweaver, an alliance that is likely to solidify HomeSite's position as a leader among HTML text editors for Windows. HomeSite includes specialized toolbars, templates, and wizards to make it easy to use. Version 3.0 is keeping up with the latest HTML standards, supporting Cascading Style Sheets and Dynamic HTML.

HotDog Pro by Sausage Software

www.sausage.com
I have to confess that my favorite thing about HotDog Pro for Windows (aside from the name) is the playful and creative company staff. The Web site is worth a visit, even if you just read about how they run around the office in bunny slippers and play foosball in the lobby. But seriously,

HotDog is a competitive HTML text editor, supporting the latest HTML tags and enabling you to add tags easily.

Image Programs

When it comes to graphics, Adobe Systems, Inc., dominates the market, producing some of the most popular and sophisticated image programs available to consumers. Every graphic designer and illustrator I know owns a copy of Adobe Photoshop, despite its $600 price tag and steep learning curve. If you are looking for a serious graphics program, Photoshop is the clear choice. However, if you don't have the budget, or the time to learn such a complex program, you may be better off with Adobe's more limited photo-editing program, Photo Delux. For creating buttons, banners, and other Web graphics, consider Jasc's Paint Shop Pro, Microfrontier's Color It!, or Microsoft's Image Composer.

Adobe Systems, Inc.

www.adobe.com

Adobe Systems is probably the leading vendor of image-creation and editing programs. Adobe makes Photoshop, Illustrator, and PhotoDeluxe, and many others. See Adobe's Web site for a complete list of programs. Below is a description of those that are most widely used for making graphics for the Web.

Photoshop 5.0   Adobe calls Photoshop the "camera of the mind." This is unquestionably the most popular image-editing program on the market. With Photoshop, you can create original artwork, correct color in photographs, retouch photographs and scanned images, and much, much more. Photoshop has a wealth of powerful painting and selection tools in addition to special effects and filters to create images that go beyond what you can capture on film or with classic illustration programs.

Illustrator 8.0   Illustrator is the industry standard for creating illustrations. You can drag and drop illustrations that you create in Illustrator right into other Adobe programs such as PageMill or PageMaker. Illustrator also comes with an export feature that enables you to export your illustrations in GIF or JPEG format with a Web palette of colors so your illustrations look great on the Web.

PhotoDeluxe   Though not nearly as powerful as Photoshop, PhotoDeluxe makes many tasks easier by automating common features. The program is designed to retouch photos (removing red-eye and improving color balance and contrast), and the has ability to crop and resize. You'll also find templates and wizards to help you create greeting cards, calendars, and more.

Macromedia Freehand 7.0

www.macromedia.com/
Freehand is an illustration program that is used widely both on the Web and in print. Freehand has many excellent Web features such as support for Web file formats like GIF89a, PNG, and JPEG, and vector formats like Flash (.SWF) and Shockwave FreeHand (.FHC).

Jasc Paint Shop Pro 4.14

www.jasc.com/
Paint Shop Pro, by Jasc Software, is a full-featured painting and image-manipulation program. Paint Shop Pro is very similar to Photoshop, but it doesn't offer the same range of effects, tools, and filters. However, it costs less than Photoshop and may be a good starter program for novice image makers.

Microsoft Image Composer

www.microsoft.com/
Image Composer is a fun image-creation program. It lets you build compositions of images and apply many interesting effects. This easy-to-use program comes bundled with FrontPage and is fully integrated with the HTML Authoring tool. Image Composer was designed for creating Web graphics so it is an idea tool for the novice Web designer.

Color It!

www.microfrontier.com
This low-cost, easy-to-use graphic program for the Macintosh is a great tool for beginners, as well as those on a tight budget.

PhotoDisc, Inc.

www.photodisc.com
PhotoDisc is one of the leading suppliers of royalty-free digital imagery (primarily photographs). At the time of this writing, PhotoDisc has two CD titles in its two animation series, *Metaphorically Blinking* and *Everyday Objects Live*. These discs include compact, completely prepared animated files that are ready to drop into a Web site. All files comes in three image sizes and in both Animated GIF and Shockwave format.

Adobe Image Club Graphics

www.imageclub.com

One of the world's largest sources for other types of clip art, Image Club Graphics has just introduced its first CD-ROM collection of Web animations. Called the Animated Art Series, the first disk is titled "The Essentials." It consists of 100 moving business objects and everyday items. Like the PhotoDisc collections, these animations are photo-based. They come in four file formats: Animated GIF, 3DMF, QuickTime VR, and JPEG.

Global Presence Animated GIF Gallery CD-ROM

http://animationcreations.com/main/gal_animation.htm

If you want more than 800 animated GIFs for a modest price, you have to order them over the Internet. These are professional-caliber, useful images that have been organized into useful theme sets.

Ulead Systems, Inc.

www.ulead.com

Ulead's GIF Animation Collection I is a real bargain with 450 animations. If you're a Windows user, you also get a library manager that lets you see thumbnail libraries of the animations. Ulead emphatically states that you can use these animations, license free, for any project, whether commercial or personal.

Software Testing Tools

WebLoad by RadView, Inc.

www.webload.com

WebLoad 3.0 is one of the leading tools for testing server performance.

Silk Products by Segue Software

www.segue.com

This company keeps getting bigger and better, now offering a whole suite of tools for testing and measuring system perfomance.

SiteSweeper by Site Technologies

www.webstewpub.com/_management/sitesweeper/

SiteSweeper 2.0 is one of our favorites. It quickly checks huge sites for broken links, and provides handy reports for quick bug fixing.

HTML Conversion Programs

Take advantage of the work you've already done with HTML conversion tools. These programs and extensions convert documents designed for print, such as word-processing and desktop publishing files, into HTML. Many of them even convert your graphics into GIFs and JPEGs automatically.

Converters for Word-Processing Programs

HTML Transit (*www.infoaccess.com*)   *Converts* Microsoft Word 97 and earlier versions, Microsoft Excel 97 and 95, Microsoft PowerPoint 97 and 95, Lotus AmiPro, ASCII, Adobe FrameMaker, Interleaf, Rich Text Format (RTF), WordPerfect (DOS and Windows), and Write for Windows 95 and NT

HTML Transit by InfoAccess is by far the most powerful conversion program for word-processing files. Capable of converting hundreds or even thousands of pages at a time, HTML Transit can automatically create a linked table of contents page, break long documents into shorter ones, and set navigational links, such as forward and backward buttons. An easy-to-use wizard walks you through the setup for document conversion, meaning that you can be up and running with this program as soon as it's installed on your hard drive. And, after you've set up your preferences for conversion, you can save them, making updating your site easy if your original document is changed later.

WebConvert (*www.webconvert.com*)   *Converts* MicrosoftWord, Lotus Ami Pro, WordPerfect, Wang WPS, and ASCII for Windows 95 and NT

WebConvert is a versatile conversion program able to handle single pages or piles of files at a time. It's not as sophisticated as HTML Transit, but it's about a fourth of the price and offers some of the same features.

RTFtoHTML 4.18 (*www.sunpack.com/RTF/*)   *Converts* ClarisWorks, WordPerfect, Microsoft Word, and other word-processing programs for Macintosh, Windows, DOS, and UNIX

RTFtoHTML 4.18 from Sunrise Packaging is a great utility that converts documents saved in RTF (Rich Text Format) to HTML. *RTF* is a file format developed by Microsoft and now widely used by most major word-processing programs on the MacOS, Windows, and UNIX platforms. The goal of the Rich Text Format is to provide a common file type that almost all word-processing programs can use to share information. Because this program converts from RTF, it can handle a wide range of programs.

Converters for Desktop Publishing Programs

Most business already have promotional materials designed in desktop publishing programs, such as QuarkXPress and PageMaker. Brochures, newsletters, and other documents provide graphics-rich material for your Web site. Using these conversion tools can save you the tedious chore of manually converting these files into HTML. That leaves you with more time to work on altering the designs to take advantage of the Web.

BeyondPress 4.0 (*www.astrobyte.com*—now *www.extensis.com*)   *Converts* QuarkXPress for Macintosh

Extensis's BeyondPress is a QuarkXPress XTension that converts XPress files into HTML and graphics into JPEGs and GIFs. BeyondPress adds a Document Content palette under the View menu and lists all the elements of an XPress document so that you can specify what is exported and turn large XPress files into multiple HTML pages. One of the most useful features of this program is the ability to map XPress styles to HTML styles. This can be set globally and can be overridden, enabling you to alter the style of any individual element while leaving the rest set with the global style. Image-conversion capabilities include the ability to scale, set transparency, create image maps, and convert images into GIFs or JPEGs. Using the XTension's Preferences, you can customize each article you export. In addition to a list of HTML options included in BeyondPress 2.0, you can create and add HTML styles.

HexWeb XT 2.5 (*www.hexmac.de*)   *Converts* QuarkXpress for Macintosh, Windows, and Windows NT

HexWeb XT by HexMac International is not as powerful as Beyond-Press but it is available for both the Macintosh and Windows. Unlike BeyondPress, HexWeb XT does not map style sheets to HTML code and lacks many of the other more sophisticated features of BeyondPress. The program is limited to matching point sizes to header tags and converting basic formatting such as bold and italics. HexWeb XT provides basic image conversion and can be used to set links by specifying elements in the original document. Header and footer elements that are repeated on every page can be defined in settings. One feature BeyondPress lacks is the Hex-Web Index that automatically generates a table of contents file after all HTML articles have been exported.

CyberPress–Bundled with PageMill (*www.extensis.com*)   *Converts* Quark-Xpress for Macintosh

CyberPress, by Extensis, is a light version of BeyondPress that's bundled with Adobe PageMill.

HTML Author—Bundled with PageMaker (*www.adobe.com*)   *Converts* PageMaker 6.5 for Macintosh and Windows

HTML Author, by Adobe Systems, Inc., is a plug-in bundled with PageMaker 6.5 to convert documents into HTML. Although Adobe showed great foresight when it first packaged this program with Page-Maker 6.0, the first version of HTML Author was a limited conversion program capable of handling only the simplest designs. The upgrade that ships with 6.5 adds the ability to convert graphics and does a better job of converting designs created in PageMaker, but it still chokes if your layout is too complex.

WebWorks® Publisher 2000 (*www.quadralay.com*)   *Converts* FrameMaker and word processing programs for Macintosh and Windows

WebWorks by Quadralay is a conversion program designed to handle FrameMaker documents. The program is highly configurable and provides for arbitrary file splitting, TOC conversion, and table conversion. Handling graphics internally or exporting them for individual handling is the user's option.

Quarterdeck WebAuthor (*www.quarterdeck.com*)   *Converts* FrameMaker and word-processing programs for Windows

Quarterdeck WebAuthor is a limited HTML editor as well as a converter for FrameMaker and many common word-processing files.

Multimedia and Animation Programs

At the more advanced end of the software spectrum, you'll find multimedia programs such as Macromedia Director, the number one choice among professional CD-ROM developers. You'll also find a new batch of software products designed specifically for creating multimedia for the Web. These programs produce impressive results (animations, video, and audio), but if you have never done this kind of work, you'll need considerable training to use them.

Macromedia Director

www.macromedia.com/

As the industry leader, the Director 6 Multimedia Studio provides everything you need to create professional multimedia projects, from corporate presentations and engaging Web pages to interactive advertising kiosks and CD-ROM titles. Director files can be converted to Shockwave files for the Web, using Macromedia's Afterburner (which is free to registered owners of Director).

Macromedia Flash

www.macromedia.com/

Flash is an all-purpose animation tool with a simple interface and interactive components. Developed for the Web, Flash creates vector-based animations that are scaleable in many resolutions, load quickly, and look fantastic! Flash animations require a plug-in to be viewed on the Web, but the Flash plug-in is part of the Shockwave suite and takes less than two minutes to download and install.

Emblaze WebCharger by Geo

www.emblaze.com

This Java-based software package was designed specifically for developing streaming multimedia content for the Web. Your viewers don't need a plug-in to see your work, but they do need a Java-enabled browser. Emblaze features advanced compression technology, video and audio support, and the ability to import most popular graphics formats.

Adobe Premiere

www.adobe.com/prodindex/premiere/main.html

You can create high-quality digital movies and videotapes with Adobe Premiere. This powerful editing program lets you combine video, animation, still images, and graphics to create engaging video experiences. Adobe Premiere now comes with an animated GIF plug-in, which converts video and movie sequences into a series of GIF files that can be saved in the animated GIF format that is commonly supported on the Web.

Adobe After Effects

www.adobe.com/prodindex/aftereffects/main.html
Adobe After Effects is a powerful tool for composing and creating 2-D animation and special effects for film, video, multimedia, and Web sites.

MetaCreations Final Effects

www.metacreations.com/
Final Effects is a plug-in for Ulead's MediaStudio Pro. Final Effects gives you twelve new video-editing effects for creating exciting computer video.

GIF Animation Programs

The following programs enable you to create GIF animations. These small applications range in price from $20 to about $50; most can be downloaded for a free trial. These tools enable you to create animations on a frame-by-frame basis, and then export them as a single GIF89a, which is the standard file format for Web animations. Although these programs are similar in function and price, I tried to rank them by putting the best programs at the top of this list.

GIFmation 2.1 (*www.boxtopsoft.com*)   BoxTop Software, Inc. (Mac and Windows)

Ulead GIF Animator 3 (*www.ulead.com*)   Ulead Systems (Windows)

GIF Construction Set (*www.mindworkshop.com*)   Alchemy Mindworks, Inc. (Windows)

GIFBuilder 0.5 (*http://www.pascal.com/mirrors/gifbuilder*)   Yves Piguet, Institut d'automatique (Macintosh and Power Macintosh)

Microsoft GIF Animator (*www.microsoft.com*)   Microsoft, Inc. (Windows 95 and NT)

Java Development Tools

No matter how good the tools are, it's important to understand a little bit about Java before attempting to use these tools. Like multimedia programs, Java development tools have a steep learning curve. Even the simplest Java tools require that you have some familiarity with the Java programming language.

Symantec's VisualCafé

www.symantec.com
VisualCafé is an elegant Java authoring tool that provides a complete environment for developing full-scale Java applets and Java Beans.

Jenernet's JenAva JG

www.jenernet.com
JenAva JG is a full-featured entry-level Java source code applet/application generator. Its point-and-click WYSIWYG environment gives those new to Java an easy interface. This is a shareware product and costs $5 if you decide to keep it.

Shareware Programs

If you're looking for a shareware program or other utility, these sites can help you find what you need. Shareware, also called try-out versions or time-out versions, is software you can download for free and use on a trial basis. If you decide you like the program, you pay for it and get a registration number. Without a registration number, most shareware programs stop working after about 30 days. Some shareware programs have limited features, lacking the ability to save your work or to use advanced options until you get a registration number.

Shareware.com

www.shareware.com
Sponsored by CNET, this searchable database is the most widely used resource on the Web for obtaining the latest shareware applications. Each program is tried and rated by staff before becoming available.

ZDNet Software Library

www.zdnet.com
ZDNet's Software Library has an extensive Web application section and a great search engine. It has lists of both shareware and regularly priced applications.

Softseek

www.softseek.com/_other/SIA.html
This is a privately maintained site that features some interesting applications.

IBM Global Software Solutions Guide

www2.software.ibm.com/solutions/isv/igssg.nsf/LanguageSelector/?OpenForm
Looking for a program to solve an unusual business need? Search IBM's Global Software Solutions Guide; you may find that just what you need has already been created. This powerful search engine checks for programs all over the world in multiple languages.

Hardware Guide

This guide is designed to help you make an informed choice about buying computers, digital cameras, and other computer equipment.

Buying a Computer

People frequently ask me what kind of computer they should buy. My best advice is to start by thinking about what you want a computer to do. If all you ever plan to do is use word-processing programs and maybe an accounting application, you don't need the fastest, most powerful machine on the market. However, if you want to create high-resolution graphics or play the hottest, latest video games, you will need a powerful machine. Make sure you choose your computer based on your needs. You don't need to buy a big rig when a pickup truck would be more than enough. But, if you have to make ten times more trips because the pickup doesn't have enough capacity, then it might be worth investing in the big rig in the first place. Assess your needs, and then start looking at computers. Spend what you can afford to get the best machine you can, and you will probably be happy with it for a long time.

The next thing to consider is whether you should get a computer that runs the Macintosh or Windows operating system. That decision should be based on two factors. First, what computers do your friends and colleagues use? If you need to trade files with your accountant, your designer, or other people, the best solution is to have the same operating system. If you find that your accountant uses a PC and your designer uses a Mac (a likely scenario), consider with whom you work most often and whether either of them could provide you with files that you could read on the other platform. Although Windows is by far the most common system and the one your colleagues are most likely to use, the Macintosh is much more versatile when it comes to sharing information. Most files created on a PC can be opened easily on a Macintosh as long as the software is available for both platforms.

That brings me to the second consideration: What software do you want to use? Unfortunately, because Windows is the dominant system, more and more software companies are designing programs only for the PC and no longer creating upgrades for the Macintosh versions. Some companies have never made versions of their software for the Macintosh. Before you buy a computer, investigate the software you want and make sure it will work on your new machine.

Comparing RAM, Hard Drives, and Processor Speeds

When you compare computers you may find yourself overwhelmed with the list of numbers and letters manufacturers use to describe their computers, odd statements like Pentium II, Pentium MMX, 133 Mhz, 16 MB RAM, and 2 Gig HD are all used to distinguish speed and memory of computers.

If you are still wondering what all that stuff means, the following should help you sort through your choices.

1. *HD*   The hard drive is the storage system in a computer. The size of the hard drive determines how much information (programs and other files) you can keep in your computer. Think of this as long-term memory (or storage), while RAM is short-term memory.

2. *RAM*   Random access memory enables your computer to run software programs. The more RAM, the more complex programs you can run and the more programs you can run simultaneously. Newer programs and upgrades require more and more RAM. Think of this as short-term memory in your computer. When you open a program, such as MS Word, you copy it from the hard drive (the storage area) into RAM (the short-term, high-speed memory) so that you can use it.

3. *Processor Speed*   Two variables determine processor speed— whether the computer has a Pentium II processor or one of the older ones, such as a 486, and the processor speed in megahertz. Today, most computers use Pentium processors (note that Pentium II is faster than the MMX). A good target processor speed for a desktop these days is about 166, but the faster the better. Most desktop computers run faster than laptops so you may have to settle for a slower processor in a laptop.

These three variables—HD, RAM, and processor speed—should be your primary concern when comparing computer systems. In all three cases, the larger the number the better, but you can always upgrade if you buy a computer that has room for expansion. Usually, that means the computer has more expansion slots and space for another hard drive if you ever want to add one. You also want to make sure there is room for more RAM, the easiest variable to increase, as long as you have the room. And then don't worry too much about your choices. Whatever you buy will be obsolete in the next three to five years anyway.

Buying Hardware: Desktop Computer Recommendations for Windows

Before you read the recommendations here, let me preface this by saying that hardware changes almost as fast as software does. The best computer this week may be outpaced next week by the competition. Use this list as a guide to help you determine which computer companies are likely to produce the best machines, but be sure you get an updated report. You can find computer reviews in many computer magazines on-line and at the magazine rack. You can also learn more about buying a computer in *PCs for Dummies*.

According to *PC Magazine*, the best hardware vendors for 1998 were Dell, IBM, and Quantex, followed closely by Gateway, Hewlett-Packard, and Micron. All six of these vendors scored above average in the areas of reliability, repair, and technical support. Gateway, Hewlett-Packard, and Micron received average because many of their units needed repair after twelve months.

Dell (*www.dell.com*)   Dell computers has risen to the top of the market, selling more computers than any other hardware company in the business. Dell covers all of its systems with 24-hour, 7-day-a-week, toll-free technical support and a 3-year-parts, 1-year-labor warranty.

Dell Computer Corp., Round Rock, TX; 800-388-8542, 512-338-4400; fax, 512-832-4329.

Gateway (*www.gateway.com*)   Another well-respected computer company, one of Gateway's claims to fame is its offer to custom-build computers. That means you can call their 800 number and describe the system you want (how much RAM, how fast you want the processor, etc.) and Gateway will build it and ship it to you. You may also be delighted to learn that it will arrive in a cardboard box that is painted to look like a cow.

Gateway 2000, Inc., North Sioux City, SD; 800-338-0169, 605-232-2000; fax, 605-232-2023.

Micron (*www.micronpc.com*)   Ranked in the top six computer manufactures (by *PC Magazine* as well as others), Micron produces a long line of desktop computers. Although there have been some problems with computers needing early repairs, the company does provide excellent technical support.

Micron Electronics, Inc., Nampa, ID; 888-634-8799, 208-893-3343; fax, 208-893-7333.

IBM (*www.us.pc.ibm.com/desktop*)   One of the oldest companies in the business, IBM is not known for being the cheapest, but its history makes it likely to be a reliable.

IBM PC Co., Research Triangle Park, NC; 800-426-2968, 919-558-5221; fax, 800-426-3395.

Quantex (*www.quantex.com*)   Quantex was rated one of the top three computer manufacturers by *PC Magazine,* making it a serious contender as you compare systems. Many of their mid-range machines include the Microsoft Office Small Business Edition 97 and the Microsoft Plus! Pack.

Quantex Microsystems, Inc., Somerset, NJ; 800-346-6572, 908-563-4166; fax, 908-563-0407.

Buying Hardware: Desktop Computer Recommendations for Macintosh

You can get some great bargains on Mac OS systems from vendors who are leaving the Mas OS market, such as Motorola, Power Computing, and APS Technology. I limited my recommendation list to computers from Apple and UMAX because both continue to sell Macintosh computers and offer warranties and support.

Apple G3 (*www.apple.com*)   The latest from Apple Computer, the G3 is a fast, powerful machine, operating at a minimum configuration of 300 Mhz with 32 MB RAM.

Apple PowerMac (*www.apple.com*)   The PowerMac series ranges from the 6500 to the 9500, getting progressively more powerful and expensive as the numbers increase.

SuperMac (*www.umax.com*)   UMAX Computer has a long line of Super-Macs, from the low end to the high end in terms of speed, performance, and price.

Laptop Computers

Laptops are consistently more expensive than desktop machines, so be prepared to spend more to get the same power and performance in a portable computer. The versatility of a laptop accounts for its price. As a small business owner, you may find that one laptop computer can serve many needs and save you money because you don't have to buy multiple machines. Because they are portable, laptops can be carried easily from home to office. They can also be shared among employees and taken to clients' offices for demos or working on location. As you consider which laptop is best for you, look for the following features:

♦ Lightweight (not more than 8 pounds—they get heavier in airports and at conferences)
♦ Active matrix screen for clear color and display
♦ At least an 800 x 600 display
♦ A lithium-ion battery, or something that gives you at least three hours of life on one charge
♦ Two PCMCIA slots (one for a modem and one for a network card, if you need one)
♦ Both a floppy and a CD-ROM drive (some are swappable, some external)
♦ A keyboard and mouse device that is comfortable for *you* (borrow one and try it out, or go to a store and type on one long enough to get a good sense of how it feels)

Windows Notebooks

IBM (*www.ibm.com*)   Some of the best laptops on the market are created by IBM. The Thinkpad has a good history of reliability and performance, and the price has dropped dramatically.

Compaq (*www.compaq.com*)   The maker of great all-around laptops, Compaq offers a competitive price and some fun features, such as a CD player that will play music CDs, even when the computer is not turned on.

Micron (*www.micron.com*)   Micron computers offer superior service and support options, good performance, very flexible modular designs, and the option to get an excellent active-matrix screen.

NEC (*www.nec.com*)   NEC offers a good price for a solid laptop. Even if you don't want to pay for the active-matrix screen, you'll find the Versa's passive-matrix screen is excellent.

Macintosh Powerbooks

One of the most useful tools in my arsenal of software and hardware is an Apple Macintosh 3400c Powerbook. This beautiful machine makes an excellent demonstration system when I meet with clients, and it's ready to handle almost anything I throw at it. As a Web developer, clients give me files in a range of software formats from both the Windows and Macintosh operating systems. Mac has lots of conversion features built in, so I can insert a floppy disk or a Zip disk from a PC and easily read the files on my Mac. I've loaded this little wonder with software and am delighted to say that I can open almost anything you could give me on this machine. If you are a small business owner and want to buy one computer that can handle many tasks, this is an excellent choice. To learn more about Macintosh laptops, visit the Apple Web site.

Modems

When it comes to modems, as a general rule, the faster the better. But in addition to speed, consider the software that comes with your modem. Most modems come bundled with fax software, but some programs are complex and difficult to use; others are intuitive and user-friendly. If possible, get a demonstration of the software or read the program description on-line before you buy a modem.

3Com and U.S. Robotics   3Com and U.S. Robotics have merged to form one of the largest networking companies in the world. The combined force of the two companies makes this a serious contender in the modem market. You'll find they produce a long list of modems for the Macintosh and Windows operating systems.

Global Village (*www.globalvillage.com*)   Not only does Global Village make great modems at a variety of speeds, it produces some of the most user-friendly software, especially for sending and receiving faxes from your computer.

Digital Cameras

This is one of the most volatile hardware categories, with new models appearing on the market nearly every day. The good news is that they get cheaper and more powerful all the time. The bad news is that it's hard to recommend a good camera today because tomorrow it's likely to be outshined by some other model. The following cameras are included to help you start researching the best digital camera for you.

Olympus D-320L (*www.olympusamerica.com*)   The Olympus D-320L won *MacWorld*'s best of show award for its high-quality image and competitive price. Olympus is one of the few digital camera producers that is creating a tool with the kinds of features you expect in a traditional camera. The D-320L features 1024 × 768 resolution, an all-glass aspherical F2.8 autofocus lens, video out, three levels of compression , exposure controls, and autoflash with red-eye reduction and force fill.

Kodak DC210 (*www.kodak.com*)   This little camera fits comfortably in your hand and boasts a nice collection of features. True megapixel CCD enables it to capture one million (1152 × 864) pixels per image, and the color LCD display lets you review and preview your pictures immediately (you can even delete on the spot the ones you don't like). The zoom lens (29 mm to 58 mm) is also a macro capable of getting as close as 8 inches. The built-in flash includes red-eye reduction options.

Agfa ePhoto 307 (*www.agfa.com*)   The ePhoto stores 36 images at the camera's highest resolution of 640 × 480 and 72 pics at 340 × 240 pixels in its 2 MB of internal memory.

Epson PhotoPC   The PhotoPC 500 can handle 30 shots at 640 × 480-pixel resolution and 60 in the low-resolution 320 × 240 mode. It's also expandable—you can add a 2 MB or 4 MB memory card, and you can keep up to 65 or 100 high-resolution pictures, respectively.

Digital Video Cameras

Kodak DVC323 (*www.kodak.com*)   This is the camera we use at Red Sky, and it's a winner.

Buying More RAM

At some point, when you start using more programs, especially if you work with graphics, you are going to want more RAM for your computer. The good news is the cost of RAM has plummeted, making upgrading your system cheaper and easier than ever. When you buy RAM, make sure that you get the right kind for az DCVB/` for your computer. Many varieties of RAM exist, and computers are increasingly sensitive. If you get the wrong RAM, you can cause problems.

ChipMerchants (*www.thechipmerchant.com/*)   In addition to offering the best prices I've ever found for RAM, this site features a great chart to help you pick the right RAM for your computer. You can order on-line or by phone.

Index

CD-ROM Warranty

Limited Warranties and Limitation of Liability

Macromedia

Macromedia warrants only that the Media upon wich the Macromedia Software is supplied is free of defects. Macromedia's and the publisher's sole obligation is to provide replacement software. EXCEPT AS SET FORTH IN THE FOREGOING LIMITED WARRANTY, MACROMEDIA DISCLAIMS ALL OTHER WARRANTIES, EITHER EXPRESS OR IMPLED, INCLUDING THE WARRANTIES OF MERCHANTABILITY, FITNESS FOR A PARTICULAR PURPOSE AND NONINFRINGEMENT. IN NO EVENT WILL EITHER PARTY BE LIABLE FOR COSTS OF PROCUREMENT OF SUBSTITUTE PRODUCTS OR SERVICES, LOST PROFITS, OR ANY SPECIAL, INDIRECT, CONSEQUENTIAL, OR INCIDENTAL DAMAGES, HOWEVER CAUSED, AND ON ANY THEORY OF LIABILITY ARISING IN ANY WAY OUT OF THIS AGREEMENT OR THE TERMINATION THEREOF, WHETHER OR NOT SUCH PARTY HAS BEEN ADVISED OF THE POSSIBILITY OF SUCH DAMAGE, AND NOTHWITHSTANDING ANY FAILURE OF ESSENTIAL PURPOSE OF ANY LIMITED REMEMDY PROVIDED IN THIS AGREEMENT. The parties agree that this provision will not limit Macromedia's remedies for the infringement of its intellectual property.

Microsoft

The Microsoft® Project 98 120-day Trial Edition and FrontPage® 2000 45-day Trial Edition programs were reproduced by Addison-Wesley under a special arrangement with Microsoft Corporation. For this reason, Addison-Wesley is responsible for the product warranty and for support. If your diskette is defective, please return it to Addison Wesley Longman, Inc., which will arrange for its replacement. PLEASE DO NOT RETURN IT TO MICROSOFT CORPORATION. Any product support will be provided, if at all, by Addison-Wesley. PLEASE DO NOT CONTACT MICROSOFT CORPORATION FOR PRODUCT SUPPORT. End users of these Microsoft programs shall not be considered "registered owners" of a Microsoft product and therefore shall not be eligible for upgrades, promotions, or other benefits available to "registered owners" of Microsoft products.

Addison-Wesley Computer and Engineering Publishing Group

How to Interact with Us

1. Visit our Web site

http://www.awl.com/cseng

When you think you've read enough, there's always more content for you at Addison-Wesley's web site. Our web site contains a directory of complete product information including:

- Chapters
- Exclusive author interviews
- Links to authors' pages
- Tables of contents
- Source code

You can also discover what tradeshows and conferences Addison-Wesley will be attending, read what others are saying about our titles, and find out where and when you can meet our authors and have them sign your book.

2. Subscribe to Our Email Mailing Lists

Subscribe to our electronic mailing lists and be the first to know when new books are publishing. Here's how it works: Sign up for our electronic mailing at **http://www.awl.com/cseng/mailinglists.html**. Just select the subject areas that interest you and you will receive notification via email when we publish a book in that area.

3. Contact Us via Email

cepubprof@awl.com
Ask general questions about our books.
Sign up for our electronic mailing lists.
Submit corrections for our web site.

bexpress@awl.com
Request an Addison-Wesley catalog.
Get answers to questions regarding
your order or our products.

innovations@awl.com
Request a current Innovations Newsletter.

webmaster@awl.com
Send comments about our web site.

mary.obrien@awl.com
Submit a book proposal.
Send errata for an Addison-Wesley book.

cepubpublicity@awl.com
Request a review copy for a member of the media
interested in reviewing new Addison-Wesley titles.

We encourage you to patronize the many fine retailers who stock Addison-Wesley titles. Visit our online directory to find stores near you or visit our online store: http://store.awl.com/ or call **800-824-7799**.

Addison Wesley Longman
Computer and Engineering Publishing Group
One Jacob Way, Reading, Massachusetts 01867 USA
TEL 781-944-3700 • FAX 781-942-3076